Care Work in
Crisis

Reclaiming the Nordic Ethos of Care

EDITED BY
SIRPA WREDE
LEA HENRIKSSON
HÅKON HØST
STINA JOHANSSON
BETINA DYBBROE

Studentlitteratur

Published by
Studentlitteratur AB
Lund, Sweden
www.studentlitteratur.se

Art. No 33235
ISBN 978-91-44-05253-3

© The authors and Studentlitteratur 2008

Cover design by AB Typoform

Printed in United States of America 2008
Lightning Source

Contents

List of tables

Contributors

Petra Ahnlund
Ph.D., Researcher
Department of Social Work
Umeå University, Sverige

Katarina Andersson
Ph.D., Researcher
Department of Social Work
Umeå University, Sverige

Karen Christensen
Associate Professor
Department of Sociology
University of Bergen, Norway

Betina Dybbroe
Associate Professor
Department of Psychology and Educational Research,
Roskilde University, Denmark

Lea Henriksson
Adjunct Professor, Academy Research Fellow
Institute for Social Research
University of Tampere, Finland

Håkon Høst
Dr. Polit., Senior Researcher
NIFU STEP—Norwegian Institute for Studies in Innovation,
Research and Education
Oslo, Norway

Stina Johansson
Professor
Department of Social Work
Umeå University, Sweden

Helle Krogh Hansen
Ph.D., Researcher
VIA University College, Research & Development Department
Risskov, Denmark

Anne Liveng
Ph.D., Researcher
Institute for Psychology and Educational Research
Roskilde University, Denmark

Suvi Nieminen
Ph.D. Candidate, Researcher
Tampere School of Public Health
University of Tampere, Finland

Saila Sormunen
Ph.D. Candidate, Researcher
STAKES, National Research and Development Centre for Welfare
and Health
Helsinki, Finland

Laura Tainio
Graduate Student
Department of Sociology
Åbo Akademi University, Finland

Päivi Topo
Adjunct Professor, Academy Research Fellow
STAKES, National Research and Development Centre for Welfare
and Health
Helsinki, Finland

Kari Wærness
Professor
Department of Sociology
University of Bergen, Norway

Sirpa Wrede
Adjunct Professor, Academy Research Fellow
Swedish School of Social Science
University of Helsinki, Finland

Foreword

This book marks an important goal in long term collaboration. Looking back at years of lively networking that for some of us started already in 1999, it is time to acknowledge our debts, both to colleagues and to institutions that supported our work.

The practical work with this book began in 2006, but it would not have been possible without the Nordic networks where we, over the years in somewhat different constellations, have taken part. The most long-lived of these received seed money from the *Committee for Nordic Research Councils for the Social Sciences* (NOS-S) in 2002. This grant made it possible for us to arrange a few meetings and seminars. While in the end our plans for a large-scale Nordic project were not successful, we nevertheless got an impetus to make a joint contribution to the field. This book cannot replace publications that would have shed comparative light on the present recruitment crisis in the Nordic societies and on the historical and present tensions in care work organisation. However, a more structured project would perhaps not have allowed or stimulated the open debate and discussion our meetings came to involve, apart from the formal presentations based on our individual ongoing research projects. The end product is a book that, while maintaining an academic ambition, addresses broader societal debates. It is our hope that this collage of Nordic studies highlights the social shaping of care work, offering fruitful perspectives for both more inclusive academic approaches and political debates on care.

Associate Professor Ole Johnny Olsen from University of Bergen was project leader in the NOS-S project. In addition to being a wonderful host to our early meetings, Ole Johnny is a generous scholar who made valuable contributions also in the later meetings. Another great friend and a scholar is Professor Kari Waerness, who has been a long-term partner in our collaboration. With the strength of her insight and devout spirit, she helped us to raise the Nordic ethos into a critical perspective on care work. We also wish to acknowledge several valued colleagues who, while not involved in this book, at different points in time took part in related networking, contributing to the development of the ideas and insights on which the book is based. Thank you Annegrethe Ahrenkiel, Hanne Marlene Dahl, Rannveig Dahle, Lars Evertsson, Tine Rask Eriksen, Marte Feiring, Camilla Hutters, Kristín Björnsdottír, Steen Baagøe Nielsen, Svein Michelsen and Thorgerdur Einarsdóttir.

Finally, we wish to thank our individual funders who have made our work with this book possible. Sirpa Wrede acknowledges the support of the Academy of Finland (grants #207066, #211270, #118395). Lea Henriksson acknowledges the support of the Academy of Finland (grants #73186, # 207402, #214430) as well as that of Jenny and Antti Wihuri Foundation. Håkon Høst acknowledges Stein Rokkan Centre for Social Studies at University of Bergen for grants that made it possible to work with the book. Stina Johansson acknowledges the support from Rådet för Arbetslivsforskning (#2000-0243), European Commission (# HPSE-CT-2001-00091) and from the research profile 'Care Work and Social Gerontology' at Umeå university. Betina Dybbroe acknowledges the support of the Danish Research Council of the Social Sciences and of the Danish Union of Nurses.

Helsinki, Tampere, Oslo, Umeå and Roskilde 5 May 2008

The editors

INTRODUCTION

Care Work and the Competing Rationalities of Public Policy

*Sirpa Wrede, Lea Henriksson,
Håkon Høst, Stina Johansson
and Betina Dybbroe*

Traditionally women in the Nordic countries, like elsewhere, had been responsible for providing the care that was needed by dependent family members. From the 1960s onwards, however, Nordic women were increasingly often entering paid employment. This development gave rise to what could be called a *care gap*. The emerging Nordic welfare states responded to this challenge by investing in the public provision of day care for children and care for the elderly and the disabled. This type of care was socially defined, unlike the care that was linked to medically defined needs. Even in the public sphere socially defined care remained women's work. Social care services expanded rapidly in the 1970s and continued to grow in the 1980s. In addition to the gender logic, the logic related to low social position can be discerned in the formal organisation of care, as a deeply embedded element of *dirty work* persisted in socially defined care in the welfare state (e.g., Widding-Isakssen 1994). The institutional framework that emerged, nevertheless, entailed certain recognition of the values of care work and an investment in care understood as a social entitlement (Simonen 1990, Julkunen 1991).

This book is concerned with what has happened with that frail recognition of socially defined care in the processes of institutional and cultural change since the 1990s. We argue that the revision of the investment in socially defined care has in part disrupted the idea of a Nordic social service model. This reorientation seems to be the most far-reaching in Finland (Anttonen et al. 2003) and in Sweden (Szebehely 2003), while the retrenchment in Denmark and Norway has not been an equally prominent trend (Dahl 2004, Rauch 2007). Here we are not primarily concerned with analysing the economic investments in the care sector, or with comparing welfare state models. Instead, our focus is on the *cultural* rather than the institutional change of care work.

The empirical context for the majority of the studies of care work presented here is elderly care. The studies contribute to an understanding of how service policy and education shape care work, but we generally adopt *a bottom-up perspective* to the world that care workers, their educators, administrators and clients inhabit. By centring the perspective of the grassroots we want to draw attention to the fact that the world of care is inhabited by caring and suffering people, not by numbers. Elderly care offers what can be identified as a critical case of socially defined care: from the perspective of instrumental rationality, caring for the elderly constitutes 'non-productive care', as no economically measurable result for the society is produced (Wærness 1980).

In the following, we first provide some illustrative background data about the Nordic societies to help the reader to locate this at present very privileged region in the global map of social development. The argument of the book is that institutional changes result from changes in the *political ethos* framing care, where emphasis currently lies on efficiency. In contrast, in the 1980s a welfare state ethos of universalism was a part of a wider political and cultural move towards greater egalitarianism in Nordic societies (e.g. Allardt et al. 1981, see Christiansen & Markkola 2006).

Historical and structural affinity: the Nordic context

In recent studies, the argument is that the legal frameworks, organisational solutions and service design in Nordic care services vary so much that the concept of 'Nordic model' is problematic. In elderly care, for instance, the level of resources and institutional support are so different that no distinct 'Nordic model' can be discerned (Szebehely 2003). When a comparative study of socially defined care was made using social service universalism and care defamilialisation as key dimensions, it supported this interpretation (Rauch 2007). Elderly care is a particularly good example of the problems of discussing a 'Nordic model' in socially defined care. Denmark is the only Nordic country that has introduced a service guarantee for frail elderly (Rauch 2007). Its investment in home care is clearly above the average Western European and the Danish service intensity is at a high level. In comparison, Norway achieves a high level of elderly care universalism only in the case of securing access. In terms of service intensity Norwegian home care is comparatively low. The Swedish elderly care system, again, has such heavy restrictions of access that 'it is far from being particularly universal or defamilialising' (Rauch 2007, 260). Figures from Finnish elderly care place it in the same 'non-Nordic' group with Sweden. Finnish home care for the elderly is slightly higher in volume but lower in intensity than Swedish home care (Kröger 2007).

With reference to *the institutional level* as described above, it might be correct to argue that a Nordic 'model' to define citizen's right to elderly care never existed. However, we argue that at *the broader cultural level* the idea of a Nordic model is relevant. In debates on international politics, the Nordic countries were singled out as a special case in the 1930s (Christiansen & Markkola 2006) and in the post-war period of the Cold War, Nordic collaboration offered a unique framework for voluntary policy exchanges and learning (Allardt et al. 1981, Kettunen 2006). In previous literature, the foundation for the shared Nordic welfare vision or ethos has also been linked to a sense of community, a deeply felt *'felleskap'* in the Nordic societies that is rooted in ancient civic culture (Hernes 1988). For feminist legal scholars arguing in this vein, the political project of building a universalist welfare state expressed a *communitarian* (as distinguished from liberal) *ethos* that came to give direction to the development of its legal and institutional framework (e.g., Svensson et al. 2005). What emerged was a broadly shared vision of aiming at accessible and equitable, socially defined care on the basis of social rights. The vision that guided the expansion of the Nordic welfare states was concerned with 'shaping the state into a political vehicle aimed at achieving equality and prosperity' (Allardt et al. 1981). Historical scholarship shows, however, that the self-conscious use of the term 'Nordic model' is of late date. The academic usage dates back to the 1960s and the political to the 1980s. At that time welfare policies in the Nordic countries were already subject to revisions (Christiansen & Markkola 2006, 9). Here we maintain that in the post-war period the Nordic communitiarism evolved as an egalitarian and to some extent *care-friendly* ethos.

Despite such empowering dynamics, it is important not to portray this period as a lost 'golden age' for socially defined care. The recognition it acquired was always ambiguous and in some cases meagre, if compared with that given to, for example, medical needs or concerns for social security. It is also evident that when socially defined needs for care were recognised, hierarchies always remained, reflecting societal values about the group needing care. Day care for children and services for people in working-age who temporarily are in need of care emerged as more legitimate than those of the handicapped or the elderly, groups that, in an instrumentalist perspective, are of little or no importance to the productivity of society (Wærness 1980, 1984).

Because of the history of welfare policy convergence, the Nordic countries have provided a specific case for the literature on comparative social welfare (e.g., Esping-Andersen 1990). The Nordic countries have also become discussed from a gender perspective as countries where women's economic dependence of men has become targeted as a problem in the state arena (Sainsbury 1996, Lilja Mósesdóttir 2001, Pfau-Effinger 2004).

Such comparisons often treat their cases as fixed. However, the Nordic region has been subject to similar transformative social change as other regions of the world. Currently, the Nordic countries are nation states with open economies. The opening of economies began in the early 1980s as a response to supranational pressures to remove hindrances from the free trade (Bergh & Erlingsson 2006, Schienstock 2007).

Table I Background data on the Nordic countries

	POPULATION (MILLION)	BIRTHS PER 1,000 POPULATION	<15	65+	PERCENT URBAN	GNI PPP PER CAPITA (US $) 2006	POPULATION DENSITY PER SQ. KM
Denmark	5,5	12	19	15	72	36,110	127
Finland	5,3	11	17	16	62	34,810	16
Norway	4,7	13	19	15	78	43,920	12
Sweden	9,1	12	17	17	84	34,780	20
Western Europe	187	10	16	17	75	32,740	169

SOURCE: POPULATION REFERENCE BUREAU, WASHINGTON D.C, 2007.

When changes in the Nordic region are discussed, economic restructuring often emerges as a leading theme. Most importantly since the 1980s, political debates have questioned the viability of the Nordic welfare state, with reference to the dependence of the Nordic countries of the fluctuations of global markets. The argument is that in the global context, Nordic national economies need to be cost-effective and competitive in relation to other, historically less generous states. Another key argument concerns demographic change. The countries have small populations that are aging rapidly. Facts like those included in Table I above have been interpreted as an indication of the growing need for care services, the cost of which would bring a publicly funded welfare state to a fundamental crisis. This type of prognoses have provided the specific impetus for the critics of these historically so successful welfare states (Korpi & Palme 2003). However, if we consider the gross national income in purchasing power parity, we see no sign of a relative decline of the Nordic region (see Table I). In contrast, if this measure is taken as an indicator, all of these countries are among the richest in the world.

Reflecting the beneficial social development in the region, Nordic people can expect to live to become nearly 80 years of age, or in the case of most Nordic women, even older than that (Population Reference Bureau 2007). This means that the potential number of those in need of care is increasing at the same time as the traditional free labour force available to provide care informally has dwindled, as, in the long-term, all Nordic countries have become more or less examples of dual-provider models (Leira 1993, Lilja Mósesdóttir 2001, Pfau-Effinger 2004).

The care gap has further problematic dimensions: a large number of the people needing care live in areas where the 'pool' of potential caregivers is particularly small in relation to those in need of care. The persistent pattern of urbanisation is that of the old remaining in rural communities when the young move away. Consequently, while there is a high proportion of elderly also in the cities, a high proportion of the aged live in the more scarcely populated rural areas. As seen in Table I, in Finland, Norway and Sweden there is a combination of small population and large territory, a circumstance that challenges effective production of services (e.g., Copus 2007).

In all of the Nordic countries, the universalist welfare states issued policies aiming at creating mechanisms of solidarity between regions. These mechanisms have been threatened by the recent strive to decentralise the public sector (e.g., Copus 2007, 17–18). Equal regional development no longer represents as central value as before in the Nordic countries, giving rise to increasing within-country heterogeneity, for instance, in terms of access to services (Neil & Tykkyläinen 1998). There is Nordic research evidence suggesting that the frail elderly are cared differently, depending on whether they live in urban or rural areas, with the rural elderly being more dependent on informal care (Nordberg 2007). The quoted study suggests in part structural reasons, related to local disparities in service provision.

Table II Demographic data and estimates for population change

	Rate of natural increase (%)	Net Migration Rate per 1,000 Population	PROJECTED POPULATIONS (MILLIONS)		
			mid-2025	mid-2050	Projected Population Change 2007–2050 (%)
Denmark	0.2	2	5,6	5,5	1
Finland	0.2	2	5,6	5,7	9
Norway	0.4	5	5,2	5,8	24
Sweden	0.2	6	9,9	10,5	15
Western Europe	0.1	1	191	187	0

SOURCE: POPULATION REFERENCE BUREAU, WASHINGTON D.C, 2007.

It is interesting to reflect upon why the affluence of the region is not in greater extent reflected in the present ethos of welfare policy. Some experts identify a sense of austerity that fuels a process of welfare-state regress (Korpi & Palme 2003). The present projections for population change in the region offer some insight into the concerns that currently drive policy. The rate of natural increase is very low, suggesting acceleration of the pace of population aging. It is important to note, however, that the calculations are based on a very moderate level of immigration, also in the long term (see Table II). Furthermore, immigration is seen more often a challenge than a solution to the welfare state: for instance, current research emphasises the burden that the integration of the immigrants places on public resources (e.g., Nannestad 2007).

It is beyond our scope to deepen the discussion of the above-described macro-level developments or to speculate on their impact on the demand or supply of welfare services in general or socially defined care in particular. This background is offered to underline the fact that the social shaping of care work is tied to such larger developments. At the same time, it needs to be remembered that all prognoses, even the seemingly objective, of the structural, economic and social conditions of social care services in the future carry ideological and cultural underpinnings. Furthermore, even the most rigid structural conditions, such as future demographic developments, are constantly influenced by the political choices made by the decision makers of today. Most importantly, nothing can free us from the moral responsibility for how we approach the problems causing suffering and inequality today.

A Nordic ethos of care: an ambiguous history

The building of a welfare state is a piecemeal activity, characterised by multiple struggles and negotiations. Above we suggested that the recognition of socially defined care was a late addition to welfare policy and never as fully endorsed as other areas of social provision. Kari Wærness (1980) has presented a particularly powerful feminist critique, drawing attention to the above mentioned hidden assumptions on productivity in welfare policy. Furthermore, she argued that the care orientation associated with traditional femininity was commonly devalued and portrayed as irrational in the welfare state rhetoric (see also Eliasson & Szebehely 1991).

Instrumental rationality was always a salient element in welfare policy, and remained so even in the 1970s and the 1980s, when the rhetoric of 'having, loving and being' emphasised a humanistic approach to welfare (Allardt 1975). The emphasis on the values of democracy, solidarity and mutual responsibility helped, however, another, competing rationality, the *rationality of caring*, to claim some ground in the welfare state (e.g., Wærness 1980). The concept 'the rationality of caring' refers to a rationality that is contextual and descriptive, rather than formal and abstract. It recognises that good care builds on personal knowledge and certain ability and opportunity to understand what is specific in each situation where help is required (Wærness 2005, 25).

Finnish sociologist Raija Julkunen (1991) has pointed out that the existence of competing rationalities is itself a core feature of modernity. Rationality of caring is congruent with the modern ideas of motherhood that first emerged in the late

19th century bourgeois family. Reflecting the inherent gender hierarchy in modernity, the caring rationality is constantly at odds and threatened by the 'real', instrumental modernity (Julkunen 1991, 82).

There is a huge literature on the impact of the Nordic welfare state on gender relations, arguing that when the patriarchal state stepped in as a party into care, women were not emancipated to equality. However, an important shift occurred when private patriarchy was replaced by a public one (Hernes 1987, 1988). Women's full-time involvement in the labour market came to be most far-reaching in Finland (Pfau-Effinger 2004). There the organisation of paid care most steadily took the shape of occupations (e.g., Simonen 1990, Anttonen et al. 1994). From the point of view of care workers, the transformation of jobs into occupations can be seen as a beneficial process, but the change of gender culture in care has been more complex. Particularly efforts to professionalise care have been subjected to a feminist critique. Professionalisation has implied that masculine assumptions about rationality have structured the way care came to be framed in the welfare state (Wærness 1980, 1984, Johansson U. 1997, Henriksson 1998, Dahl 2000). Accordingly, the professionalisation of social care in the welfare state resulted in a series of separations and exclusions, where the 'irrational' and 'dirty' aspects of care became framed as *non-professional* and therefore inferior work (Gough 1987, Widding-Isakssen 1994, Tedre 1999, Dahle 2003).

Alongside with the cultural critique of professionalism it is important, however, to consider the impact of the universalist welfare state on the institutional matrix surrounding care work. In the public care services, care workers gained new occupational mandates that do not exist in the conditions of the market (e.g., Wærness 1984, Simonen 1990, Evertsson 2000). In the institutional context of the 'service state', the professionalism of occupations providing welfare services came to be attached closely to the state and its policies (Johansson S. 1997). It has been argued that the equality-driven *welfare*

ethos supported the institutionalisation of occupational jurisdictions in care and that this ethos empowered both users
and members of the professional groups providing the services (Henriksson et al. 2006). While social inequalities were not
erased, they were alleviated through both organisational and
cultural change in the 1970s and 1980s and the position of
women-dominated occupations improved in relation to the
professions that were traditionally male (Julkunen 1991). For
the universalist welfare state, education emerged as the key
strategy of reform in the care sector. However, the academisation of nursing has been more prominent development than
that of socially defined care (Johansson 2002).

The rationality of efficiency

The last quarter century has been marked by the ascension
of neoliberalism—market deregulation, state decentralisation, and reduced political intervention in national economies (Campbell & Pedersen 2001). Since the 1980s, the Nordic
welfare regimes have been reordered under the influence of
this ideology. As a consequence, the professional mode of organising work has been challenged by managerialism that
builds on implementing ideas from business management
to the production of welfare services. Influenced by the concerns raised by conservative governments in the United States
and the United Kingdom, policy makers everywhere in the
high income countries and in the Nordic countries adopted
such models. Different variants of organisational models that
separate the producer and the provider in service production
were in the year 2003 implemented in 82 % of the Swedish
municipalities and in one third of the Danish municipalities.
In Norway, only one in ten municipalities has adopted such
models. However, as the first municipalities to implement the
idea were the big cities, in 2004 already a half of the population lived in areas where that model was used (Vabø 2005).

The neoliberal turn constituted what was identified as 'a
break in the professional project of the welfare state' (Julkunen

1994) or 'the market professional discourse' (Hugemark 1994). From the beginning, the managerialist attack on welfare policy hit care occupations more severely than other welfare professions (Julkunen 1991). In the Nordic context care workers in paid care emerged as a key target for policies aiming at increasing the effectiveness of the public sector due to their large numbers and the key roles they play in the provision of publicly-funded care services. Managerialism in the care sector constitutes a new disciplinary order to be imposed on paid (and unpaid) care providers. In cultural terms, the reconfiguration of the care sector is expressed in new rules and vocabularies, borrowed from business management, that emphasise quality control and effectiveness. In public discourse, economists became the experts in questions addressing the efficiency of the welfare sector (Hugemark 1994, Julkunen 2001).

The efficiency drive has deep-going consequences but these are not always easy to detect. On the basis of her observations from all four of the countries, Mia Vabø (2003) argues that the rationality of caring orientation of elderly care personnel, both care managers and care workers, at present may contribute to the concealment of the defective steering power of the reforms. Rationality of caring is one of the cultural resources that the managers of the relatively powerless groups of care workers can exploit. This inward management style overstretches the capacity of the workers and creates an environment which is not supportive or caring of individual members of the staff (Davies 1992, Wrede & Henriksson 2005, Wrede 2008).

Nevertheless, the associated changes are complex and culturally embedded. Recent scholarship shows that neoliberalism has resulted in much more diverse and contested changes than was appreciated by the early critics. There is no convergence toward a common set of neoliberal institutions, nor are states unable to influence the direction of change (Campbell & Pedersen 2001). Accordingly, the Nordic countries differ in terms of how pervasive a shift the rise of neoliberalism has been in the respective public policy. The two extremes appear to be Denmark and Finland. The impact of neoliberalism on the Danish public sector has from the perspective of the care sector been characterised as New Public Management 'Light' (Dahl 2004). Even within elderly care, our critical case, a system corresponding to the image of a Nordic model continues to be at place: a service guarantee exists and home care is provided free of charge (Rauch 2007, 258). On the other hand the organisation of, for instance, elderly home care is clearly structured along managerialist ideas also in Denmark (Vabø 2003). The other Nordic states do not measure up to Denmark's level in elderly care. In the cited comparison of elderly care services, Norwegian elderly care 'only to a certain extent' corresponded to the idea. With the stated criteria, both Sweden and Finland fail to come even close a Nordic model, as both have cut services heavily, narrowing down their scope and intensity and no service guarantee exists.

Finland appears to be farthest away from this ideal, even though the differences to Sweden are complex. However, in terms of service intensity, Finland lags behind.[1]

Increasing inequalities in access to services and social security has led several Finnish experts to polemically characterise the ideological change as a shift from the welfare state to the 'competition state' (Heinonen 1999, Sipilä 2005).[2] Other experts emphasise that expenditure in the social sector has not decreased and that the currently 'internationally acclaimed' Finnish model has been successful in combining economic growth, education, employment and social policy, as well as transition to knowledge society and sustainable development (Saari 2006, Schienstock 2007).

In Sweden and Norway the impact of neoliberalism has been discussed in less pessimistic terms than in Finland. In Norway, for instance, a recent book argues that changes in the scope of services are much less radical than is often appreciated, suggesting a great degree of stability in Norwegian government (Mydske et al. 2007). It also needs to be kept in mind that Norway did not follow the Nordic model in socially defined care to the same extent as the other countries (Rauch

2007). While the level of services has not generally been cut in Norway, also there neoliberal ideas have been implemented by deregulating public services and improving the economic efficiency of the public sector (Vabø 2005, Mydske et al. 2007). Similarly, when the stability of the Swedish welfare state is discussed (Bergh & Erlingsson 2006), it is social security and not social care that is in focus. In that macro perspective, welfare state resilience is commonly raised as the relevant interpretation, with reference to social security systems such as pensions (e.g., Taylor-Gooby 2001). Studies of elderly services present a different picture of the resilience of the Swedish model (Rauch 2007). Furthermore, as already indicated above, managerialism has commonly been implemented in the Swedish public sector, suggesting, as in the case of the other countries, a cultural change where the rationality of efficiency has become a salient logic in formerly socially defined care. In words of Hanne Marlene Dahl (2005), a changing ideal of care may very well be a form of retrenchment.

Education as a strategy for regulating care

While the ideas about organisation of care are one important influence on care work as well as on care workers and care recipients, the ideas concerning education are another influence of equally vital importance. In all the Nordic countries, education emerged as a key strategy for regulating the care sector when training programmes for the assistant groups were established in the post-war period. From the beginning, these were closely connected to hospitals or nursing homes, and they all seem to have had good recruitment (Høst 2006). Particularly many adult women with families were interested in these so-called 'lower-skill' jobs. For them the expanding care sector offered secure and often flexible jobs. This was particularly true for socially defined care where the requirement for formal competence was late to appear, particularly in the case of elderly home care (Wærness 1980, Simonen 1990, Törnquist 2004). Even in the universalist welfare state, it was common that care workers in elderly home care only had taken short training courses (Szebehely 2003).

The care work educations became gradually more integrated into the national education systems, a development that resulted in increasing expectations on formal competence in socially defined care. The rise of the universalist welfare state played a central role also for this development (Johansson 2002). A key institutional change that resulted from these developments was that the regulation of care educations became administratively detached from the planning of the care sector at the level of central government. In Finland this took place in 1968 (Klemelä 1999, 295). A similar reform was implemented also in Norway (Høst 2006). In Sweden this institutional arrangement was reached through the 1977 reform of higher education which aimed at an integration of all vocational training into the higher education.

Welfare states of the Nordic type invested large resources in education, including vocational education (Hega & Hokenmeier 2002). There are, however, both national systems and the style and the extent of integration vary. Care workers have the shortest education in Sweden and longest in Finland (Kröger 2007). Yet in Sweden the educational base of care managers has undergone academisation (Johansson 2002). The most far reaching integration is found in Sweden where the vocational educations have been replaced by broad educational programmes which do not give any kind of vocational specialisation or title (Törnquist 2004, Høst 2006). In the other end, we find the Danish SOSU-programmes which are established as an autonomous system parallel to the national vocational education system. In spite of this outside position the SOSU-programmes are coupled to the nurse education. However, they have also sustained strong ties to the field of work (Ahrenkiel et al. 2006, Høst 1996). While the Danish education reform has been judged as quite successful, the Swedish is seen as problematic in several ways. The education has problems in recruiting young people and the relevance of the education is questioned as well (Ahnlund & Johansson

2006). Norway and Finland hold a position in between these examples. Common for all countries, however, are tendencies towards a large distance between the education and the social care and nursing sector. This may in turn threaten to lower the standard of the practical skills if not further education is arranged in the workplace. However, in periods of retrenchment there is a risk that it is not given priority.

In a situation where the changes in the demographic structure, discussed above, point towards a fast increase in the demand for care and nursing staff, recruitment is problematic in all Nordic countries. Few people choose to work in elderly care. The efforts to turn the education programmes into adolescent education in order to increase the formal level of qualifications among personnel in elderly care have met large problems in all Nordic countries, and the status of the programmes seems to decrease (Høst 2006). These trends make the consideration of the state of care work culture and the structural constraints shaping it particularly relevant.

Care work in crisis

Summing up, greater efficiency has emerged as a key concern for the policy makers in the Nordic welfare states. Our argument is that the pursuit of efficiency needs to be critically addressed, as a cultural shift in care work that has many different expressions and dimensions. According to Stein (2001) efficiency has become a cult when we no longer ask the questions 'efficient at what?' or 'for whom?' This 'cult of efficiency' (c.f., Stein 2001) is based on instrumental rationality, as the present efficiency drive is abstract and lacks consideration for context and the particular. In our effort to reclaim the Nordic ethos of care, we attempt to draw attention precisely to these considerations.

This book contributes to a bottom-up examination of at least three related expressions of the cultural crisis of care work that all have consequences at the structural level of care institutions:

1) crisis of recruitment of personnel for care work,
2) crisis of educational models and knowledge base
3) crisis of lacking valuation of care work.

We are aware of a great *intra-country* as well as *inter-country* variance that extends to the level of the workplace and to educational programmes. Thus, we do not talk of one 'Nordic care work crisis', but of a set of multiple crises in the complex and multilevel field of care. We wish to address the multitude of *disconnections* that are currently occurring, expressed, for instance, at the macro level in the lack of coordination between educational policies and service policy. We find evidence of further disconnections at the meso and micro level between management ideas lacking rooting in the care context and the practical organisation of care work.

We believe that the analysis of the current trends shaping paid care work in the Nordic countries is of interest not only to a wide Nordic audience but to both academics and others interested in paid care work, residing outside of the Nordic countries. The economic, political, structural and cultural challenges the Nordic countries have faced and face so acutely in coming years are shared by most of the high-income countries. Policymakers making decisions about the future direction of care service and education policy are placed as the 'switchmen of history' who determine whether they choose to reclaim socially defined care or whether that part of the unique Nordic ethos is lost.

Aim and scope

This book grew out of a Nordic research network that initially focused on the recruitment crisis in care work. The collaboration took the shape of series of workshops, where we discussed concepts and interpretations and exchanged stories and information about trends and developments in the individual countries. It is through these exchanges that the notion of crisis in care work first took shape as a meaningful frame for a shared book.

By collecting the qualitative evidence about the value of socially defined care and its current predicament, we the editors wish to reclaim that specific Nordic ethos that made room for the rationality of caring. We do *not* make a claim for the reinstatement of some specific model to organise care, even though we share a view that key services should be publicly funded and provided on the basis of a social right. What we defend here is the specific humanistic Nordic ethos that gave impetus to a policy convergence underpinning *care-friendly* as well as *care-worker friendly* institutional developments in the welfare services.

The book covers developments in care work in four Nordic countries—Denmark, Finland, Norway and Sweden, building on a number of qualitative case studies that together provide so-called 'thick description' of the world of care. We believe that by bringing these insights together we can provide a richer and more dialogic account than would be possible, had we confined ourselves to more specifically defined themes and sought to redact the research materials into comparable figures.

Several chapters in this book examine the impact of the cultural shift associated with managerialist reforms. Some chapters examine the shaping of formal care work at the macro level but the majority of chapters focus on the grassroots level of care where the two competing rationalities create a tension. Our shared view is that it is particularly important to help voices from the grassroots to be heard, to challenge the currently dominating discourse that often presents the structuring of the services as a 'rational' campaign of streamlining care in an effective way (Vabø 2003, 85).

The studies that form the foundation for the book have their separate, independent histories and do not advance a shared interpretation or agenda. The aims of the different chapters and authors vary: some of us seek to make *the lived experience of care workers or those cared for somehow visible*, while others focus more on uncovering *how politics structure* that *experience*. But even though interpretations may vary, these analyses are shaped by a shared conviction about *the value of the human experience*, be it that of the person cared for, or the care worker.

In order to emphasise the aim of the book to offer culturally and institutionally embedded accounts, the book is organised in four parts, one for each larger Nordic country[3]. Hopefully, our decision to keep the countries separate helps the reader to grasp a more multifaceted understanding of the dynamics in the similar but not identical countries. The more detailed presentations of the chapters are given in the short introductions found in the beginning of each part.

Each country section has an emphasis on some specific analytical dimension. In the Danish part, this broad perspective is learning, reflecting the background of the authors in education studies. In the Finnish part, attention to welfare state restructuring underpins sociological analyses of the shaping of work and occupations in the context of service policy. The chapters in the Norwegian part are inspired by the modernisation perspective and focus on long-term developments in care occupations. Finally, the Swedish part most consequently focuses on elderly care as a social service, developing the analysis primarily from the point of view of social care research.

Notes

1 Finland was not included in Rauch's study, but comparable data from other sources (Szebehely 2003, Kröger 2007) allows us to discuss it together with the other countries.
2 The concept 'competition state' was introduced by Philip Cerny (1990).
3 Unfortunately we did not have contacts to Iceland at the time when this book project was launched.

References

Ahnlund, P. & Johansson, S. (2006) Omvårdnadsutbildning som mål eller medel? *Socialvetenskaplig tidskrift* 13(3), 212–227.
Ahrenkiel, A. G. et al. (1996) *Evaluering af de grundlæggende social- og sundhedsuddannelser.* København. Amtsrådsforeningen: Kommunernes landsforening og Undervisningsministeriet.

Allardt, E. (1975) *Att ha, att älska, att vara. Om välfärd i Norden*. Lund: Argos.

Allardt, E., Andrén, N., Friis, E.J., Gíslason, G., Sparre Nilsson, S., Valen, H., Wendt, F. & Wisti, F. (Eds) (1981) *Nordic Democracy. Ideas, Issues, and Institutions in Politics, Economy, Education, Social and Cultural Affairs of Denmark, Finland, Iceland, Norway, and Sweden.* Copenhagen: Det danske selskab.

Anttonen, A., Henriksson, L. & Nätkin, R. (1994) *Naisten hyvinvointivaltio*. Tampere: Vastapaino.

Anttonen, A., Baldock, J. & Sipilä, J. (Eds) (2003) *The Young, the Old and the State. Social Care Systems in Five Industrial Nations*. Cheltenham: Edward Elgar.

Bergh, A. & Erlingsson, G. (2006) Resilience through Restructuring: Swedish Policy-Making Style and the Consensus on Liberalizations 1980–2000. *Ratio Working Paper 110*. The Ratio Institute: Stockholm.

Campbell, P. & Pedersen, O. (Eds) (2001) *The Rise of Neoliberalism and Institutional Analysis*. Princeton: Princeton University Press.

Cerny, P. (1990) *The Changing Architecture of Politics*. Sage Publications: London and Newbury Park.

Christiansen, N.F. & Markkola, P. (2006) Introduction. In Christiansen, N. F., Petersen, K. Edling, N. & Haave, P. (Eds) (2006) *The Nordic Model of Welfare. A Historical Reappraisal*. Copenhagen: Museum Tusculanum Press.

Copus, A. (Ed.) (2007) *Continuity or Transformation? Perspectives on Rural Development in the Nordic Countries*. Stockholm: NordRegio.

Dahl, H.M. (2000) *Fra kitler til eget tøj: Diskurser om professionalisme, omsorg og køn*. Århus: Politica.

Dahl, H.M. (2004) A View from the Inside: Recognition and Redistribution in the Nordic Welfare State from a Gender Perspective. *Acta Sociologica* 47(4), 325–337.

Dahl, H. M. (2005). A changing ideal of care in Denmark: A different form of retrenchment? In Dahl, H. M., & Eriksen, T. R. (Eds) *Dilemmas of Care in the Nordic Welfare State*. Aldershot: Ahsgate.

Dahle, R. (2003) Shifting boundaries and negotiations on knowledge: interprofessional conflicts between nurses and nursing assistants in Norway. *International Journal of Sociology and Social Policy* 23(4/5), 139–158.

Davies, C. (1992) Gender, history and management style in nursing: towards a theoretical synthesis. In M. Savage and A.Witz (Eds) *Gender and Bureaucracy*. Oxford: Blackwell Publishers.

Eliasson, R.-M. & M. Szebehely (1991) Äldreomsorgens särart och särbehandling. *Socialmedicinsk tidskrift* 68(2–3), 69–77.

Esping-Andersen, G. (1990) *The Three Worlds of Welfare Capitalism*. Cambridge: Polity Press.

Evertsson, L. (2000) The Swedish Welfare State and the Emergence of Female Welfare State Occupations. *Gender, Work and Organization* 7(4), 230–241.

Gough R. (1987) *Hemhjälp till gamla*. Arbetslivscentrum: Stockholm.

Hega, G. & Hokenmaier, K. (2002) The welfare state and education: A comparison of social and educational policy in advanced industrial societies. *German Policy Studies* 2(1), 2002.

Heinonen, J. (1999) Kohti yksilöllistä pirstoutumista vai demokraattista yhteisöllisyyttä? *Yhteiskuntapolitiikka* 65(3), 270–278.

Henriksson, L. (1998) *Naisten terveystyö ja ammatillistumisen poltitiikka*. Tutkimuksia 88. Helsinki: Stakes.

Henriksson, L., Wrede, S. & Burau, V. (2006) Understanding professional projects in welfare service work: Revival of old professionalism? *Gender, Work & Organization* 13(2), 174–192.

Hernes H. (1987) *Welfare State and Woman Power*. Universitetsforlaget: Oslo.

Hernes, H. (1988) Scandinavian citizenship. *Acta Sociologica* 31(3), 199–215.

Hugemark A. (1994) *Den fängslande marknaden. Ekonomiska experter om välfärdsstaten*. Lund: Arkiv förlag.

Høst, H. (2006) *Kunnskapsstatus vedrørende rekruttering og utdanning til pleie- og omsorgstjenestene i nordiske land*. Notat 4–2006. Rokkansenteret: Universitetet i Bergen.

Johansson S. (1997) Hälsoprofessioner i välfärdsstatens omvandling. In E. Sundin (Ed.) *Om makt och kön i spåren av offentliga organisationers omvandling* (pp. 69–102). SOU 1997:83. Stockholm: Fritzes.

Johansson S. (2002) *Den sociala omsorgens akademisering*. Liber: Stockholm.

Johansson U. (1997) Den offentliga sektorns paradoxala maskuliniseringstendenser. In Sundin, E. (Ed.) *Om makt och kön—i spåren av offentliga organisationers omvandling*. SOU 1997:83. Kvinnomaktutredningen. Stockholm: Fritzes.

Julkunen, R. (1991) Hoiva ja professionalismi. *Sosiologia* 28(2), 75–83.

Julkunen, R. (1994) Hyvinvointivaltiollisten professioprojektien katkos. *Tiede & Edistys* 19(3), 200–212.

Julkunen, R. (2001) *Suunnanmuutos. 1990-luvun sosiaalipoliittinen reformi Suomessa*. Vastapaino: Tampere.

Kettunen, P. (2006) The power of international comparison. A perspective on the making and challenging of the Nordic welfare state. In Christiansen, N. F., Petersen, K. Edling, N. & Haave, P. (Eds) *The Nordic Model of Welfare. A Historical Reappraisal*, pp. 31–65. Copenhagen: Museum Tusculanum Press.

Klemelä, K. (1999) *Ammattikunnista ammatillisiin oppilaitoksiin. Ammatillisen koulutuksen muotoutuminen Suomessa 1800-luvun alusta 1990-luvulle*. Turku: University of Turku.

Korpi, W. & Palme, J. (2003) New politics and class politics in the context of austerity and globalization: welfare state regress in 18 countries, 1975–1995. *American Political Science Review* 97(3), 425–446.

Kröger, T. (2007) Vanhuus, hoivatyö ja hoivaköyhyys. Presentation at Vanhuus, hoiva ja sosiaalityö –meeting, Verso, Lahti, 30/3/2007. verso.palmenia.helsinki.fi/asp/datastore/download.asp?ds_id=115&Krger+070330.pdf Retrieved January 23, 2008.

Leira, A. (1993) Mothers, markets and the state: A Scandinavian 'model'? *Journal of Social Policy* 22(3), 329–347.

Lilja Mósesdóttir (2001) *The Interplay Between Gender, Markets and the State in Sweden, Germany and the United States.* Aldershot: Ashgate.

Mydske, P.K., Claes, D.H. & Lie; A. (Eds) *Nyliberalisme—ideer og politisk virkelighet.* Oslo: Universitetsforlaget.

Nannestad, P. (2007) Immigration and welfare states: a survey of 15 years of research. *European Journal of Political Economy* 23(2), 512–532.

Neil, C. & Tykkyläinen, M. (Eds) (1998) *Local Economic Development. A Geographical Comparison of Rural Community Restructuring.* Tokyo: United Nations University Press.

Nordberg, G. (2007) *Formal and Informal Care in an Urban and a Rural Elderly Population. Who? When? What?* Stockholm: Karolinska institutet.

Pfau-Effinger, B. (2004) *Development of Culture, Welfare States and Women's Employment in Europe.* Aldershot: Ashgate.

Population Reference Burau (2007) *2007 World Population Data Sheet.* Washington D.C: Population Reference Bureau.

Rauch, D. (2007) Is there really a Scandinavian social service model? A comparison of childcare and elderlycare in six European countries. *Acta Sociologica* 50(3), 249–269.

Saari, J. (Ed.) (2006) *Suomen malli—murroksesta menestykseen.* Helsinki: Yliopistopaino.

Sainsbury, D. (1996) *Gender Equality and Welfare States.* Oxford: Oxford University Press.

Schienstock, G. (2007) From path dependency to path creation: Finland on its way to the knowledge-based economy. *Current Sociology* 55(1), 92–109.

Simonen, L. (1990) *Contradictions of the Welfare State, Women and Caring. Municipal Homemaking in Finland.* Acta Universitatis Tamperensis ser A vol 295. Tampere: University of Tampere.

Sipilä, J. (2005) Minkä instituutioiden varaan uskallamme turvamme rakentaa? *Sosiaaliturva* 93(9), 14–16.

Stein, J.G. (2001) *The Cult of Efficiency.* Toronto: Anansi.

Svensson, E.-M., Pylkkänen, A. & Niemi-Kiesiläinen, J. (Eds) (2004) *Nordic Equality at a Crossroads: Feminist Legal Studies Coping with Difference,* pp. 23–61. Aldershot: Ashgate.

Szebehely, M. (2003) Den nordiska hemtjänsten—bakgrund och omfattning. In M. Szebehely (Ed.) *Hemhjälp i Norden. Illustrationer och reflektioner.* Lund: Studentlitteratur.

Taylor-Gooby, P. (2002) The silver age of the welfare state: perspectives on resilience. *Journal of Social Policy* 31(4), 597–621.

Tedre, S (1999) *Hoivan sanattomat sopimukset. Tutkimus vanhusten kotipalvelun työntekijöiden työstä.* Joensuu: Joensuun yliopiston yhteiskuntatieteellisiä julkaisuja 40.

Törnquist, A. (2004) *Vad man ska kunna och hur man ska vara.* Diss. Lärarhögskolan i Stockholm: HLS Förlag.

Vabø, M. (2003) Mellan traditioner och trender. In M. Szebehely (Ed.) *Hemhjälp i Norden. Illustrationer och reflektioner.* Lund: Studentlitteratur.

Vabø, M. (2005) New Public Management i nordisk eldreomsorg—hva forskes det på? In: M. Szebehely (Ed.) *Äldreomsorgsforskning i Norden. En kunskapsöversikt* (pp. 73–111). TemaNord 2005:508.

Wærness, K. (1980) Omsorgen som lönearbete—en begreppsdiskussion. *Kvinnovetenskaplig tidskrift* 1(3), 6–17.

Wærness, K. (1984) The rationality of caring. *Economic and Industrial Democracy* 5(2), 185–211.

Wærness, K. (2005) Social research, political theory and the ethics of care in a global perspective. In H.M. Dahl and T. R. Eriksen (Eds) *Dilemmas of Care in the Nordic Welfare State. Continuity and Change* (pp. 15–32). London: Ashgate.

Widding-Isakssen, L. (1994) *Den tabubelagte kroppen. Kropp, kjøog tabuer i dagens omsorgsarbeid.* Bergen: Universtiy of Bergen.

Wrede, S. (2008) Educating generalists: flexibility and identity in auxiliary nursing in Finland. In E. Kuhlmann and M. Saks (Eds) (2008) *Rethinking professional governance. International directions in health care* (pp. 127–140). Bristol: Policy Press.

Wrede, S. & Henriksson, L. (2005) The changing terms of welfare service work: Finnish home care in transition. In H.M. Dahl & T. R. Eriksen (Eds) *Dilemmas of Care in the Nordic Welfare State. Continuity and Change* (pp. 62–79). London: Ashgate.

DENMARK

INTRODUCTION TO PART I

Crisis of Care in a Learning Perspective

Betina Dybbroe

Denmark presents some special features of the Nordic experiences of crisis of care. The crisis is profoundly shaped by the interrelatedness of: deteriorating quality *in* and *of* care; the lack of political strategies for the provision of care; and the lack of ability to attract and preserve qualified occupational groups in social and health care. The ethos of care has traditionally been that of equal access to and equal quality of public services. There has been a resistance to privatisation as well as to leaving responsibility for caring to families and to civil society. Since 2002–2003 this approach to care has been undergoing change. However, health care workers still remain strongly identified with the welfare state in Denmark.

In the following, I point out some of the contradictory and paradoxical developments unfolding in the field of social and health care in Denmark. Social and health care services and the caring sectors (in relation to the ill, disabled, and elderly, and to rehabilitation, reproduction etc.) have been expanding since the end of the 1990s (Pedersen 2005). Elderly care remains a major activity, amounting to 15 % of public service expenditures, with a yearly net increase of 1.6 % since 1995 (Pedersen 2004). In the year 2007, 203,000 persons received elderly care, amounting to an increase of 2.2 % per year since 1977. It is estimated that this figure will rise dramatically in the coming years due to the 'ageing society' (Strategiske Forskningsråd 2006, Meijer 2004).

Changes in politics of care

At present social and health care is politically constructed primarily as a social and health economy. All activities are measured with reference to the costs for society, instead of taking into account the welfare generated for society. This became visible when in 2006–2007 a reform of governance, financing and costs (*Strukturreformen*) took place, changing especially the structures of the social and health care sectors. The public, the NGOs representing the elderly and the patients, and the relevant trade unions expressed the need for developing the social and health care sectors. The government perceived its task differently, opting for solutions that lower the established standards. At the institutional level, leaders put pressure on the employees to perform at a lower standard, or 'worse' (Finansministeriet 2007, Ahrenkiel et al. 2007).

During the past five years Denmark has been moving towards a more neoliberal version of New Public Management. In the public sector, New Public Management now also includes privatisation, corporatism and more external production control, and a redistribution of resources from general economic frames and instead to specific targets. Within the organisation of care, this means that elderly people are no longer allocated time for care but are provided with specific, politically prioritised services. The most notable change, if compared with the New Public Management programmes of the 1980s and the 1990s, is the break with professional output control through performance measurements and quality management (Knudsen 2006) and stronger centralisation.

There is a contradiction between the way political discourses frame care work (focusing on change, transformation and the disruption of past procedures, attitudes and professional and occupational rationalities of work) and the professional interpretation of care work. Transformation is seen inside a horizon of *growth, renewal, rationalisation, discontinuity to the past and bettering* (Finansministeriet 2007). The quality of care must be improved, patients must get better, the flow must accelerate, routines have to be renewed, etc. The dominant political discourse is in conflict with the continuation of professional caring practices and with the rationality of care inherent in the *socially necessary practice* (Becker-Schmidt 2003) of managing birth, loss, decay, irrationalities and continuations of vital life processes of patients and clients. It creates a paradox for the caring occupations. Another paradoxical aspect, is that the dominant discourse of transformation is institutionally directed at making an impact on practice through described *things, tasks, procedures and manualisation* (Knudsen 2004), approached as artefacts or symbols. The work to be transformed, however, is conducted between humans and by humans, i.e. through subjective professional decisions and inside relations to citizens and individual persons. Care workers have to manage these conflicts and paradoxes of rationalities professionally in their day-to-day work as ambiguities of practice and with ambivalent approaches. A means to achieve this is by submitting oneself to the discourse of transformation of the social and health care system. Other means to achieve it is to defend the professional ethos and professional borders, i.e. also the working conditions of the professionals.

Professionalisation and deprofessionalisation in care work

The Danish Quality Model (being implemented in social and health care 2007–2008) outlines and instrumentalises the effort to control and make the Danish social and health system effective. The model has the notion of the social and health care worker as a performer to be regulated through risk management, standardisation and the manualisation of professional knowledge to the extent that the professional does not have to know very much. The guideline for the occupational groups in social and health care outlines negotiation, listening, humbleness and cost-consciousness as equally important as professionalism (Finansministeriet 2007). This can be understood in the perspective of dequalification and deprofessionalisation, as work is becoming less dependent on the learning and development of the care worker, and more dependent on political and institutionally directed constructions of caring practice.

The notion of quality in the model goes against the grain with the successful process of educational professionalisation that took place through the creation in 1992 of the *social and health care helper* with 14 months of education, and the *social and health care assistant* with an additional 18 months of education. These training programmes were flexibly integrated into the general professional educational system. Since the year 2001, social and health care assistants have been allowed also to continue their education, studying for a nursing degree. In 2007 the social and health care assistants acquired authorisation that qualifies them both for hospital work and for work in elderly care. In contrast to the other Nordic countries, the assistants have had access to all types of nursing work, and their real competencies have been greatly acknowledged. Approximately 60 % of the assistants work in elderly care and 40 % in hospitals (Pedersen 2004). Through the national educational reform, the so-called CVU reform, nursing education has become integrated into the general programme of higher education. A bachelor's degree was established, and Centres of Professional Knowledge set up in order to develop a professional knowledge base in nursing.

Crisis of quality and the declining interest in care work

The rhetoric of the Danish Quality Model as well as the politically negotiated Quality Reform of 2007 emphasise the need for developing a better quality of care. Paradoxically, however, the rhetoric does not acknowledge and try to come to grips with the sources of the crisis of quality of care. Yet there are clear indications of deteriorating quality of and in care for the sick, elderly and disabled. Furthermore, the quality of working life has deteriorated, with consequences for the subjective meaning of work for the social and health care workers in these sectors. Many care workers in elderly care have to leave the workforce, because they are worn out before the usual retirement age (Hansen 2006). A recent inquiry into job satisfaction in elderly care showed that 60 % of the employed, less than 40 years of age, wanted to move to another job (FOA 2007). Only 50 % of social and health care assistants and helpers remain in the sector until retirement (Pedersen 2004).

An even more serious problem is that these jobs are becoming less popular amongst all occupational groups in care. There is a shortage of qualified workers in both nursing and social and health care. Approximately 2000 nursing jobs were vacant in January 2008 (1500 in January 2007) according to statistical information from the Union of Nurses (DSR 2007). Approximately 20 % of the jobs for qualified social and health care workers were filled with unskilled personnel in 2007 according to the Danish Confederation of Public Employees (FOA 2007). The need for social and health care workers is estimated to be at least 8000 more in the coming 10 years (Finansministeriet, 2007), excluding the positions presently filled by lesser skilled workers. In contrast, the current political strategy of the government addresses the need for a better quality of care by downplaying qualifications. The focus in recruitment is on lower skill groups and on the reorganisation and revision of care work, aiming at an increasing delegation of work to lower skill groups.

The social and health care occupations constitute groups that are fundamental to the creation and maintenance of welfare. The centrality of these occupations to welfare is not only related to the quantity of care receivers and the broad range of services provided, but also to the professional identities and qualifications of the social and health professionals and care workers. The professional qualifications of the social and health care workers correspond to the political and ethical standards of the Nordic welfare model. Furthermore, people in these occupations have identified themselves professionally with that model. Therefore the present recruitment crisis in Denmark is an important part of the crisis of welfare services.

Learning in care

The following three chapters, constituting the Danish section of this book, are examples of research into care as work and working life from the perspective of practice and the subjectivity of the care worker. This has been part of qualitative learning research into changes in the welfare-creating sectors and occupations that has been carried out at Roskilde University over the last 15 years. The three contributions conceptualise *learning* as an integral part of the working of the individual, and of the collective working environment. The concept of learning connects the experiences of the worker as a learner with her expectations for the future, both as an individual and as a member of a collective group of workers/professionals. A horizon of expectations is created from experience. The articulation and activation of this horizon enables specific steps in learning. However, the possibilities for such articulation and activation are dependent on the historical and cultural context and the specific *learning space* occupied by the worker. The learning space is actively created through a process of framing. Framing is shaped by power structures, but also by the activity of the agents/learners. The learning concept has its roots in the concept of subjective and collective horizons of experiences and learning (Ziehe 1998) that suggest different forms of learning, understanding and action.

The three chapters aim at creating knowledge about the practices and practitioners in care from a psycho-societal perspective in order to analyse the impediments to and possibilities of learning and becoming active agents of change in care.

Chapter 1 by *Betina Dybbroe* focuses on processes of occupational identification and learning in nursing and points out how these are framed through a process involving political, social and structural factors. Placing the spotlight on the experiences of three nurses, Dybbroe argues that paradoxes in work in the health sector create paradoxes of learning that dismantle learning spaces within work.

In Chapter 2 *Anne Liveng* analyses everyday interactions in elderly care from the perspective of social and health care helpers. The analysis demonstrates that subjective meaning in care is a prerequisite for not only quality in care, but also the willingness and the ability of care workers to stay in care work. Liveng shows how impediments to creating meaning and strong occupational identifications in work are related to hierarchical structures framing care work.

Chapter 3 is by *Helle Krogh Hansen* who considers the space for self-reflection and learning in elderly care in all three occupational groups found in Danish elderly care: social and health care helpers, assistants and nurses. Through the perspective of experiential learning and practice-based knowledge, Krogh Hansen probes into the possibilities of learning in care work, arguing that such possibilities are presently unused and downplayed. Thus Krogh Hansen illuminates how the occupational groups might become agents of change in care through the organisation of the everyday practice of elderly care as a learning environment seen from a lifelong learning perspective.

References

Ahrenkiel, A., Dybbroe B. & Sommer, F. (2007) *DSR tillidsrepræsentant i et forandret sundhedsfelt*, Roskilde: Roskilde University.

Becker-Schmidt, R. (2003) Introduction, and theorizing gender arrangements. In R. Becker-Schmidt (Ed.) *Gender and Work in Transition, Globalization In Western, Middle and Eastern Europe*. Opladen: Leske & Budrich, (pp. 7- 48).

DSR (2008) The Danish Nurses' Organization. www.dsr.dk/PortalPage. aspx?Menu/itemID=10

Finansministeriet (2007) *6 skarpe om kvalitetsreformen*, Copenhagen: Sekretariatet for Ministerudvalget.

FOA (2007) The Danish Confederation of Public Employees www.foa.dk/ sw7255

Hansen, H. K. (2006) *Ældreomsorg i et pædagogisk perspektiv*. Ph.d.-afhandling. Roskilde: Roskilde universitetscenter.

RUC Statistics from https:\\indberetninger.uvm.dk/pls/www.ndb

Knudsen, M. (2006) Performance Measurements performer selv. *Social Kritik—Tidsskrift for Social Analyse og Debat*, nr. 104 (maj), 6–19.

Kvalitetsreform (2007) *På vej mod en kvalitetsreform*, Kvalitetsreform— Sekretariatet for ministerudvalget, http://www.kvalitetsreform.dk/ page.dsp?page=315 Retrieved in October 2007.

Meijer, M. (2004) Forklædt som ældrebyrde. *Social Kritik—Tidsskrift for Social Analyse og Debat*, nr. 94 (juni), 56–59.

Pedersen, E. B. (2004) *Social- og sundhedshjælpere og –assistenter. Antal, flow og årsager til frafald under og efter endt uddannelse.* Arbejdsmedicinsk klinik, Bispebjerg Hospital, FOR-SOSU rapport nr. 1. Copenhagen: AMI.

Strategiske Forskningsråd (2006) *Det aldrende samfund*, Videnskabsministeriet, Copenhagen.

Tronto, J. (2004) Care as the work of citizens: A modest proposal. In K. Wærness (Ed.), *Dialogue on Care*. Bergen: Bergen University.

ONE

A Crisis of Learning, Professional Knowledge and Welfare in Care

Betina Dybbroe

This chapter contributes to the understanding about the crisis in paid care work in the Nordic countries by highlighting the crisis of learning and professional knowledge in care in Denmark, here viewed as linked both to the critical conditions in and of care and to the crisis of recruitment. The theme of crisis of learning and professional knowledge concerns all four countries, as the ideology of New Public Management in its different versions has been universally implemented. In all of the Nordic countries, this meant taking practical steps towards creating an 'economy of health', in which strategies to improve and widen qualifications in health care are seen mainly as costs and not investments in the future welfare state. All of the Nordic countries therefore experience aspects of dequalification of the work force in the professional and semi-professional groups. The dequalification process has several implications, concerning the jobs themselves, the shortage of qualified social- and health care workers, as well as the failing recruitment strategies. The key consequence in focus here is the short supply of quality learning environments in the workplaces.

The chapter builds on two recent research projects on nursing (Andersen, Dybbroe & Bering 2004, and Ahrenkiel, Dybbroe & Sommer 2008) that shred light on the development of occupational identity and learning, closely linked to the changes in the conditions and the frames of the social and health care sectors. Here I explore the crisis empirically through subjective and intersubjective experiences and dynamics, relating these to the contextual and structural factors that actively contribute to the framing of education and learning in care.

Before exploring the learning crisis, I shortly discuss the long-term crisis in recruitment facing the Danish care occupations that has taken a turn during the last few years.

Recruitment crisis—a symptom

The recruitment crisis in Danish social and health care is currently both a public concern and a widely recognised problem among politicians. The number of graduates from the new social and health care educations (established in 1992) increased until the late 1990s, but a rapid decline began in the year 2000 (see table 1, see also Dybbroe 2003, Christiansen 2003). All care educations have lost in popularity among the young people, if compared with other educations for the young under 25, and recently this decline has accelerated. In the year 2005, the intake for nursing education decreased by 9 % if compared with the year before. This decline in intake coincided with renewed investments in enlarging the workforce in order to keep up with the public demand for elderly care and in an effort to expand hospital treatment (Pedersen m.fl. 2006). Consequently, the slight decrease in the number of graduates had a severe impact, with the number of non-qualified employees in elderly care increasing rapidly.

Table 1.1 Recruitment to the social and health care occupations in Denmark—central figures[1]

NUMBER OF INTAKES

	1992	1995	1999	2000	2001	2002	2003	2004	2005	2006	2007
SOSU-helper	5.309	6.588	7.321	6.966	6.457	6.471	6.244	6.449	6.516		
SOSU-assistant	1.655	3.471	4.197	4.340	4.064	3.201	3.442	3.224	3.391		
Nurse	2.435	2.880	2.694	2.628	2.785	2.768	2.871	3.080	2.850	3.002	2.729

NUMBER OF GRADUATES

	1992	1995	1999	2000	2001	2002	2003	2004	2005
SOSU-helper	3.930	4.695	6.828	5.964	5.480	5.275	3.621	4.616	4.695
SOSU-assistant	909	1.815	3.529	3.418	3.406	3.487	2.522	2.512	2.398
Nurse	1.732	1.697	2.048	1.884	1.932	1.920	1.867	1.953	2.604

(continue on next page)

NUMBER OF DROPOUTS

	1992	1995	1999	2000	2001	2002	2003	2004	2005
SOSU-helper	569	827	1.227	1.353	1.256	1.296	1.501	1.601	1.514
SOSU-assistantAssistant	151	400	834	738	822	724	723	766	751
Nurse	508	676	877	1224	885	917	923	826	844

SOURCE: MINISTRY OF EDUCATION 2003 AND 2007.
ON THE BASIS OF INSTITUTIONAL REPORTS TO STATISTICS DENMARK.

1 All figures are with some reservations as the method of compiling the statistics vary from year to year.

The proportion of dropouts in social and health care educations was traditionally at the same level as for other professional and semi-professional educations, holding at approximately 20 % (Pedersen, E.B., 2005). In recent years, however, the number of dropouts in care educations has been increasing drastically: The percentage to complete the social and health care helper education has decreased from 85 % to 75 % in the years 1996–2005. The percentage of dropouts from nursing education has been particularly high: 47 % in 2000, 32 % in 2003, 25 % in 2005, and 35 % in 2006.[1] While there are several background factors that in part explain the high level of dropouts, the numbers remain very high if compared with other fields. The overwhelming majority of dropouts happen during the clinical and institutional practice periods. This is a recent development and one that especially stresses the need to examine the learning possibilities and professional development in the workplaces.

There is further a notable decline in applicants with nursing as their first priority. Nursing education was in the 1970s and 1980s still one of the most popular educational choices of young women, whereas now only about 40 % of the applicants have nursing as their primary educational choice (Ministry of Education: Uddannelsesguiden, 2007). The declining interest coincides with the decrease in the volume of applicants. It is evident that the nursing profession has lost its former attraction among potential young recruits. However, the most important problem is the job dropout among the newly educated. The large proportion of dropouts in this stage is a shared problem in nursing and social and health care. Only a half of the newly educated social and health care assistants and helpers take jobs in this sector after graduation (Pedersen m.fl. 2006).

The recruitment crisis is aggravated by three factors: Firstly, it is difficult to change the strategies of the new cohorts of school leavers in a situation, where 25 % of the cohort does not acquire any vocational competence (Ministry of Education: Indberetninger om uddannelsessøgende 2003). The second factor is related to the current expansion of economy, giving rise to a stronger competition for the young well educated school leavers. Presently, all professional occupations providing welfare services are losing applicants. Less than 5 % of the young people in each cohort choose a social- and health care or pedagogical vocational education. The third factor is demographic and welfare-political, i.e. the rapid ageing of the society. A recent prospective estimation of the needed manpower, not taking changes in the demands and tasks for future work force into account, stated that, by 2015, the number of new health professionals needed is 9.400. An additional large number of new social- and health care workers are needed (FTF 2007 b).

A further concern is that it is becoming exceedingly difficult to meet the need for *qualified professionals*. A growing number of qualified professionals are leaving the sector. At the same time, an increasing number of young people lack the basic qualifications needed even to be able to gain access to the social and health care educations. The decreasing interest in these educations and the high number of workers and students leaving the sector is not, however, politically addressed (FTF 2007 b). Furthermore, the transition from education to work, vital for the shaping of a care worker's qualification, is currently largely ignored by policy makers. The key neglect in education policies is the lack of attention to the conditions for working practice and the life strategies of the young generations.

A qualification strategy for welfare?

Like the other Nordic countries, Denmark has made a sizable investment in the development of qualifications for care work. The occupational groups in these sectors mainly consist of three categories: 1) nurses and other health professions with a bachelor degree, 2) social and health care assistants with a recently established authorisation and a 2 ¾-year long education, and 3) social and health care helpers with 14 months of education and long practical experience. At present, one of the slogans uniting several political bodies, as well as some trade union organisations, is 'More hands to social and health care', indicating that what is lacking is practical caring labour. This discourse detaches care work from education, professions and formal qualifications.

The political focus is on attracting new labour-market groups to the jobs in social and health care sectors. In the background is the low level of unemployment in Denmark, 3,3 % in the year 2007 (Ministry of Education: Uddannelsesguiden, 2007). The current political discourse is narrowly framed by a labour market perspective and builds on a low ranking of jobs and educations in the social and health care sectors. As a result, the attractiveness of these jobs is declining among the traditional target groups for recruitment, forcing policy makers to direct recruitment to new, more peripheral and lower skill groups, and the contents of the jobs have to be revised so as to fit lower skill groups (Minister of Employment 2007). Paradoxically, at the same time as decision makers are focusing on 'more hands', the media is waging a separate debate about care, where scandals about quality in care in institutions are discussed in terms of the deterioration of quality of care and general conditions in these sectors. A number of revelations in the media of scandalous quality in the caring institutions in 2006–2007 created public and political critique of the ethics and standards of staff in health care institutions.

A critique from the trade unions representing the professional groups in the health care sector (nurses, physiotherapists etc.) demanded wider access to all the health educations, more possibilities for continued education, and further professionalisation as part of the solution to the recruitment crisis (Sundhedskartellet 2007). Their strongest argument was against lowering of professional standards. The unions demanded that the 'hands' need to be qualified and professionally educated. Investing in the professionals (i.e. nurses) as well as semiprofessionals (i.e. social and health care assistants) was suggested as part of the solution and not a part of the problem. Contradictory to this the government has opposed these claims, arguing for quality without further costs (Minister of Employment 2007).

Recent research supports the argument that there is a relationship between conditions in care work and the willingness and ability of care workers to stay in these jobs (e.g., Hansen 2006, Liveng 2007, Andersen & Dybbroe 2004, Wethje & Borg 2003). The research indicates that *conditions, structures and framing* in social and health care work, not the jobs and the work itself, are becoming exceedingly unattractive. The studies further suggest that care workers experience a threat against their *professional standards* (Baagøe Nielsen & Dybbroe 2008). At present, care workers do not have adequate possibilities, in the form of qualifications, learning possibilities, professional authority and working conditions, to properly perform the tasks that are expected of them. Research further indicates that public sector organisations are not able to organise learning possibilities for their employees (Gustavsson 2006). From this perspective, the recruitment of workers with lower qualifications than earlier has the potential only to accelerate the crisis.

But how are the inadequate possibilities for learning affecting knowledge, reflection and learning in the everyday life of care work? How are the professional identities of care workers changing due to changes in conditions and possibilities? And how do care workers today create meaning and the desire to stay on in the welfare-providing sector and in care work? These questions are the basis for an analysis and critique of the crisis in welfare provision. In the next section, I move on from the discussion about policy developments at the macro level to consider the developments in care work from the perspective of the people providing care. This provides insight into the ways *subjective horizons of experiences and learning* are composed and how these, in their turn, are related to the everyday life of care and nursing as well as other practices of life.

Learning to be professional

The life history of the care worker, including her experiences and knowledge, form her subjective context for learning. New demands, challenges and circumstances must fit in, be rejected, or change her knowing and life historical orientation. Experiences from the life history, not only as individual but as part of social and historical contexts shape the individual's horizon of expectations and knowledge,, forming her approach to work, working culture, learning and the workplace, i.e. forms her professional identification. Her experiences may be included or excluded in the culture, the organisation, the knowledge base of the actual work process. Her subjective horizon of experience will in part become meshed with the collective horizon of experiences and learning (Lorenzer 1980), that is, the collective 'ways' of doing, reflecting and developing practice, for instance of how to cope with death or handle an emergency. This will also include shaping common or generalised experiences and expectations: of what the nursing standard should be, about the meaning of welfare for patients and on the relation between care workers and politicians etc. Learning in the workplace will therefore include both adaptive and transformative processes, and the learning space can be seen to be more enabling or constraining learning (Ellström et al. 2008). Learning in the work place thus always has both an individual and a collective side.

In the following, I present an analysis of life-historical interviews with three nurses. Examination of these three different horizons of learning in care work helps me to high-light the crisis of learning and professional knowledge from different angles.

IDENTIFICATION AND A REFLEXIVE COMMUNITY

Birthe, who was interviewed in 2006, belongs to the one third of the nursing working population who is between 40–49 years of age (FTF 2007a). When Birthe became a nurse in the 1970s, nursing was in a rapid process of professionalisation, helping nurses to acquire a strong position on the labour market. For Birthe, adaptation to nursing practice and to the nursing community became intertwined with the building of a personal professional identity. Even though her learning process occurred in the context of an emancipatory project to improve the terms of employment for nurses, Birthe's identification with her occupation was ambivalent, as a revolt against the still central discourse of the occupation as "a calling".

The professional discourse of the time was full of tensions and contradictions, claiming a high level of professionalism both at the level of skills and in terms of moral and ethics, and in the nursing school that Birthe attended both sides were emphasised. Teaching bound theory together with practice so that theoretical themes were linked to specific areas of nursing work. Teachers in the nursing school had a mentor role for students, and apprentice-based learning played a big role. The relation between teachers and students was close, and occupational identification was built up as something similar to educational identity. The object of learning and work was the same, and work was introduced to students as a learning environment with no borders to school. This affinity of education and work helped Birthe to almost 'slide' into working as a graduate. She did not experience that transition as especially challenging or threatening.

> We were in the ward and we were one or two days in school, and what we learned in the classrooms, i.e. if we learned about the liver, then the teachers knew that it was related to other things and

> tried to tie it together so we could relate to it, and then we learnt that on a specific ward and section there was a patient, whose condition was like this and this, and we could go down and look around...

'The time it takes' was a guideline for how much emphasis should be given to showing students the processes of work and giving students insight into patients´ own experiences of illness. The latter were to be acquired by listening to the patients, implying a practice of locating patients whose condition would illustrate the theme the students worked on in the classroom. Birthe built a strong identification with her work, portraying herself as a 'craftswoman'. It is a part of her professional thinking that practice always has to be adequate to the task and the need.

> A carpenter will not saw crooked because he is in a rush, because then it won't fit into the next notch, will he? You have to, I think, for yourself, you owe to do a good piece of work and get a good result out of it...

Birthe's words illustrate the viewpoint of a strongly identified nursing worker who learns through the community of practice she is in, and who stresses proficiency in specific tasks, problems, methods of working, i. e. particular manners of working, that are perceived to be the right way etc. This style of learning has been identified as *adaptative learning* (Ellström et al. 2008) Although Birthe is an example of a learner formed through the older, more adaptive educational system, she has been able to continuously incorporate her own experiences, i.e. involving herself in transformative learning. She reacts against the contradictions in work, i.e, the discrepancy between the discourse about the important role of the patient, and the factual indifference towards the patient as a person and citizen. She finds it a big challenge to include patients, and will not accept asking patients how they feel, without time to do anything with the answer. In her early identification with the occupation she learned always to connect words with action. Therefore her biography is full of examples of workplaces she has criticised and left, and things she has tried to change in everyday practice.

In Birthe's experience, a regrettable change has occurred in her work situation.

> There is no education at the moment. Everything *has gone out*, everything is *back to zero*- no courses…there isn't any money to continue developing anything right now. I mean right now *we are standing still*, we are standing *absolutely still* …and maybe there are some things, where you could say, could that have been avoided, if we hadn't had to *dash on like that*

The phrasing is symbolic, drawing the picture of stopped movements (*standing absolutely still*), but also of time standing still (*back to zero*) and light that has *gone out*, implying that her present situation, as well as that of her colleagues, was best characterised by darkness, as expressed by the notion 'professional black-out' that she uses in the quote. At the same time there is a lot of *dashing* for something else, disconnected to learning and development. The rest of the interview conveys that she links this experience to changes in the workplace of more tasks and more complexity, larger work areas and self-financing units, as well as more hierarchical management. These new organisational and economic measures are framing work, and getting the care workers to move too fast, while at the same time they experience standing still in their own development.

From a learning perspective, Birthe and her colleagues are presently not part of a reflecting community, and their experiences of the changing situation are individualised and not shared. As a learner, Birthe is highly dependent on an enabling learning environment and when she is faced with a lack of expectations to maintain high quality she is at a loss, unable to keep the new experiences inside her horizon of experiences. Her own high standards and experience of making words into action are slowly pushed away from her perspective on everyday work. She feels constrained by the experience of a professional standstill. Neither the organisation, nor the care worker collective are able to secure her the experience of providing good care. Birthe expresses her fear that nurses in hospitals currently work under a too heavy time pressure. This fear contributes to the forming of her horizon for expectations of the future. She fears that work will become undignified. The space and time for learning are disappearing for her.

LIFE HISTORICAL EXPERIENCES CLASH WITH WORKING LIFE EXPERIENCES

The second nurse is Nanna who graduated in 1999. She was interviewed in 2004. She is one of the 12 % of the working nursing population who is under 30 years of age (FTF 2007a). Nanna was building her professional identity at a time of big transformations in social and health care work, and at a time of increasingly severe recruitment crisis. She remains among the two thirds of nurses who did not dropout during education or during the transition to work. She even wants to continue to work. Nanna is engaged both in her work and in her family and life outside of work. She interacts dynamically with her work, the patients, colleagues and the organisation and takes part in the transformation of the health sector, not just being reactive, but proactive. Like in many other life histories of young nurses, an open professional identification process can be identified in Nanna's account.

Commonly in life-historical interviews, informants use phrases that suggest identification with some of the important professional roles in nursing. In a previous study, we identified four common narrator positions expressing nursing roles: 'the very caring nurse', 'the housekeeper', 'the medical assistant' or the 'organiser and manager' (Andersen et al. 2004). Rather than positioning herself in this way, Nanna positions herself *against* such images:

> It's usually *nice girls*, that become nurses... well I do consider myself a nice girl, but I am also quite *coarse*, you know *I trample* on

people, and they *fall* straightaway. And of course I apologize if I have molested them, but you know, I haven't got that, I don't know if it's because I don't have that feeling of things… I really have that with the patients, there I am really very, but if I have an opinion about something, then I say it… but nurses are nice girls who say the right things and smile at the right places… and that's never really been my style, it's probably true, I am not really the epitome of a nurse.

Nanna confounds here two Danish proverbs:1) *trampling onto people's toes, and 2) people fall for me straight away*[2]. In other words, she is coarse and hurts people, but she is also close to people and they like her very much. The linguistic mix-up expresses her experiential mix-up. She feels pressure to conform to the role of the nurse, which to her means rejecting the way she 'really' is. Nanna refuses to be a 'nice girl', but at the same time, from her own perspective, she is an intimate and a good person and carer. Thus, she can preserve her dignity by positioning herself against the 'obvious' positions for nurses in the context of the hospital as patriarchal institution, while at the same time constructing a professional identity that meets professional standards.

Nanna's ability to transform the relevance of gender in the context of the hospital is possible only because she employs her life history as a context. She creates a transformative learning space at work by bringing in her societal experiences as a young woman and by drawing from the changed gender socialisation of her generation. Nanna is building a work role and a professional identity in an innovative and transformative way, without taking any professional identity for granted or as a preconception.

The 'nice girl' is a gendered stereotype that strongly has an impact on Nanna. Even though Nanna does not explicitly identify it, the symbolism of the ward as a home where the chief physician is the father and the nurses are daughters is the 'missing link' here. Patriarchy of the health system is however a strong and open reference in other parts of Nanna's story. From this perspective, Nanna is trying to do away with the 'nice daughters' in the hierarchy and establish a counter-professional identity. Nanna has three strong narratives of fighting against the hierarchy. The longest of these accounts is a story about protesting against management and organising a strike, the other two stories are about resisting male doctors. In these situations, Nanna articulated her expectation of being recognised as a partner in symmetrical relations at the workplace, but she was met with offences. One situation was an open professional argument that took place after a doctor had strongly corrected Nanna, in front of a patient, whom they had been working with. Nanna experienced the doctor's expectation that she would submit herself to his authority as next-to a violation, that for her was beyond acceptance.

> He had simply put me in a situation which was deeply disgraceful… where I confront him with it and say to him: you will never do that again in front of a patient, I will simply not allow it, I think it's so filthy… And point was taken, so actually it did better the relation to that doctor greatly.

Her action against the male doctor is a significant moment for Nanna, and as a learning experience it is an experimental practice that transcends 'normal' practice. Experimental practices take place in order to create a new balance between the desirable and non-desirable sides of a challenge that threatens subjectivity. Acting in a new way requires that one finds inner energy to do so. This sort of practice and experience can transform professional identity, and seems to have done so for Nanna. The story is thus one of her turning points, a significant experience of transformative learning, which has influenced her practice and her professional identity. However there are other aspects of working life in which Nanna does not find it so easy to act, in order to restore imbalances. She is confused as how she should understand the importance of her professional work, when following a strike against bad working conditions, the management forced the employed back to work. Here Nanna expresses her irritation with the double-sided messages about the value of care work that she perceives to be dependent on the context.

> I think *it* ought to be valued as highly as *they* actually do, when *we* are in a crisis… I mean then *we* are really indispensable… *we* shouldn't strike, because *that* won't do in relation to *our* patients, because actually *you* are really, really necessary in order to make *this* run. But on the other hand, [we] shouldn't be so necessary that *you* need to get any money for *it. That*'s a lot of bullshit!

The many positions and rationalities active in the workplace are present as voices in the inner dialogue taking place in Nannas narrative. Work is positioned as a thing *it,* and *this,* but it is also a *we,* as working identity. Nanna even expresses a threatened professional identification through the discrepancy between *you* and *it,* as she is giving voice to the management.

Nanna's account conveys ambivalence and dilemma of identification with her work. Which version of 'work' should she identify with? With the work that has high value for her personally, or with the low value her work is given in terms of salary? Or should she identify with the views of her patients? For Nanna it is necessary to work with patients, but in her view the management, the politicians and the public do not share the responsibility. The patients are thus constructed as the domain of the workers, '*your*' patients. Nanna's statement makes visible the gravity of the problems of the professionals when they, reacting to the double-sided messages of the management, find the different understandings of their work incompatible. Taking responsibility for the patients in a professional way may mean doing work of high value, in adequate conditions and frames, but it may also imply working with a concept of necessity, that is not professional and has low value. This type of paradox actively frames the learning space and shows how difficult it is to learn under such conditions. It upsets professional identification.

The importance of expansive and transformative learning spaces in the workplace is evident in Nanna's story. Currently, the context of care clashes with many of the expectations of care workers. Such clashes are made even more severe by the fact that the potential for learning is currently neglected. Assuming gender as well as professional symmetry, young nurses expect to have equal opportunities and rights. Furthermore, they expect opportunities for personal development and space for being, at the same time, an individual and a care worker. Nanna provides us an example of how, in this 'life-strategic' perspective, professional learning and knowledge in the workplace involves managing and creating conflict. Young care workers are met by contradictory demands for socialisation, in work and outside work The imbalance between these incompatible demands from the working culture and institutional context does not encourage the nurses or care workers to learn and create transformation.

CONTRADICTIONS IN WORK CREATING DILEMMAS OF LEARNING

Ditte who is a nurse in her thirties is one of the 30 % of the nursing working population between 30 and 39 years of age. She was interviewed in 2007. Ditte did her basic occupational education in the 1990s and has since taken two specialist educations in nursing and a number of long continued education courses, in all, amounting to seven years of professional nursing education. She is innovative in her approach to nursing and in learning, and she identifies with specialist as well as general tasks in nursing. She is an example of the young, well-educated nurses who are focused on developing nursing professionally in practice and not as research. However, she draws on the existing professional knowledge base:

> I will say as ordinary nurse, it demands, it really demands, that somebody sits down and keeps up with recent development, and reads the new PhD thesis. I don't think it is very interesting to work if your attitude is: we have never tried that before, it won't work. No, we have got to, we have got to develop ourselves and otherwise I don't find it interesting to be an employee.

Ditte has chosen to work as a basic nurse, with no specialist functions, because she identifies professionally with the clinical and basic elements of nursing (i.e. observation, mobilisation, communication and everyday hygiene):

> I have learnt [so much] about general care in the medical ward, and had all my anatomy revised by being here for two years. In anaesthesia we just stood there watching anaesthetics, and said, well, a little for that and a little for that, and really I didn't know what was happening and how the individual processes of the patients developed.

Workplace learning is of professional interest to Ditte, both in terms of teaching and tutoring colleagues and students in the workplace, and in relation to her own development as a practically professional nurse. In her view, professionalism is created through practice. It is here transformative and expansive learning takes place. In her job she has had the opportunity to become responsible for workplace education and learning in a larger area of the institution.

Ditte talks about how to recruit nurses to the medical unit where she currently works, and makes a contrast between her current work in general medicine, and the work she left in the anaesthetic ward:

> [Here] *I only work 8 hours at a time*. I used to be working both 16 and 24 hours, and I am not doing that again…so I am really happy about just having 8 hours, because although things may be *tough* here, then I do have, then it *does have an end*. And in that way I think you could recruit more, because in some ways, then it is, the way it goes on [in my old ward is like] a production unit, then it is *production*, production, production. There is *no development* of how you receive a patient, and who and what do we do with the anxious, and what we do with those that cannot have the mask. I mean there is nothing, there is production, production, production, and I think there could be some students you could attract to a medical unit, if they knew, that this is what it is about, and you will not be *hunted down*, when you get off work.

But in another part of the interview Ditte tells us about her present work in the medical unit:

There are never enough people on the job, a high percentage of absence due to illness, and what comes in first then… In the future I think we will become *hunted down*, you know, we are called in already any minute, if they are lacking people in duty. *People have to work 16 hours.* Those are the stories of old, but it isn't right that those things aren't changed; it shouldn't be true that these things still go on… And don't think we aren't working *'accelerated patient flow-through'* as they are doing in the chirurgical units, we also do that here. *It's out the door*, and I must admit, it is unbelievable what we send home to be taken care for in the patients' own homes. But *that's the way it is*, and there are lots of mistakes…

Here Ditte describes her present workplace in nearly the same language as she describes her old: early discharge is a part of the logic of accelerating the 'flow-through' of patients according to a production plan. In both places working hours exceed the eight-hour working day. Neither of the units provides time for development. But Ditte does not discuss the similarity of her two workplaces, instead she stresses the differences between them. The contrast she creates in the narrative allows her to express that her experience of work is actually contradictory. Her present working situation is seen in two perspectives: in a wish-orientated idealising perspective, which draws on her professional identity and on the experiences of the difference between the former, more uninteresting and the present, more interesting work. The new work becomes the realisation of what quality in nursing is really all about to Ditte. But from another perspective, her old work and her new work are the same. She speaks in a language that reflects the Taylorisation of her work, where hospital nursing work is divided into small units, and divisions of labour following this dequalifies work and detaches it from professional judgement. From the second perspective she talks about her work in the language of a hard-working labourer who can identify only weakly with the contents of work and is more concerned with the conditions she works in.

This contradiction gives rise to ambivalence in relation to work and a learning dilemma for Ditte. On the one hand work is attractive and engages her to go on developing and setting professional standards. On the other hand work is almost disgusting (*it is unbelievable what we send home*) and very difficult to identify with. Similar to Nanna, Dittes learning dilemmas are directly related to changes in working conditions and linked to the many double-sided messages of the health system. To be engaged in learning and creating learning possibilities for others in this situation is very difficult. What should the students and young graduates be suggested to adapt to or learn? In order to encourage transformative and expansive learning the given situation must be counteracted. Which students will follow that road? As already pointed out by Thunborg (2001) the health services have always created learning dilemmas. The use of some qualifications has not been allowed and some are not affirmed when the situation in a ward changes, or when patients or technologies change. Care workers encounter situations where they think they know how something should be done, but are not allowed or encouraged to do it. They can also face the dilemma of not knowing how to do something but being asked to do it (i.e. in emergency situations).

Ditte regrets that many young nurses resign during their transition to work, finding clinical practice difficult. Another element in the disillusionment of young nurses is that the more theoretical standards in nursing, upheld by the new graduates, are not recognised in the workplace. According to Ditte, who is responsible for educating and tutoring young nurses in her institution, many of them focus on nursing management after the initial disappointment with clinical practice. Thus they do not try to master the practice of clinical nursing. From a learning perspective, this can be seen as a defence mechanism against the ambivalences that the contradictions in work create. Ditte is an example of how dilemmas in learning can result in the exclusion of experiences, in this case of the changing and worsened conditions in work. Ditte clings on to a story about the differences between her two workplaces, which becomes a representation of the contradictions in nursing work in general. By emphasising the good conditions in her present workplace, Ditte can maintain a certain tolerance towards the very ambivalent experience of work as learning space.

Subjective and shared experience of dequalification

This chapter has shown that if we are to understand the crisis of learning and professional knowledge in care in Denmark, it is relevant to reflect on the *horizon of experiences and learning* (Ziehe 1998). This reflection involves an inquiry into how we understand this horizon as being present in the learning space that the social- and health care work constitutes for care workers. The horizon of learning is always present as the publicly articulated and established goals of learning and, in the case of work, this could be: the existing demand for competencies when introducing new technology, new procedures in a specific work etc. The horizon of learning is, however, also created through the subjective experiences and the commonalities in these in a specific working culture. A working culture encompasses the themes identified as professional themes in a specific workplace. The shaping of the subjective learning horizon is related to the predominant professional experiences and discourses, that the care worker encounters in the workplace. In the case of hospital wards, the horizon of learning is influenzed by themes related to the curing paradigm and to the work procedures of the shared 'production line'. This institutional horizon both limits and facilitates experiences and learning. And at the same time the learning space can be framed so as to enable or constrain learning, which defines the scope for learning, particularly for transformative learning.

There are a multitude of potential horizons for the transformation of work and workplace knowledge, meaning that there is not just one transformative space inside the workplace, but several separated spaces of transformation. These spaces are related to and framed by the different 'invitations' for transformation that take place in the workplace, and to the life-historical subjective contexts of learning that also are active in the space. The learning space can be understood in relation to the lived experiences of a *life*. Recognising the complexity of a life as a basis for experience means attention both to the lifewide experience and to the *lifelong* learning of the individual. In a life-historical perspective, the learning of care workers extends across physical space, administrative sectors and social spheres (Becker-Schmidt 2003). Care workers carry their shared experiences of the working process and their individual life-historical experiences into the work they perform. Furthermore, their 'unbordered' life experiences shape their space for learning in mental, emotional and physical ways. Unavoidably, they establish spaces of learning and transformation that extend across borders between work and life outside, and between past and present. An example of this is the way Nanna transforms the gendered role and the identity of the nurse by breaking with those called for by the workplace structure, and takes her life as a young woman in present day society into the work place. Other examples are provided by the way all three, Birthe, Nanna and Ditte reflect their relation to working with patients in professional as well as personal ways. Here they take in their life-historical experiences as a citizen and as a person, although this is not what is called for inside the professional frame. By employing their life histories as a context, professionals are thus able to establish other than the professionally constructed horizons for learning and transformation of work.

While the life-history perspective makes visible the great potential for renewal and development that is brought to care work by the care workers themselves, it is evident that the crisis in learning and professional knowledge smothers rather than supports the establishment and preservation of such horizons for learning, that could accommodate the experiences of the social and health care workers. When young graduates entering the workplace, meet contradictions similar to those described by Nanna, Ditte and Birthe, they may recoil and retract from their commitment to the occupation. The three professionals, whose stories form the empirical foundation for this chapter, have remained within nursing, but their stories provide insights into a dangerous landscape of contradictions and double-sided messages. The analysis of these stories further suggests that nurses are constantly forced to juxtapose their strong professional ambitions with the harsh reality of the workplace. Less-engaged nurses do not avoid these paradoxes and contradictions. Rather, their strategies may be much more defensive, such as withdrawal from clinical practice. The lack of engagement may also lead to adaptation to the austere conditions of the workplace and, in this way, contributing to the weakening of professional knowledge and identification.

This analysis has shown that there is a contradiction between the ways that the care workers conceive, create and enact their tasks, and the quality standards and the ways these are framed by the present organisation of social- and health care work. Currently, these contradictions are becoming so fundamental, that they exclude experiences and knowledge from practice and deconstruct space and time for learning. The lack of space for learning in the workplace creates stressful ambivalences in the professionals, impeding learning. The second analytical point raised is, that the deterioration of learning possibilities implies that occupational identities are threatened and weakened. This development has great relevance for the future of care, as it has an impact on how professionals identify with their work and the workplace. Furthermore, it is likely that the loss of learning possibilities is reflected in the growing number of dropouts from care work.

Notes

1 The figure for 2006 is taken from a newsletter from the Danish Union of Nurses, and they indicate that the figures will be published shortly in a report from the Ministry of Education, as the analysis is still in progress. However the figures have been part of the discussions between

the trade unions and the government about the future in the social- and
health sector.

2 In Danish the confusion or mingle is quite apparent: *'[jeg vader ind
i folk med træsko på for et godt ord'* The two proverbs are: 'jeg vader
lige ind i folk med træsko på' (I walk straight into peoples hearts, or they
fall for med straight away) jeg træder på folk for et godt ord (I step on
people's toes).

References

Ahrenkiel, A., Dybbroe, B. & Sommer, F. (2008) *Tillidsrepræsentant
i DSR –udfordringer og svar.* Dansk Sygeplejeråd, Center for
Arbejdsmarkedsforskning, CARMA, Aalborg Universitet, Institut for
Psykologi og Uddannelsesforskning, Roskilde University.

Andersen, V. Dybbroe, B. & Bering, I. (2004) *Fællesskab kræver fællesskab.*
Hillerød: Dansk Sygeplejeråd, Frederiksborg Amtskreds.

Baagøe Nielsen, S. & Dybbroe, B. (Eds) (2008) *Flere hænder? Velfærd,
kvalitet og rekrutteringskrise i omsorgen.* Mpower, Vejle.

Becker-Schmidt, R. (2003) Introduction, and Theorizing gender
arrangements. In R. Becker-Schmidt (Ed.) *Gender and Work in
Transition, Globalization in Western, Middle and Eastern Europe.*
Opladen: Leske & Budrich, (pp. 7- 48).

Borritz, M. (2006) *Burnout in Human Service Work- Causes and
Consequences. Results of 3-Years of Follow-Up of the PUMA Study among
Human Service Workers in Denmark.* PhD. Thesis, Copenhagen:
National Institute of Occupational Health.

Christiansen, Ipsen S. m.fl. (2003) :Omstillinger i Københavns
Kommunes Hejemmepleje, delrapport 1–4. CASA and Københavns
Kommunes BST.

Dahl, H. M. (2004) A changing ideal of care in Denmark: a different
form of retrenchment? In H. M. Dahl & T. R. Eriksen (Eds), *Dilemmas
of Care in the Nordic Welfare State, Continuity and Change* (pp. 47–61).
Aldershot: Ashgate.

Dybbroe, B. (2003) For hvem har sundhed værdi og mening? *FOFU-Nyt*
2003 (1–2), p. 7–13.

Dybbroe,B. (2006) Omsorg i skæringspunktet mellem arbejde og liv.
Menneskearbejde- Tidsskrift for Arbejdsliv 2006 (1), 67–81.

Ellström, E., Ekholm, B. & Ellström, P-E. (2008) Two types of learning
environment: Enabling and constraining a study of care work.
Journal of Workplace Learning, 20(2), 84–97.

FTF—The General Federation of Public Employees (2007a) Tal der taler,
www.FTF.dk

FTF—The General Federation of Public Employees (2007b) Ubalancer på
det offentlige arbejdsmarked frem imod 2015, Notat May 2007 www.
FTF.dk

Gustavsson, M. (2006) Organizing for learning opportunities in a resource squeezed public sector organisation. Conference paper for Research Conference Linköping University- Roskilde University, April 2006 at Linköping University.

Hahr, E. (2007) Sygeplejeuddannelsen. Notat, October: www.DSR.dk

Hansen, H. K. (2006) *Ældreomsorg i et pædagogisk perspektiv*. Ph.d.-thesis, Roskilde University.

Hjort, K. (2004) Viden som vare. In K. Hjort (Ed.) *De professionelle*. (Pp. 73–101). Roskilde: Roskilde Universitets Forlag.

Holm-Petersen, C., Asmussen, M. & Willemann, M. (2006) *Sygeplejerskers fagidentitet og arbejdsopgaver på medicinske afdelinger*, DSI, Copenhagen.

Liveng, A. (2007) *Omsorgsarbejde, subjektivitet og læring*. PhD. Thesis, Roskilde University.

Lorenzer, A (1980) Die Analyse der subjektiven Struktur von Lebensläufen und das gesellschaftlich Objektive. Revised version in H. Dahmer (Ed.) Analytische Sozialpsychologie. Bd 2, pp. 619–631. Suhrkamp, Frankfurt am Main.

Ministry of Education (2003) Indberetninger om uddannelsessøgende. Uvm.dk/pls/www.ndb

Ministry of Education (2007) *Uddannelsesguiden, Statistik*. www.ug.uvm. dk

Minister of Employment (2007) *6 skarpe om kvalitetsreformen*. Copenhagen: Sekretariatet for Ministerudvalget.

Nielsen, S. B. (2004) Når unge vælger uddannelse og job. In S. B. Nielsen & B. Simonsen (Eds), *Unges valg af uddannelse og job- udfordringer og veje til det kønsopdelte arbejdsmarked*. Roskilde: Center for Ligestillingsforskning ved Roskilde Universitetscenter.

Olesen, H. S. (1996) Tacit knowledge and general qualifications. Concepts of learning in everyday life and formal education when work changes. In H.S. Olesen (Ed.), *Adult Education and the Labour Market III*, ESREA, Roskilde University and University of Leeds.

Olesen, H.S. (2004) Professioner som (trold) spejl for arbejdet i den udfoldede modernitet. *Tidsskrift for Arbejdsliv* 2004 (1), 77–95.

Pedersen, E.B. (2005) *Social- og sundhedshjælpere og –assistenter. Antal, flow og årsager til frafald under og efter endt uddannelse*. Arbejdsmedicinsk klinik, Bispebjerg Hospital, FOR-SOSU rapport nr. 1 AMI, Copenhagen.

Pedersen, K. M. m.fl.(ed.) (2006*): Sundhedsvæsenets økonomi, organisation og ledelse*. Gads forlag.

Sundhedskartellet (2007) *Kvalitetsreform: 7fiks punkter til fremtidens sundhedsvæsen*, www.sundhedskartellet.dk

Thunborg, C. (2001) Lärdilemman inom hälso- och sjukvården. In T. Backlund, H. Hansson. & C. Thunborg (Eds) *Lärdilemman i arbetslivet. Teoretiska och praktiska perspektiv på lärande*. Lund: Studentlitteratur.

Wethje, A. & Borg, V. (2003) *Sygeplejerskers Arbejdsmiljø, trivsel og helbred* (SATH). *Sygefravær, intentioner om jobskifte samt intentioner om ophør fra arbejdsmarkedet.* Copenhagen: Dansk Sygeplejeråd and Arbejdsmiljøinstituttet.

Ziehe, T. (1998) Goodbye to the 70ies. In E. Prescod (Ed), *Zapping Through Wonderland. Social Issues in Art for Children and Young People.* Amsterdam: KIT Publishers.

TWO

Neglected Opportunities
for Personal Development:
Care Work in a Perspective of
Lifelong Learning.

Helle Krogh Hansen

The tasks of care workers providing welfare for the elderly are multiple and complex. In some cases the actions involved are multifaceted. In other cases the complexity arises from the fact that the activities involve providing care to very ill, demented, or dying people. At other times the complexity is due to the fact that the care is provided to people who have a particular lifestyle characterised by psychological or social problems. The work is demanding because the care workers are expected to handle the tasks efficiently and subject to a time schedule. They are also under contractual obligation to live up to certain standards. At the same time they are obliged to respect the recipients' individual needs. This involves providing social and pedagogical support in order to fortify the care recipients' self-care and quality of life. In addition, the care workers have a role as buffer between care recipients and the system (e.g. Meijer 2004, Thorsen 2003). In the buffer role the individual caregiver is expected to handle the problems associated with the so-called 'burden of the aging population', which creates a lack of confidence in the welfare system. The buffer role can repeatedly position the care workers in dilemmas, because they understand the recipients' needs, as well as society's wishes (of which they might or might not approve) with regard to limiting social expenses (Hansen 2006).

In Denmark, many care workers have to leave the work force, because they are worn out before the usual retirement age (Jensen & Hansen 2002). Furthermore elderly care employees are faced with the problem that, in comparison with other professional groups, it is relatively difficult for them to get compensation for work related injuries (Dahl 2002).

In spite of the physical and psychological stress loads the care workers are in general still pleased with their jobs. The reason is that they experience it as a meaningful occupation, where the human relations are a decisive factor, and because they wish to provide comfort to others (for example Christensen 1998; EVA 2001; Szebehely 2003). This orientation towards the care recipients is, however, also a problem, because the care workers feel that they are placed in an untenable position between two diametrically opposed demands: they must provide quality care to the care recipients (who usually need more attention than the caregiver is expected to provide). At the same time they must take care of themselves and show responsibility and loyalty to colleagues (who must work harder if they themselves do not go beyond the call of duty, or who might think that if you put in a lot of work, you force the pace and thereby undermine the rights achieved). Christensen (1998) describes the position of diametrically opposed demands as the two roles of the helper: the carer's role in relation to the client, and the role as employee, work colleague, and professional person. Szebehely (2003) also points to the dilemma of the care work's conflicting roles and contends that the employees must be contract oriented and flexible, while also displaying orientation towards tasks and relations. However, the work is also experienced as meaningful. It provides care workers with development potential, through which they—the present generation of care workers—develop independence and identity.

In this chapter I shall contend that one should consider a care relation as a pedagogical possibility in the sense that it might contribute to personal development and quality of life for both parties in the care relationship. The focus is on the carer. Here the carer's learning processes at work are considered from the perspective of lifelong learning. The argument is that such an understanding of care work enhances the quality of care, as well as supports the modern citizen's demand that a job should provide a subjective experience of being meaningful and developing. In this way a pedagogical perspective on the care of the elderly is also an expression of the effort made with regard to the problems of recruiting and keeping a workforce in the sector.[1]

In the following I shall present some examples from my own empirical research concerning learning potentials in care work. Then I shall move on to consider the tensions inherent in care work from a pedagogical perspective. I further discuss the concept of 'exemplary learning' and examine it with a focus on some of the needs and potentials associated with learning, which I found in my research.

Learning processes in care work

The discussion presented in this chapter is based on a study where I investigated Danish care workers' understanding of care work and the way they perceive themselves as care workers, including how and under which conditions they handle the daily care relations (Hansen 2006). An important element in the research was to let small groups of care workers observe, comment, and discuss some filmed examples of care praxis. The groups were controlled as little as possible in order to see what was observed and commented on spontaneously, as well as which issues would cause discussion in the groups—and how. All the participants' comments and discussions were recorded on tape and video. A critical hermeneutical interpretation of the material showed some essential, formative ideals, motives, conditions and possibilities in concrete and practical elder care. This provided me with the possibility to identify learning potentials located subjectively, individually, and collectively in care staff as part of their complex and conflictual work and living conditions.

Among some of the care workers who observed and commented on my films, there was for instance a spontaneous and heated discussion about the use of gloves when assisting with personal hygiene. The discussion began during a film sequence where a social- and health care helper helps an elderly man in a shower. The group of five female spectators focused their attention on the fact that the care worker was not wearing gloves. 'I could not have done that,' one of the spectators commented and explained to the other people in the group that if she herself had been a care recipient, she would have preferred that the caregiver had worn gloves in such a situation. Her comment was: 'I feel that you cross a line by not wearing gloves. You get too close to me. If you are wearing gloves, then there is a layer in between, you know what I mean—wearing gloves creates a distance between us and I don't feel that you touch me directly…'

There was not consensus in the group with regard to this attitude. Some of the women felt that one should always use gloves when assisting with personal hygiene. Others felt that gloves should only be applied in certain situations. One of the women expressed this in the following way: 'I only wear gloves with patients who have skin problems or the like… when I wash them below I always wear gloves and also when I apply remedial ointment, but not when applying ordinary moisturising lotion… no.'

This remark prompted the first woman to protest: 'It is not because I do not want to touch them,' and a third woman in the group seconded her: 'You do it for the client's sake.'

However, the woman who only wanted to apply gloves in certain situations was not convinced: 'It can also be the other way round. It depends on who it is… if I was lying there and someone put on gloves, just because they were going to touch me, it could also be like that…'

The observers' discussion became long and intense, but regardless of whether or not the women spoke for or against a general use of gloves, they, as a matter of consequence, resorted to arguments, which were entirely supported by the ideal of taking the elderly people's emotions into due consideration. Indirectly they were, however, clearly also voicing their own concerns regarding touch. I interpret this as an expression of the fact that the women for various reasons repress and place a taboo on their own feelings and needs, which are strongly affected in the care work. At one point the discussion nevertheless touched upon the question of the significance of the gloves with regard to protecting the care workers against the intimate contact. This aspect of the situation was only sporadically voiced in explicit terms. However, the attentive listener would soon realise that the participants themselves inadvertently opened up a discussion of ambivalent emotions related to the encounter with the aging body.

The forceful psychic energy inherent in the discussion is an example of the fact that care personnel needs to talk about the body, touching, aging, and death, as well as about taboos in the care work and about societal expectations to the care workers. All these issues are relevant material for learning processes in the field.

'Occupational identity' is yet another example of a theme, which appeared in my research as a good point of departure for learning through experiences from one's own work. The term occupational identity expresses my categorisation of a number of different statements and discussions which occurred among the observers in my research, when they were asked to talk about anything that came to mind, while they watched my films about care work. As it happened, one of the groups had a long discussion prompted by a take in the film, where a nurse refers to a social- and health care helper as a home help person. In this discussion the women voiced the concern that it is annoying, even hurtful, to be called a home help person, when one is trained as a social- and health care helper or assistant. Furthermore they found it even more hurtful when nurses, who are acquainted with care training, do not use the right terms. The following excerpt from the discussion shows some of the issues at stake:

> HD: 'That [home help] is an old concept, you know.'
> SI: 'It is an old concept and that is why we have to move on.'
> KG: 'In fact it would almost be the equivalent of her using the term 'domestic help', I think. That would be just as offensive to me.'
> HD: 'Actually, they are home help staff who worked as domestic help.'
> KG: 'Yes, precisely.'
> HD: 'They helped the clients clean, especially if the housewife was not capable of doing so herself, and washed their clothes; that is what it was like then. Today we also do the nursing.'
> KG: 'Yes, precisely.'
> HD: 'And a home help person does not do that, because a home help person is not trained to do so.'

Formally speaking, the term 'home help person' as a reference to an occupation became obsolete in 1992, when an educational reform merged five Danish care and nursing training courses into two new educational branches of which one was an education as social- and healthcare helper (a 14 months training programme) and the other was as social- and health care assistant (20 months further training). In my view the word 'home helper' is strictly speaking a nice term compared to the system-oriented terms 'social- and healthcare helper' and 'social- and health care assistant'. However, this term is, like the women say, an outdated concept. It reminds them of the domestic help persons, who cleaned, and they wish to distance themselves from this role. Social- and health care helpers and -assistants embrace the (basic) nursing aspect and this is an important element in their occupational identity. In the section above relating their discussion, I have only included a small extract of a debate, which touched on many subjects. It clearly indicated that stories about the lives of housemaids, domestic helpers, and home help persons, etc. are both interesting and relevant as narratives about a certain practice. Due to the combination of historical distance and the topicality of the themes, the narratives are saturated with reflections and invitations, which endow the battles won, the issues under threat, and the battles worth fighting with transparency and actuality.

Reading the excerpt above, it is evident that it is important to the women, that they, as opposed to the home help corps, embrace the nursing aspect. These women do not react to the fact that their broad interdisciplinary competences are rendered invisible when they are labelled home help staff, a term in which issues related to social functions and health disappear. What actually matters to them is the fact that they have embraced the nursing aspect, which has higher status than other tasks. This raises the question whether it is advisable that it is a nursing orientation, which should attract the new generation of employees, or whether it were advisable that other aspects related to the care work get a better image?

My research further indicates that occupational identity is related to the individual's life and subjective ascription of meaning to his or her work. Above and beyond these issues there are questions related to traditions and structurally determined definitions of which competences are allocated to various occupations, what tasks they are actually capable of performing, and which tasks they wish to perform. In a further perspective the theme also encompasses very basic cultural assumptions about gender, care, and the societally constituted view on the elderly, since the contents of the education for elderly care reflect the views on the elderly peoples' needs and wishes held by contemporary culture.

As a final example of a theme, which developed during the discussions among the participants in my research, I shall mention the question of giving and receiving recognition. The need for recognition and problems associated with this need surfaced in the context of various values, ideals, reasons, and feelings related to injustices such as those expressed in the following discussion, which I referred to above: 'Nor do I think that the education is given recognition, you know... and—how should I put it—given credit and exposure if it continues to be called 'home help'.'

When questions of recognition arise in the care workers' reflections on their daily experiences, there is fertile ground for learning processes that create insight into the motives behind actions such as doing something—consciously or unconsciously—with the ulterior motive of achieving recognition and status. At the same time the question of recognition invites a critical stance with regard to the possibilities of achieving recognition from colleagues and management. This would be a precondition for avoiding a situation, where the individual care worker experiences a dependence on the recognition dispensed by the care recipient, thereby unconsciously creating a state of dependence. Insight into motives develops this type of competence which Honneth (2003a; 2003b) calls 'sense of moral context'. This refers to an understanding of the fact that your own, as well as other people's actions are not transparent and completely controllable and cannot be interpreted from the point of view of universal principles. Instead they should be understood in the context of the individual's relations in the past, the present, and the future. This process expands the horizon, describing what and whom one can recognise, tolerate, and respect.

When care workers discuss for example problems of recognition of their professional competences and personal qualifications (a subject often touched upon by the participants in my research), it is an obvious pedagogical task to get them to associate their discussion with an investigation of how needs for recognition, and problems related to achieving recognition, are related to personal issues, professional traditions, relations to colleagues, the conditions of the care work, and societal relations in general.

The tensions of care work in a pedagogical perspective

The examples mentioned above are concerned with physicality, encounters with age and death, occupational identity, the societal position of care work, and the need for personal and professional recognition. The themes reflect the fact that the care work concerns three basic dimensions in most people's lives. Firstly there is always a social dimension in a care relation, since the relation is intrinsic to one of the parties' work in such a way that social status and peace of mind are at stake. Secondly there is a psychodynamic dimension, since conscious as well as unconscious drives are affected. Thirdly there is an existential dimension, since the care touches on questions related to fear of death, dependency, and meaning of life (cf. Schibbye 2005).

In a wider perspective the three dimensions—people's relations to work, desire, and death—encompass the entire range of themes, which I found via empirical analysis of the care workers' understanding of themselves and their work. In my in-depth hermeneutical interpretations the comments from the participating care workers demonstrate that a good deal of struggle is brought to bear on problems associated with paid care work, including the question of occupational identity and societal recognition (of a low wage occupation traditionally associated with a woman's job, but as a paid work to a great extent evaluated within the status paradigms associated with male symbols, reflecting a medical world. The women are thus split between on the one hand experiences gained in a life history of good care performance, and on the other hand those aspects, which give status and support the efforts to bring professionalism into the care paradigm).

My research has also shown that there is a great struggle to deal with the psychodynamics and existential challenges associated with care relations, i.e. more or less conscious, ambivalent, and tabooed emotions, which arise in the contact sphere with old, ill, and dying bodies, as demonstrated in the first example. This problem is reinforced through expectations that the care worker, as woman and professional person does not harbour negative feelings towards these issues, and that she without any problems can control and ignore her own emotions and needs. I am particularly interested in the consequence that both the giver and the recipient of care are positioned in what I call a 'state of existential loneliness'. By this term I mean that both parties in the relation come to ignore, repress, and distort perhaps the most important issue in their relationship, namely the experience of deterioration, bodily decay, dependency, and death, and that this happens at the cost of the possibilities of applying the relation to clarify existential questions and personal development. In other words, my contention is that both parties in the relation are let down, because problems and emotions are individualised, tabooed, negated, and levelled out in such ways that the care personnel is afforded very limited possibilities of personal expression via dialogical presence and recognition. In short and general terms I ascribe the existential loneliness to the fact that the tasks, roles, and relations of the care worker as well as the care recipient are defined and valued in ways, which do not involve the concern for existential questions (cf. the investigation carried out by Borg et al. (2005), which indicates that care personnel to a great extent experience a demand that they hide their feelings). The important questions, which are a good point of departure for learning and personal development in care education and work, will often concern relations which involve anxiety, conflict, taboos, and ambivalence. Such learning processes are obviously difficult to organise. However, perhaps these themes offer an ideal opportunity to learn more about oneself and each other.

According to Honneth (2003b) the learning associated with such themes occurs through the articulation of impulses to take action. This requires anxiety free settings. This means that one should give care personnel the possibility to express and process the feelings and needs, which guide their actions at work. I agree in principle, however, I do not think that one can completely circumvent anxiety. As already mentioned, we are not transparent to ourselves. For this reason each and every one of us is an inexhaustible source of anxiety. Instead of attempting to create anxiety free learning environments, one should attempt to create environments, which can contain anxiety, i.e. by talking about it, and countering it with open attempts to understand it, while also providing support for creative exploration of individual and collective motives for action. Such processes should, however, not develop into therapy as such. Anxiety free articulation of impulses for action is a pedagogical ideal, and a point of orientation for significant learning processes. It is, however, not a project that could be honoured completely. A concrete plan of action could involve the establishment of learning situations, based on the understanding that progression and regression are two sides of the same coin. This means that supervisors, teachers, and others, who have a responsibility in the fields of education and working life, should not only accept the students' will and engagement. Supervisors and teachers must also be able to relate to and understand those learning potentials textured in the students' resistance and lack of motivation. There should also be room for ambivalent emotional expressions, where the learning ambitions are not to make the feelings of anxiety go away, but to diminish the fear of getting in contact with anxiety.

In my view it is a fundamental assumption that any care relation involves invaluable potentials for learning that provides insight and change. These potentials can unfold, when care personnel are encouraged to show interest and openness to the challenges created by the shared interface. This presupposes that those responsible in the fields of education, as well as in the daily practice, understand and support the fact that learning in a relation is a reciprocal process. This means that if the care in any way honours ideals such as equality and humanity, the care work changes both parties in the relation (Dybbroe 2006). Furthermore the potential stresses that the caregiver's, as well as the care recipient's lifelong learning and development should be supported. By doing so, one takes into consideration the motives that inspire care workers and encourage them to remain in the field.

The learning potentials to which I am referring here are embedded in the nature of the care relation, i.e. in the meeting occurring between two people located in widely differing situations, but who to some extent share the practical and cultural circumstances of caring (one of them because care giving is an occupation and an identity, and the other because he or she is dependent on the care and is defined by virtue of this need). The meeting provides both parties with an opportunity to learn something new about themselves and the other. Learning processes with the potential to create change should provide increased insight into subjective as well as individual relations and into the historically constructed care conditions. The learning processes should (as part of the insight) liberate disciplined and disciplining psychic energy. This means that care personnel individually and as a group should be offered assistance to liberate some of the bound up psychic energy blocking their insight into their own feelings and attitudes in the care relations, a block that impedes their nuanced and critical insight into guiding cultural, social, and existential aspects of the care work.

Insight into the complexity of care, as well as liberation of psychic energy, presuppose that you, or anyone directly or indirectly implicated in the possibilities of learning, accept that the subjective meanings of concrete experiences from every day life, including emotional ambivalences, are very important sources for relevant learning for care workers. One has to accept that the learning processes should afford the care workers the opportunity to gain insight and create change in their own (occupational) lives. If the learning does not (also) target the care workers themselves, their quality of life, their experiences, their emotional and physical relations, there will be a risk that the learning translates to instrumental actions and empty or distorting rhetoric. At the same time the learning should be brought into the care relations partly as an inherent quality with a focus on the care personnel's competences for taking concrete action, and partly as learning potential for care recipients as well. The latter statement is intended to convey the fact that the competences, which the care workers attain, should be a part of the care relations in such a way that the recipients of care also become a part of this learning, i.e. that both parties are learners as well as teachers.

Lifelong exemplary learning

In order to further emphasise the special demands of care work and the particular needs and learning potentials associated with the occupation, I shall proceed with a discussion of the diametrically opposed logics, which become part of the orientation of the care personnel. By extension I shall introduce the concept of 'exemplary learning' and present some reasons that justify its application in care training and learning in professional life.

As a result of my analyses and interpretations of care workers' comments on my films about care for the elderly, I have come to the conclusion that some of the complexity and the conflicts in care work can be explained by the fact that the practical care of the elderly is constituted in a field of tension between three reciprocal systems of logic. One is an ideological logic, where the care for the elderly is normatively constituted as an ethical, humanistic, and pedagogical project. This logic, which can be found in political slogans and in the educational programmes, expresses wishes and expectations that the care workers reflectively apply themselves, offering nurture and care, including social and pedagogical actions. The other logic is a rational, service minded logic, which demands an efficient solution to a societal problem, presented in such a way that the recipients are perceived as consumers, and where the relation between system and consumer is contractual. And while the ideological logic upgrades care as paid work, the rational, service oriented logic downgrades care as paid work, which of course influences the possibilities of recruitment of workers who wish to remain in the occupation.

The third logic I have chosen to call subjective ascription of meaning. The term is indicative of a subjective logic, which against all odds and in spite of the ideological as well as the rational logic shapes the care workers' actions. This logic is determined by the individual's gender and personal history, and it is of course moreover formed by the two other systems of logic, while also going beyond those. With the term subjective ascription of meaning I mean partly that the individual caregiver subjectively interprets any situation, relation, and experience, and partly that any caregiver uses her so-called practical common sense and her feelings in every concrete situation. In so doing she sees a deeper sense in the work, which primarily consists in contributing to the other person's life with something good and by virtue of this action knowing in her heart that it is an effort which is useful to society. When she subsequently explains her actions, she constructs—with the help of the two other systems of logic—some practical, professional rationales, which completely justify her actions. In more psychodynamic terms one could describe the subjective ascription of meaning as a construction created during processes of transference, since every subject through her internal world colours her picture of the external world and through internalisation or introjection of the external world constructs her own internal world. The transference, which can be said to be the main source of the subjective ascription of meaning, is present as an element for everyone and in all relations throughout one's entire life. This does not, however, reduce the world to a subjective construction. The objective reality is there, but the subject's experience of the meaning of reality originates within (Chodorow 1999).

Concerning the subjective ascription of meaning in a learning perspective, one could say that it expresses the condition that every subject on the basis of a personal perspective of signification, which constructs emotional patterns and stylistic preferences (basic assumptions), interprets objects and the meaning of events. The personal perspective of meaning is founded during childhood socialisation and changes (through processes of learning) continually throughout life in interactions with the societal conditions (Mezirow 1990).

In an overall perspective the three systems of logic can substantiate and legitimate the system at large in such a way that its immediate representation is relatively logical and harmonious. It is, however, hard work for the care workers to get the various demands posed by these systems of logic to add up. As a result care workers' as well as care recipients' basic human needs are occasionally violated. For this reason care workers must be encouraged to understand the contexts shared between political, personal, psychodynamic, and existential aspects of care work. They should develop what I shall later refer to as a sociological mode of thinking, and they should be supported in their efforts to address the modern paid care occupation—precisely as a paid work challenged by diametrically opposed logical systems and demands—but also as a prospect of self-development, and as a widely respected opportunity to unfold the need to have a meaningful relationship with other people.

These ideas are rooted in Oskar Negt's paradigm of 'exemplary learning'. Negt takes his point of departure in Wagenschein's concept of the exemplary principle, where students learn about holistic concepts through a good understanding of individual aspects (parts) of the subject. However, in Negt's paradigm, the holistic concept is 'the totality of a society's production and reproduction process that is organised through the sharing of work and seen in its historical dimension; the 'parts' is the sociological fact, which is relevant to the life of society, the classes, and the individual human beings' (Negt 1981:44). Accordingly the whole is not in Negt's paradigm (as it was in the original exemplary principle) a subject or an issue. On the contrary, the holistic concept is the totality of the societal production and reproduction processes, which should be seen in their historical dimensions. This part is the empirical, social fact relevant to the learners. This relevance is not limited to the learners as individuals. It also concerns the occupational groups of care workers as wider collectivities and the society in general.

Learning should hence take its point of departure in socially experienced facts (the parts), which concern the learners as subjects embedded in societal relations (the whole). A precondition for the learners' self-understanding as individuals shaped by and shaping society and history is that they acquire a sociological mode of thinking (Negt 1981). This consists in transgressing the usual scientific (professional) divisions, thereby becoming aware of structural connections, and changing a non-political conception of social relations to a political understanding. Through this sociological mode of thought, learning which otherwise might seem chaotic, can become motivating and build potential for change.

Negt emphasises that one should not confuse or equate exemplary learning with case methods in the teaching. He does, however, suggest that in exemplary learning one should work with cases from occupational life. Cases can originate from and describe people's objective situation in their workplace whether it be e.g. about accidents at work or court cases relating to work: 'Above and beyond the function as 'approach', the case studies offer the possibility (...) of establishing a disciplinary interpretation of certain case conditions through collective learning processes, in which all learners participate. This may later make it easier to control what has been learned.' (1981:46).

In the quote above Negt does not explain what he means by controlling what has been learned, so I shall choose to consider this as a possibility—when talking about 'real' cases from everyday life—to establish what actually happened or may happen in the case at hand. Alternatively I shall see it as a possibility to maintain that there should be a connection and a social reality in the case (that insights and suggestions do not dissociate themselves from concrete reality in disconnected or idealistic ways).

Building on Negt's above-discussed ideas on exemplary learning, I introduce the notion 'lifelong exemplary learning' to conceptualise the prospects for educational processes in care work. By modifying Negt's concept I wish to emphasise the lifelong aspect. Negt talks about exemplary cases. I prefer the expression 'an exemplary theme', because this concept suggests more flexibility with regard to the content. The issue is not necessarily that someone formulates a case, but that something is described in a thematic way. (For a detailed discussion of the theoretical approach and its foundation, see Hansen 2006.) Inspired by Negt, I have formulated criteria, which define an exemplary theme as a theme that:

- Originates from the learning subjects (for example from givers and recipients of care)
- Has subjective meaning to the learning subjects
- Is supported by psychic energy
- Goes beyond the individual and the subjective to the collective and societal level
- Is suitable for reflections, which create a critical consciousness and emancipation

The understandings of care and of the care work's ideals, possibilities, and problems, which I have found in my research, show that there is a need for learning processes, which can help care personnel deal with emotions in new ways, and understand themselves and the work in a larger societal context. The problems show that the learning processes must engage with quotidian life and its subjective meanings. However, to prevent the process from becoming therapeutic, and in order not to reinforce the present tendency to cumbersome individuality, subjectivity, and intimacy (Ziehe 1989, 2003) it is essential that the learning goes beyond the individual and his or her subjective emotions and experiences.

Conclusion

There are many explanations to the crises in the care work sector in the Nordic countries: the multiple stress loads and the opposed demands of care work, the relatively low status it is ascribed in society, and its bad reputation due to press reports on quality issues in elderly care all bear some of the blame. The situation calls for change. This chapter has raised the argument that a tenable strategy in recruiting and keeping care workers within elderly care must encompass perspectives for the organisation of the care work. The care organisation should offer the care workers more adequate support with regard to coping with the various demands and stress loads, including the buffer role, in which they invariably find themselves. In short, the care work must have intrinsic relevant and desirable possibilities for lifelong learning and personal development. This is necessary in order to help the present care workers to deal with the work, and to provide care work with an appealing image that will attract young people of today. As a rule this age group only applies for and remains in a job if it is experienced as meaningful, widely respected, and providing opportunities for personal development.

Care work is complex and fraught with stress loads, and care personnel must perform a balancing act between diametrically opposed roles and systems of logic. I have shown in this chapter, however, that care work offers quite significant, yet unexplored, potentials for learning. I have indicated that a strategy for recruiting and maintaining employees in elder-care should focus on the potentials of the care work in order to support the lifelong learning and development of the care personnel. Furthermore such a strategy should recognise and honour the care personnel's desire to have meaningful relations with others. The learning in the care educational system and occupation should assist the care personnel in dealing with the work as modern wage labour, as well as honour modern people's expectation to occupational life.

I have pointed out that such learning should unfold as exemplary learning processes, characterised by an application of the learners' own themes, i.e. applying their own experiences as points of departure, introducing something that has subjective significance to them, and which is supported by psychic energy. In addition there is the demand that learning based on experience must go beyond the individual with a view to understanding his or her own situation in a societal context.

Since the learning should take its point of departure in the participant's concrete quotidian, I have not been able to outline the contents of a plan or a curriculum for such learning. I have, however, suggested that one finds material for the themes of learning by increasing the awareness of direct and indirect statements about everyday life made by students or trained care workers.

It goes for all exemplary learning processes that these in one way or other must embrace the interaction between the subjective, the individual (cognitive and emotional), and the structural. Either way exemplary themes in care training and in care practice will always be concerned with the question of psychosocial forces, which motivate as well as create problems in the relations between caregiver and care recipient. In this way there will be a focus on the learners' own investigations of situations where care actions express reciprocity, solidarity and recognition, what constitutes a relation, and what positive and/or negative issues motivate the individual and the group of care workers to participate in relations with aging and ill people.

The care work sector of the future should position itself clearly when it comes to offering inherent opportunities for learning, so the individual and groups of care workers can experience personal and professional development and thereby participate actively in the development of the field. In other words, it is about engaging the care personnel actively and allowing it to influence the development of a practice that they feel like being part of.

Note

1 The care involved in the relation between the carer and the recipient of care for the elderly will in some way always involve pedagogical tasks and deal with learning and development. Whether or not the care situation is regarded as a charitable relationship, as part of medical treatment and nurture, or as a contractual service obligation, a caregiver must be able to mediate, motivate, and involve as well as support the care recipient in the building and maintenance of a number of important competences. In this view pedagogy are perceived as a tool to enable another human being to perform or understand a certain issue. This view of the role of pedagogy offers a fruitful agenda for both research and development of care work, but in this chapter I do not focus on these pedagogical aspects of care work, as I wish to address the potential of the pedagogical perspective for enhancing quality care.

References

Borg, V., Clausen, T., Frandsen, C.L., Winsløw, J.H., (2005) Psykisk arbejdsmiljø i ældreplejen. *FOR-SOSU rapport nr. 4 AMI-rapport.* Copenhagen.

Dybbroe, B. (2006) Omsorg i skæringspunktet mellem arbejde og liv. *Tidsskrift for Arbejdsliv 1/2006.* Odense: Syddansk Universitetsforlag.

Chodorow, N. (1999) *The Power of Feelings.* Yale University Press.

Christensen, K. (1998) *Omsorg og arbejde—en sociologisk studie af ændringer i den hjemmebaserede omsorg.* Bergen: Sociologisk Institut.

Dahl, H.M. (2002) En køn retfærdighed? Et spørgsmål om status og lighed med hjemmehjælpen som case. In A. Borchorst (Ed.), *Kønsmagt under forandring.* Copenhagen: Hans Reitzels Forlag.

EVA (Danmarks Evalueringsinstitut) (2001) *Social- og sundhedshjælperuddannelsen. Undersøgelse af en uddannelse i forandring.*

Hansen, H.K., (2006) *Ældreomsorg i et pædagogisk perspektiv.* Ph.d.-afhandling, Roskilde: Samfundslitteratur.

Honneth, A. (2003a) *Behovet for anerkendelse.* Copenhagen: Hans Reitzels Forlag.

Honneth, A. (2003b) *Erkännande—praktisk- filosofiska studier.* Göteborg: Daidalos.

Jensen, J.J., & Hansen, H.K. (2002) Review of literature since 1990: Psychosocial job environment, job satisfaction, gender and other diversities in care workforce, and quality of care services. Denmark. http://www.carework.dk Retrieved 7.10.2007

Meijer, M. (2004) Forklædt som ældrebyrde. *Social Kritik—Tidsskrift for social Analyse og Debat* 94, 56–59.

Mezirow, J. (1990) Hvordan kritisk refleksion fører til transformativ læring. In Illeris,K. (ed) (2000) *Tekster om læring.* Roskilde Universitets Forlag.

Negt, O. (1981) *Sociologisk fantasi og eksemplarisk indlæring.* Copenhagen: Kurasje

Schibbye, A. L. (2005) *Relationer.* Copenhagen: Akademisk forlag.

Szebehely, M. (ed) (2003) *Hemhjälp i Norden—illustrationer och refleksioner.* Lund: Studentlitteratur.

Thorsen, K. (2003) Gränser för omsorg och den gränslösa omsorgen— Om gränsdragningsprocesser i hemtjänsten. In M. Szebehely (Ed.), *Hemhjälp i Norden—illustratiner och refleksioner.* Lund: Studenterlitteratur.

Ziehe, T. (1989) *Ambivalenser og mangfoldighed.* Aarhus: Politisk Revy.

Ziehe, T. (2003) Adieu til halvfjerdserne! De unge og skolen under den anden modernisering. In J. Bjerg (Ed.) *Pædagogik—en grundbog til et fag.* Copenhagen: Hans Reitzels Forlag

THREE

A Crisis of Recognition in Care Work for Elderly People?

Looking at Professional, Bodily and Gendered Hierarchies for Explanations

Anne Liveng

Paid care work for elderly people can be analysed as inscribed in three hierarchies: A professional hierarchy, a bodily or 'dirt' hierarchy, and a gendered hierarchy. In all three hierarchies care work is ranked low. According to Kari Wærness' (1982) seminal work, Nordic literature on care has discussed the specific logic of care work as rationality of care. This kind of orientation towards the relations of care is an important motivation for women who are being trained for the basic positions in the social and health sector. Care orientation, recognised by research as a central element in the motivation of the employees in the field, seems to be under great pressure, existing in spite of political and organisational intentions (Nabe-Nielsen 2005). This 'concealment' of the motivation and rationality of care can be considered a consequence of the low ranking of this kind of work (Christensen 2003). Thus the hierarchical position has severe implications for care workers. Most importantly, the knowledge of careworkers is seldom recognised. The typical knowledge of care workers at the lowest levels of hierarchies is a product of their commitment to constructing care as a relation between specific people rather than as a performance of a set of impersonal tasks. However, neither those interested in professionalising care work, nor those concerned with care organisations generally acknowledge their specific form of knowledge as a resource for developing care.

The situation described above could be identified as a 'crisis of recognition'. With reference to a comparison of long-term developments in the advantages and burdens of specific jobs in the public sector, Hanne Marlene Dahl (2002) argues that while a higher degree of economic recognition of care work for the elderly has emerged, the rationality of care is still not properly recognised. A need for controlling the work care workers carry out in their daily care of the elderly is expressed as a part of the very way basic care work is organised. The recent initiative 'Common Language' (*Fælles sprog*) is an example of this. The Common Language initiative was launched in 1998 by Kommunernes Landsforening, which is the public employers' association in Denmark. Common Language aims at standardising ratings of the level of functioning of the individual citizen, standardising services offered by the municipality, and standardising estimation of municipal key figures. One of the consequences has been uniform time measures for the tasks carried out by social and health care helpers working in the home-based care for the elderly. As the initiative restricts the possibilities of the care worker to estimate which tasks are most important to carry out and for how long, it reduces the possibility of practicing a 'good-enough-care'. The term 'good-enough-care' is inspired by the psychoanalyst Donald Winnicott (1986), who talks about the 'good-enough-mother'. The 'good-enough-mother' is able to form a relation to her child, in which the child can develop in accordance with its age and does not get harmed. The intention is to create a concept, which does not indicate an ideal of the perfect, but still implies that conditions exist for physical and psychological growth. Transferred to the care of the elderly, the term implies that even though it is impossible to take care of every single need of the citizen, it is necessary to take care in such a way that the old person does not get harmed and is able to use whatever physical and psychological abilities he or she may have.

Unlike the Common Language initiative and other projects designing care work in such a way that it ignores the motivation and rationality of care workers, the aim of this chapter is to raise the perspective of the people working in the most humble positions in the professional hierarchy in the care sector as an important concern. My argument is that neglecting their situation does not only constitute a threat to the subjective motivation of live care workers, but also underpins a recruitment crisis which can be a threat to the future of welfare societies. Furthermore, from the point of view of the old person receiving help, the crisis of recognition of care workers' knowledge is a threat to the quality of the care.

The chapter discusses the insights of my PhD thesis, which deals with the orientation towards caring jobs among trainees at the Danish social and health care helper education (*social- og sundhedshjælperuddannelsen*), and with the trainees' being faced with the demands of the work (Liveng 2006; 2007). With the term 'orientation' I wish to point to the fact that all the 17 women I interviewed and followed in their practical work saw a job in the care sector as much more than a way to earn a living. It was a way to be able to be important by doing 'good' to others, a way of establishing relations, and to several of the interviewed the role as care taker had been a central obligation since childhood. The focus of the analysis is on the meaningfulness of care work which is connected to a theoretical understanding of care work as essentially relational work. Starting from this theoretical signpost, I work with the concept of care orientation as a way of describing the trainees' orientation towards work in the basic social and health courses. Below I present an empirical study of how the hierarchies in which care work is inscribed has an impact on care workers' everyday work and thereby on their orientation towards their work.

Care work for elderly people as low ranked in three hierarchies

To speak of care work for elderly people as 'low ranked' in as many as three hierarchies involves the risk of confirming prejudices about care work as work 'every woman is able to carry out' because of her female socialisation. Arguing that it is low ranked in a bodily hierarchy involves the risk of strengthening cultural images of the work as dirty. Confirming prejudices is not the intention of the analysis. Instead, my intention is to point to structural phenomena as an explanation of the low status of paid care work. The structural explanation helps to understand why care work for the elderly is still not considered an attractive job, in spite of campaigns to recruit staff, the introduction of educational reforms and the opinion of the general public emphasising the importance of care work.

Research carried out by the Danish trade union for workers employed in the public sector, FOA, has demonstrated that the 'image problem of the profession' is a cause of frustration especially among trainees and the newly fledged care workers in the lowest positions in the social and health sector (FOA 2006).Trainees and students who have just finished their course consider it to be humiliating that their work is held in such low esteem in society. The latest research on job satisfaction among social and health care helpers in Denmark shows that it is the youngest group of the staff who are less likely to want to continue within the sector. The low hierarchical positions of the work could be seen as factors influencing both job satisfaction of care workers already employed within the sector, but it also explains the difficulties in recruiting new staff, which is a widespread problem in the Nordic countries.

The following sections take a closer look at how the three hierarchies structuring care work for the elderly are expressed in the everyday context of work.

Social and health care helper work as inscribed in a professional hierarchy

Most obvious is perhaps the inscription of care work for elderly in a professional hierarchy. While it might be difficult to observe a gender hierarchy directly at the empirical level, the professional, medical hierarchy of the sector leaps immediately to the eye when one looks at observations of work practice.

In the following example from an observation of the social and health care helper trainee, Lotte, the professional hierarchy is demonstrated. Lotte, who is 20 years old, is in the second trainee period in which she is working in the home-based care of the elderly. Together with a qualified health care helper, Alice, she is going to take care of an old lame woman, Anne Mette, who receives help mornings and evenings. Lotte has taken the initiative to a visit by a physiotherapist in Anne Mette's house in order to get some medical devices for her. The health care helpers cannot wash Anne Mette's hair because she is not able to walk the few stairs down to her bathroom and Lotte wants to solve this problem.

Lotte and Alice have just washed Anne Mette and helped her out of bed by using a lift. During washing they have discussed her bedsores and both have been concerned about another health care helper who has coated her in cream 'below'. We are now all standing in the bedroom, Anne Mette is sitting in her wheelchair:

> The physiotherapist arrives and everybody says hello. I explain who I am and the physiotherapist comments on my PhD project. She explains that 'we' (this is the physiotherapists) think that 'they' (that is the social and health care helpers) learn far too little about the transfer of people. I come to think of Lotte telling me that the health care helpers could not attend a course in transfer of people until after they had finished their social and health course. At the same time I get the feeling that the physiotherapist is unfair speaking of the helper assistants in this way while they are present. Just like the helper assistants sometimes speak of the elderly people as if they were not there, so the physiotherapist talkes about them in this situation.
>
> Lotte tells the physiotherapist why she has called her, and the physiotherapist suggests that they should (beside the medical devices) also discuss whether they could make an exercise programme for Anne Mette, which the helper assistants could show her how to do. The physiotherapist uses some Latin words, and Lotte asks what they mean. It strikes me that they speak completely different languages.
>
> The health care helper, Alice, explains about a device they have got for washing Anne Mette's hair, but which does not work because it cannot be fastened to the bedpan chair. This question raises a lot of discussion back and forth. The physiotherapist sums up and clarifies what the two health care helpers are saying. After a while she concludes, 'Well, this is only a technical problem.' She does not have any other suggestions. So the health care helpers do not get the problem solved that they cannot wash Anne Mette's hair. And they have not been relieved from worrying about it. (18.06.04.)

The inscription of care work for elderly in a professional hierarchy is present as conditions in the daily work, which influence working environment and motivation of the employees. The professional hierarchy can, as in the example above, mean that initiatives and undertakings coming from people working lowest in the professional hierarchy are ignored. The involvement the trainee Lotte has shown in relation to the problems of the old woman does not lead to further reflections about how the problem with the hair washing could be solved or to the trying out of new technical alternatives. On the contrary her initiative is set aside and thereby also her empathy with the old woman. In short, Lotte experiences that her attention towards the client and her engagement in carrying out care as well as possible does not matter. Not only is her initiative not taken seriously—she is at the same time explicitly devalued. As a learning process it points in the opposite direction of the development of self-reflection, which is highlighted as the ideal of the social and health training and in official documents is seen as a necessary competency for trainees.

When the relation to the client and the empathy with the person concerned are important reasons for female care workers' motivation for choosing their job, ignoring this motivation means a lack of recognition. This lack of recognition does not improve their satisfaction with their job. In a historical period in which the field suffers from scarcity of labour in the field, ignorance of this motivation seems to be risky as it could lead to even lesser interest in the jobs.

The example further illustrates that what one notices and worries about as a care worker is dependent on the distance to the client. Old, lame Anne Mette getting her hair washed is apparently only important to the people who are physically near to her. This might be obvious: The people near to her are those who see and smell the dirt, those who eventually see Anne Mette's grief when she is not able to keep her body tidy anymore.

The example shows why—in a perspective of care—it is also risky not to listen to the people working in the lowest ranks of the professional hierarchy. When they are not heard, the quality of the practiced care risks being poorer than it might have been. And this is not necessarily a question of resources, even though resources of course play an important role. But the questions is as much about paying respect to and recognising that people working nearest to the clients have a different kind of knowledge and observe other aspects of the condition of the client than those working at a distance from the person.

Kari Wærness (1982, 33) differentiates between three categories of publicly financed care work:

- Care work connected to growth or results.
- Care work connected to maintenance or stagnation.
- Care work connected to situations marked by decline.

Care work leading to growth is the most attractive for professional groups. The result-oriented social and health sector primarily aims at treatment; that is to say to make the patient function so that he or she leaves the role as a patient or client. 'Institutions of growth', as for example the somatic hospitals, are in general the institutions in the sector which have most prestige. Efficiency is usually measured in frequency of discharges. Inside the institutions of growth the jobs concerned with the basic carrying out of care give the lowest wages and least prestige.

Maintenance care does not lead to self-reliance of the client, but aims at a certain level of functioning. Examples of institutions in this category are institutions for the chronically ill and the physically or mentally inhibited.

Care work connected to situations marked by decline is the least attractive. A striking relation of care in this category is caring for a dying person. Care workers in this category—and often also the recipients of care—know that the process in the short or long terms will have a negative course. Wærness speaks of this kind of care as 'result-less', as the 'effectiveness' of this work is hard or impossible to measure.

Care work for elderly people in a 'dirt' hierarchy: working with decaying and dying bodies

In all of the three categories of care work discussed above, the care nearest the client and the client's physical body is ranked lowest. The fact that basic care work with old and sick fellow human beings is ranked low cannot be separated from the closeness of the work to body and death. In this sense, the work carried out by social and health care helpers can be thematised as inscribed in a 'hierarchy of dirt'.

Lise Widding Isaksen (2003) sees work near the body as related to symbols and values which society attributes to the body and bodily dirt. Male and female bodies are interpreted differently and so are young and old bodies. Bodily care work deals with taking care of bodies which smell and leak in places one usually does not expose to anyone but one's sexual partner. Cultural classification of hygiene as strictly private makes it difficult to discuss work in this field publicly. We lack a language in which we can speak of the experiences of smelling and touching tabooed bodily liquids without feeling vulgar or touching on sexual associations (Krogh Hansen 2006). Isaksen further argues that bodily closeness and intimacy, which are not related to sexuality but solely to care, are often inscribed in images of the feminine. In intimate hygiene one most often has to work directly with one's hands. Working directly with one's hands ranks lower than working with tools between oneself and the material. Working with tools, 'marking the world', is in a society dominated by patriarchal structures, seen as productive and connected to masculinity. Isaksen identifies a hierarchy of illnesses corresponding to the cultural symbolism described above, where illnesses cured by the use of technology gain more status and receive more funds than illnesses which 'only' require long-term treatment and basic bodily care.

Working with 'decay' and particularly with dying people can bee seen as extreme forms of 'dirty work'. Both Freudian psychoanalysis and social anthropology define dirt as 'matters placed in wrong places' (Isaksen 2003:175).The fact that maintaining the body takes a hygienic effort, is an aspect of physical life which demands organisation and work. When one gets old or ill, one becomes dependent on the support of others to manage this work. But maintaining the body could not only be understood in physical terms, but also in psychological ones. Maintaining and controlling our own bodies is a part of our very individuality. Losing the ability to manage our own body could, at the psychological level, be understood as a sign of dissolution of the individual. Also for the care worker, encountering this dissolution can provoke anxiety.

In several concrete and symbolic ways social and health care workers perform 'dirty work'. When analysing my observation notes I realised there was a repeated focus on what I identify as passages. Again and again I had, without being aware of it, noticed how the health care helper trainee locked us in and out of houses and apartments. I had written about ways and hindrances to reach the elderly person needing care, about doors and gates, keys and locks, stairs and bells. While driving between the homes of the clients the trainees told me about diverse causes for nervousness, ranging from not being able to find the way to the clients to the fear of walking into a home one day, finding the client dead. The care workers talked about walking into places that were hidden from the outside world, and leaving them. I interpret the focus on the 'real' passages as a way of handling—at a symbolic level—the passages between life and death, between control and dissolution, and between clean and unclean which are present in the observation notes. In order to understand the psychological energy expressed in the accounts of such passages it is necessary to see them as having both a 'real' and a symbolic content. The task of the care worker is to observe the condition of the client and identify potential anomalies. If she finds an anomaly, she is expected to report it to the relevant expert outside of the home, such as a nurse or a doctor. But signs of anomaly are also at a symbolic level signs of decay and death—and therefore frightening.

The following extract from my observation notes focuses on the passage into the house of an old man, an almost labyrinthine task. The observation gets the character of 'scene of the crime'. Hanne, the trainee who I accompany, already in the car warns me about what is expecting us 'in there':

'The next client is an old sick man', Hanne tells me. 'He has often faeces all the way up the back of his head when I arrive in the morning. He has to get washed and helped out of bed.' The man, Peter, lives together with his wife in an old house. In the drive lies a big rolled carpet. Hanne jumps out of the car and moves the carpet so I can park in the drive. In the garden a big dog is jumping around. We have to move a wooden pallet and climb a fence in order to get near to the door. Hanne tells me that this is not to prevent the dog from running out, but to prevent anybody from getting in. From the fence and up to the door the grass is worn off, so that you walk on the bare earth. The couple's car is parked in the middle of the lawn, and things the dog has gnawed are spread all over the lawn.

Hanne rings the bell, and the wife opens, dressed in a dressing gown. She sits in the kitchen and drinks coffee and solves a square puzzle. Some rye bread is put to rise on the kitchen table. It is pretty cold. The house lies low. Here I do not consider taking off my boots, as I normally do. Hanne explains why I accompany her, and the wife asks me if I am there to control Hanne's work.

In the room where the old man lies, the air is actually warm and stuffy. He lies in the living room in a hospital bed. The furniture is pulled together to get room enough for it. There is a wood burner with piles of briquettes around. The television is on—it is placed so that he can see it from the bed. Around the bed the floor is covered with old newspapers.

When Hanne removes the blankets from Peter, he is, as she told me, literally smeared with his own shit. He has a blanket underneath his duvet, with no cover on. He wears neither underpants nor nappy, but is just lying on a sheet with his faeces running down him. Hanne washes and washes—it takes a lot of flannels before he is clean. The smell is heavy. Meanwhile the nine o'clock news begins.

Hanne and Peter talk about his wife baking rye bread. The dog enters and lies down on the newspapers while it is gnawing an old bone. Hanne washes Peter's toes—he does not like that, he says, because he has had a health care helper who was so rough that he is still completely sore.

Hanne looks at some wounds Peter has got on his arms from falling and on his heels from lying so much. The wounds look okay and dry. They both begin to explain to me how he fell. She rubs him with lotion and puts thick socks on his feet. All the time she is wearing gloves.

'Now we have to go for a walk', Hanne says 'and then you will get your reward'. She lowers the bed so that he is able to step out on the floor and she takes one of his arms. He is very skinny and completely hunchbacked. Together they walk to the door and open it into the kitchen where he says good morning to his wife. He only wears a vest and socks.

Slowly Hanne walks with him back to an armchair where a fur plaid and a sheet like the one he had in his bed is placed. Peter sits down in the chair and it turns out that he sits with his buttocks naked right on the sheet. I think it must be so unworthy. He gets a dressing gown around his legs and Hanne places his legs on a footstool. He puts his hands down under the blanket. It strikes me that he may be fiddling himself a bit. The reward for walking turns out to be a glass of sherry. (11.03.03).

The extract from the observation notes gives a strong image of everyday work in the home-based care of the elderly in Denmark. Not all clients live like Peter, nor are they all so fragile. But still the example is not extraordinary. The meetings with situations implying degrading, dissolution and decay on the one hand, control and mistrust on the other, are part of the daily work. Here it is Peter's wife who expresses the need for control. But a need for control is not only expressed by worried relatives; it is part of the very way basic care work is organised in initiatives such as 'Common Language', as was discussed above. One can discuss whether the care provided for an old man like Peter is 'good enough'. This is not my point here. My point is to draw attention to the strains situations like this put on the care worker; situations in which she is alone and has to be able to contain psychologically both the anger expressed by Peter's wife and the very despair of his situation.

Looking at the observation, the placing of 'matters in wrong places' is obvious. From the time Hanne and I arrive at the house till Peter sits in his armchair the description of matters mixed together in unusual places is a thread through the observation. The urge of the trainee to wear gloves[1] and my keeping on my boots could be interpreted as a way of setting bounds. (Krogh Hansen 2006). Setting bounds between oneself and the other person who is 'dissolving' and bounds between clean and unclean is in a psychoanalytical perspective a way of protecting oneself from the threatening dissolution.

In spite of the need to set bounds Hanne still cares for Peter. The situation causes her to feel frustration and anger, but this anger is turned towards Peter's wife, who expresses her distrust towards the helpers working with Peter: After we have left Peter's house, Hanne explains to me that she herself is the one who has taken the initiative to his little walk in the mornings, by motivating him by the 'reward'. Hanne is worried that Peter is too thin; she suggests that the wife economises on his food in the same way as she economises on the heat in the rest of the house. The wife could not be trusted: she speaks ill of the helpers behind their backs.

This epilogue of the visit at Peters house points to one of the consequences of not recognising the strains of care work for elderly people and the social and health care helpers' orientation towards care. Someone like Hanne, who wants to provide best possible care to the benefit of her client, is faced with multiple conflicting emotions. On the one hand, she experiences the anxiety caused by the confrontation with the decaying body. On the other hand, she encounters the mistrust leading to control and Taylorisation. Her resulting reaction is anger. In this case, her anger is directed towards the relative, but during my observations I also often met anger towards one's colleagues. Neither type of anger provides a fruitful basis for the cooperation which is a vital condition for the quality of care.

Care work for elderly in a gender hierarchy: devaluation of the care orientation

Why are the strains of care work for elderly people not recognised? Why is the orientation towards care and care rationality not valued as being important, even necessary, for carrying out this specific kind of work? To answer these questions one has to consider the similarities between paid care work and the unpaid care work in the private sphere primarily carried out by women. Such reproductive work is generally held in low esteem.

The German social-psychologist Regina Becker-Schmidt (2002) argues that there exists a fundamental connection between gender, work and the valorisation of fields of work. With a critical theoretical and feminist point of departure, she analyses how on the one hand gender, seen as a structural category, and on the other hand power and status are intertwined in hierarchical structures depending on their position in relation to the social spheres. Becker-Schmidt further argues that the importance of dealing with gender arrangements as relational lies in the possibilities this gives for analysing how unequal circumstances in one social sphere are connected to hierarchical constellations in another social sphere. From this perspective, individuals as well as social sectors can be viewed as elements in relation to each other. With a starting-point in the historical social division of labour, in this case in the separation of men's work in the public sphere and women's work in the private sphere, it is possible to see how the social spheres are mutually dependent. Thus, social spheres can be understood as inscribed in a gender and power hierarchy due to their gendered connotations. The gendered connotations are connected to the question of whether the sphere and its institutions are regarded as 'productive' and thereby 'male' or they are regarded 'reproductive' and thereby 'female'.

The Danish psychologist Simo Køppe (1997) describes how in the wake of the introduction of capitalist economy in North European societies an ideology was introduced which saw housework as work that was the payment in itself. Because of the gratification that women received from their work, no monetary compensation was needed. The home and the intimate sphere became the centre for emotions and humanity—the place that balanced the economical rationality of the productive public sphere. At the same time as work linked to the sphere of reproduction was economically devalued, it became ideologically upgraded. Nevertheless, following the diffusion of the capitalist way of production, power and prestige became associated with money. As the private sphere was isolated from the public sphere of social exchange, it was at the same time made dependent on and subordinate to this sphere. The economical contribution from the male head of family in the form of wages made the work of the man more prestigious than housework, because it stemmed from the sphere of social exchange, where work was paid for by money. The female work in the home was not paid for, even though it was a prerequisite for the male 'productive' work.

In a similar vein, Becker-Schmidt points out that work which historically and traditionally has existed outside the money economy of capitalist society tends to be regarded as less worth than work for which a wage is paid. Care work has almost entirely been carried out in the home—by women—and the low valuation connected to this sticks to the work even when it becomes publicly financed wage labour. In this perspective the unequal relationship between a rationality of care and an economical and technical rationality can be seen.

The above-described gender hierarchy of productive and reproductive work is inscribed in the professionalisation process where attempts to professionalise care work go hand in hand with economical-technical rationality. The following quotation is from my notes from an observation at a Social and Health Care School in October 2003. It illustrates the idea of being able to separate one's subjective motivation from the work one is doing:

> Male teacher: 'One should be able to be in other people's shoes, but also to take them off again. What do I mean by that?'

1. Female trainee: 'That you should leave the problems when you go home.'

2. Female trainee: 'Being a professional means that you do not slide into the same mood as the other person.'

   Male teacher: 'Maybe it is a prejudice, but men are normally better than women to be professional—or to be 'cold in the ass'.'

3. Female trainee: 'That is our mother instinct.'

   Male teacher: 'Yes, a caring gene... But one should not carry the problems home.'

Certainly, it can be a problem if the care worker identifies too strongly with the person she is helping, but placing professionalism on an equal footing with being indifferent is an insult both towards the orientation of care workers and towards the needs of the elderly people the care workers are supposed to give care. It gives an unrealistic image of professionalism, which—when seen in an existential light—is impossible to reach, because it sets aside the very character of the caring relation.

Entering relations of care with elderly and sick people can function as a memento mori of the temporal limits of one's own lives, thus awakening an existential anxiety. But the relation of care can also awake an existential joy (Noddings 1984). Both anxiety and joy are fundamental aspects of meeting 'The Other' in the caring relation and both require involvement. Ignoring this fact potentially leads to quite the opposite of professionalism, i.e. to a situation where the care worker tries to 'put up shutters' between what is 'personal' and what is related to work. Denying that in relational work the worker uses her feelings makes it impossible to handle the emotions in a conscious way, and thereby only leads to 'pseudo-professionalism'.

An intention to professionalise social and health care helpers by teaching them to be immune towards the influences of care work can of course originate from the considerations of their wellbeing and satisfaction with their work. But it could also be interpreted in connection with the esteem of the work in a gendered hierarchy. Putting up shutters between 'personal' and 'professional' is the logic of the public sphere, whereas the tendency to let time, work tasks, involvement and emotional states flow is the logic of the private, reproductive sphere (Dybbroe 2006). The image of professionalism just presented is in itself inscribed in a gendered hierarchy.

Conclusion

When I accompanied the trainees in the home-based care of the elderly and in old people's homes, I experienced first hand the reality of care orientation conceptualised in care theory as rationality of care (Wærness 1982). The care orientation of a care worker is expressed through a way of thinking and acting in the practical work, placing the needs of the client in focus. My analysis of life historical interviews and observations with trainees further shows that in spite of differences in age, former education and experiences with caring jobs, all of the women perceive a job in the care sector both as work and as relation. Care work awakes feelings of joy and of disgust: it is frightening and giving.

Care work is in itself full of paradoxes. One of my informants compared care work with work at a mink farm, which suggests that this work is not highly valued. At the same time she clearly considered being a social and health care helper the best job she had ever had. In fact, all of the informants consider care work as an excellent form of paid work: the working hours are flexible, there is a possibility to work anywhere in the country, and even the wages are rising. But none of the interviewees perceived the job as a social and health care helper only as paid work. Rather, at the subjective level, they experienced care work to be full of meaning (cf. Hansen et al. 1999, Krogh Hansen 2006). This meaningfulness is connected to their close contact with fellow human beings, carrying out subjectively meaningful activities. My informants discussed having close contact to others, being important to others, and being able to help and support sick or fragile fellow human beings as reasons for choosing to be qualified for care work. Perceiving care as a relation can be understood as a particular subjective work orientation, which does not undermine the importance of work as a way of earning one's livelihood. At the same time, however, care orientation entails that specific qualities are expected in the caring relation. Correspondingly, rationality of care can be considered to be a necessary strategy for orientation towards care. Furthermore, rationality of care also involves strategic action arising from the caring relation in the incidences where the practitioners of care do not withdraw because of anxiety, powerlessness or the lack of recognition in the relation.

On the basis of my analysis, the rationality of care seems to be in an unsolvable contradiction to the demands of the modernisation of the field of elderly care. At the organisational level, modernisation has implied strict time schedules and requirements of documentation of every task carried out. At the discursive level it has implied an understanding of professionalisation in which the ability to act professionally is considered in opposition to be 'personal' or personally involved. This tendency is found in other research in the field, too (e.g. Szebehely 2006).

What happens to the commitment of the social and health care helper trainees when their motivation and efforts to build relationships with their clients are belittled? My analysis shows that if the hierarchies lead to a neglect of the personal meaningfulness of the work, the care worker is put under such pressure that work loses its meaning for her. The care worker may still act in a care-rational manner and engage in a relation with the client, experiencing the giving dimensions of the relation. However, the existential joy resulting from this experience that has been described in the literature (Noddings 1984) does not necessarily appear. Instead of existential joy there is a risk that the care worker feels existential anxiety in the face of conflicting demands. Thus, the work can give rise to ambivalence between the ideal of 'doing good' and feelings of powerlessness and discomfort.

The Nordic literature on care work offers a powerful analysis of how efforts to raise the esteem of care work, such as professionalisation, involves a risk of resulting in a neglect of the logic of care and the strains and ambivalences connected to caring. My analysis bears witness to how this type of modernisation of the field has so far resulted in an atmosphere where the ideals and logics practiced by care workers have to be hidden, making parts of the competencies of care workers invisible. As a result of the silencing of the relational aspects of care, the dilemmas resulting from the reality of feelings of guilt, anxiety and aggression, ever present in the care work with old, sick people, are harder to put into words. If it is not acceptable to say that you actually care, it is even less acceptable to talk about the difficulties in caring.

During my field work at social and health schools and at work places it was evident that this misjudgment of the care relation as 'unprofessional' means that talking openly about engagement as well as about the strains and discomforts of care work are reduced to non-official spaces, like the smoking room or during lunch breaks. An alternative strategy for both modernisation and professionalisation is urgently needed, if our societies want to recruit motivated care workers.

By highlighting the orientation towards care work and the rationality of care among the trainees, I do not want to ignore the ambivalences towards the work which were also expressed in the empirical material. Parallel to the appraisal of the meaningfulness of care work there were often signs of the strains involved in the work, including anger and even disgust. Still, the orientation towards care emerges as one of the main motivations for the women to enter this field, while the rationality of care appears as a necessary condition for carrying out care for other human beings. Thus, respect for the rationality of care emerges as an important component in securing a qualitatively 'good-enough-care' for elderly people.

As shown above, in the eyes of society, care work in the field of elderly care remains dirty work that is mainly done by female care workers on the 'outskirts' of professional hierarchies. But if social and health care helpers are to be supported in their care orientation, the existential dimensions of their work have to be accepted. Further, we need to take the low social position of care work for the elderly into account and tackle the uncaring logics of modernisation and professionalisation which potentially affect us all.

Note

1 I am aware that according to hygienic considerations, the trainees are taught always to wear gloves during personal care, but I have also seen this precept broken during my observations.

References

Becker-Schmidt, R. (2002) Theorizing gender arrangements. In R. Becker-Schmidt (Ed.) *Gender and Work in Transition*. Opladen: Leske & Budrich.

Christensen, K. (2003) De stille stemmer—om kønsrelateret magt i offentlige omsorgstjenester. In L.Widding Isaksen (red.) *Omsorgens pris. Kjønn, makt og marked i velferdsstaten. Makt og demokratiutredningen, 1998–2003*. Oslo: Gyldendal Akademisk, Gyldendal Norsk Forlag AS.

Dahl, H. M. (2002) Er køn retfærdighed? Et spørgsmål om status og lighed med hjemmehjælpen som case. In: *Kønsmagt under forandring, Magtudredningen*. København: Hans Reitzels Forlag.

Dybbroe, B. (2006) Omsorg i skæringspunktet mellem arbejde og liv. *Tidsskrift for Arbejdsliv*, 8(1), 67–81.

Isaksen, L. W. (2003) Homo Fabers symbolske makt. Om kropp og maskulinitet i pleiearbeid. In L. Widding Isaksen (Ed.) *Omsorgens pris. Kjønn, makt og marked i velferdsstaten. Makt og demokratiutredningen, 1998–2003*. Oslo: Gyldendal Akademisk, Gyldendal Norsk Forlag A.

Krogh Hansen, H. (2006) *Ældreomsorg i et pædagogisk perspektiv*. Ph.d. afhandling, Forskerskolen i Livslang Læring, Roskilde Universitetscenter.

Køppe, S. (1997) *Freuds psykoanalyse*. 2. udgave København : Gyldendalske Boghandel, Nordisk Forlag.

Liveng, A. (2006) Social- og sundhedshjælperelevers omsorgsorientering og hjælperarbejdets modsætningsfyldte krav. *Tidsskrift for Arbejdsliv*, 8(1), 32–48.

Liveng, A. (2007) *Omsorgsarbejde, subjektivitet og læring. Social- og sundhedshjælperelevers orienteringer mod omsorgsarbejdet og deres*

møde med arbejdets læringsrum. Ph.D afhandling, Roskilde
Universitetscenter.

Nabe-Nielsen, K., Nygaard Jensen, J. Høgh, A., Giver, H. & Strøyer,
J. (2005) *FOR-SOSU pjece: Profil af nyuddannede social og
sundhedshjælpere og -assistenter.* København: Arbejdsmiljøinstituttet.

Noddings, N. (1984) *Caring. A Feminine Approach to Ethics & Moral
Education.* California: University of California Press.

Szebehely, M. (2006) Omsorgsvardag under skiftande organisatoriska
villkor—en jämförande studie av den nordiska hemtjänsten.
Tidsskrift for Arbejdsliv, 8(1), 49–66.

Winnicott, D. W. (1986) *Home is Where We Start From.* London: Penguin
Psychology.

Wærness, K. (1982) *Kvinneperspektiver på socialpolitikken.* Oslo—Bergen—
Tromsø: Universitetsforlaget.

PART II
FINLAND

INTRODUCTION TO PART II

Care Work in the Context of a
Transforming Welfare State

Lea Henriksson and Sirpa Wrede

In Finland, the deregulation of the money market in the 1990s was related to the deep economic crisis and associated mass unemployment, together helping the new neoliberal ideology to gain hegemony (Patomäki 2007). Far-reaching institutional changes that reorganised the division of labour between the central state and the municipalities hit care work intensely. In macroeconomic terms, Finland continues to follow the Nordic development but only to a moderate degree.

An ideology that posits work as a central societal value is deeply rooted in Finland. It underlies approaches to situations perceived as societal crises. Furthermore, deriving from the experiences of the generations who have faced wars and former depression eras, there is a readiness in Finnish culture to accept policy measures framed as responses to societal crises that in themselves may require some groups to make sacrifices for the greater good. Reflecting such cultural dynamics, the policy rhetoric surrounding what is currently recognised as a societal crisis in care creates gendered ethical appeals; new expectations and demands placed on women and care workers in particular.

This introduction sheds light on the Finnish discussions of the neoliberal policy shift. In order to identify the current claims directed at care work and its changing terms and conditions, it is important to be aware of the national policy context and the new agendas of care work, but also of the location and audiences of these debates. Discussions in various arenas are interlinked and related to the same policy shift but comprise different actors, vocabularies and impacts.

The neoliberal turn in Finland

The dominant political rhetoric states that Finnish politics aims at the deepening integration in Europe in terms of economic, social and environmental competitiveness. The former Minister of Foreign Affairs Erkki Tuomioja (2006), who is one of the vocal critics of this rhetoric, has argued that the emphasis in the recent debates is on economic integration.

In his view, the message is that the country has to forego its universal social services and employment safety, cut social security, public spending and taxes, privatise, outsource and open up for competition; in short go for the full monty of the neoliberal agenda in order to survive. Formulating a social-democratic critique of the current Finnish position, he further holds that social progress is a national issue, but it is also justi-fied in terms of the Nordic and the European goals, i.e. there is a consensus about social progress being included in develop-ment (Tuomioja 2008). In his view, the partnership in health and social wellbeing is also a precondition for the sustainable economic development of the Nordic region.

Since the early 1990's the navigating of the Finnish 'com-petition state' (Sipilä 2005, Kettunen 2006) has been about the profitability of the national economy. In economic and tech-nological terms, recent developments are reflected in what has been termed a national 'joint venture for productivity' (VATT 2007). This drive for productivity encompasses welfare services and vocational educational schemes comprising al-most half of the Finnish welfare expenditure. More open com-petition is the key principle in the process of designing the 'creative welfare society'. This authoritative view was formu-lated by the Parliamentary Committee for the Future chaired by the leading conservative politician, the present Minister of Finance Jyrki Katainen (EK 2004). The statement of the com-mittee is that the pressures of welfare services and pension expenses endanger the speed of economic growth. A major solution propagated then in this scenario is the nexus model, a welfare mix in which the public sector has the dominating responsibility for financing and control, while both private and public producers supply the services.

From a feminist perspective, the ongoing policy shift has, for instance, been critiqued with reference to democracy. It is argued that while democratic government should be about the social rights of the citizens, at present it is the gendered rights of those most capable in economic terms that are the key point of reference (Kailo 2007). At the same time, the number of total working hours of full-time employed Finnish women is the highest in Europe. Furthermore, there is a lot of evidence that the outsourcing of public services often means an increase in women's care responsibilities and workload, at the same time as their work-related social rights and pay have weakened (Eräsaari 2002, Julkunen 2004). Thus, from the point of the view of equality between women and men, Finland is far from perfect.

On the national policy level, the need for a 'broad framework' among ministries and sector administration is being addressed (MHSA 2001a, b, 2002, 2007, see ILO 2007). Governmental welfare strategy emphasises mutual solidarity in terms of the 'caring moral' as a societal resource (MHSA 2007, 22). Despite the welfare state ethos and its strong support, sectoral regulations demonstrate that the strongest social rights and shared responsibility concern the early phases of the life cycle whereas the more moderate ones are typical of the end of the cycle (Heikkilä 2005). None of the security systems ensure citizens the right to a certain service, but do safeguard their position in relation to the complicated service bureaucracy. In the legal arena, the development towards stronger service rights is on target; new treatment guidelines concerning the provision of care within specific time frames are examples of the implementation of the principle of the social guarantee (Heikkilä 2007).

The logic guiding the making of new organisational models and workforce designs is that of streamlining the 'logistics' of the 'production lines' (see Davies 2003). Seamless services, integrated care and fluent flow-through are examples of the managerialist vocabulary being implemented in the name of cost-effectiveness and quality consciousness. Production lines from hospital to home, from special care to primary care and from vocational education to work are referred to as key processes of streamlining. This agenda is rooted in the view that the disturbances to this rational management of service production are created by economic, demographic and institutional forces. For instance, rigid organisation structures with their powerful professions and the out-of-date education schemes are referred to as obstacles to flexibilisation. The demographic pressures identified by policymakers have also brought the issue of migrants as potential future care workers to the policy agenda. The national picture is, however, contradictory. On the one hand, there are calls for work-based immigration, on the other hand there is a long history of national discourse that makes it in practice difficult to tolerate and deal with diversity (Lehtonen & Löytty 2007). Health care is especially known for being a national realm (Nieminen 2007).

Whatever the vocabulary used in the political or governmental arena, the care needs of the aging population are seen as a threat to the future capacity of the Finnish welfare state to produce public services. The eroding of the mandate of public care in general and elderly care in particular has created a crisis of care and especially an ongoing erosion of the ethos of socially defined care. As a service, child care is adopting the model of primary education while care for the elderly seems to be following health care procedures (Lehto et al. 1999, Wrede & Henriksson 2005). The social, particularly in the meaning of homemaking, is becoming excluded from public services (Tedre 1999). Within the occupational realms, the expertise of social care is challenged. Academic social workers in Finland are constructing occupational boundaries and exclusive credentials (Julkunen 2004). For teachers and students at the polytechnic level, the value and the meanings of the *social* as the cornerstones of vocational expertise are becoming blurred (Niiranen-Linkama 2005).

Tension in workplaces: professionals and care recipients

In the media headlines, cost-effective health service provision is epitomised in the formula: 'For two doctors, you can get six nurses' (HeSa 24.11.2007). This example mirrors the two elementary foci of the public debate. Recipes such as these are used as criteria for cost-effective staffing and also reflect the focus of political interest on the upper ladders of the occupational scene. As a policy, the rationality of efficiency is resulting in the annulment of work-related social rights, for instance, the right to occupational development and employment safety, care workers' wellbeing and chance to control their own work. The neoliberal policy shift is thus eroding the goals the trade unions have traditionally defended and what the corporatist negotiation system has vouched for.

The Finnish section highlights the viewpoints of the care workers and the care recipients, offering insights for the reclaiming of the ethos of care that is beneficial for both parties. The question of how to retain *dignity* in care work emerges as a shared focal point. On the one hand, the issue is how to safeguard the occupational opportunities and ethical treatment of the care workers in service organisations. On the other hand, the question is about the equity of access to public services and the social rights and human treatment of the frailest care receivers. Experiences of the declining occupational pride and attraction of care work occupations are related to job insecurity, which goes together with the inflation of degrees and the devaluation of care work. Policies that count on flexible, generic-skill schemes in frontline work easily endanger and dismantle the fragile occupational agency and the terms and conditions for good care.

Finland is known for the high quality of its basic and higher education, for its technological inventiveness and innovativeness. In addition to these notions, we argue that Finnish service policy has deserved recognition for its social innovations related to care occupations. The underlying idea of socially defined care is here understood as a social innovation of the Nordic welfare state project. In Finland formally defined care occupations and the services the diverse care worker groups have been an integral part of the welfare state infrastructure. From the point of view of care recipients, the existence of this infrastructure secured the realisation of their social rights. From the point of view of the care workers, the chapters show the relevance of these institutional characteristics for their occupational projects and identities.

Two of the chapters in the Finnish section focus on the macro level and two on the micro level of care work. Chapter 4, authored by *Lea Henriksson* and *Sirpa Wrede*, examines the reorganisation of elderly care through policy reform. Chapter 5, by *Päivi Topo* and *Saila Sormunen*, shows what kind of an impact different modes of organising care work have from the point of view of the elderly clients. Chapter 6, by *Laura Tainio* and *Sirpa Wrede*, focuses on the work role, examining how it structures the workplace ethos from the point of view of care workers. Finally, in Chapter 7, *Suvi Nieminen* and *Lea Henriksson* examine the reconfiguration of the care-work labour force, drawing attention to the policy context and the patterns of incipient ethnification. Together, the chapters offer insights into the social impact of care work and its organisation on both care recipients and care workers.

Overall, the Finnish section shows that the recent developments of narrowing down both the scope of welfare services and the groups they are provided to, in association with the reorganisation of care work, have contributed to a major turn in care services. The fragmentation of care work cultures threatens to erode the social innovations achieved through previous policies. We argue that at the core of socially defined care in its Finnish formulation has been the strong occupational commitment and agency of care workers, fuelled by the welfare ethos underpinned by the stated aim of equity of access to public welfare services. Thus, the retrenchment and the curtailment of the service system for the care recipients parallel the erosion of the welfare ethos and the occupational agency of the care workers. Furthermore, the work-related social rights of the care workers are affected, as discussed in Chapter 4.

The jurisdictional claims of occupational groups, having different amounts of social power and authority, are raised simultaneously in different societal arenas (Abbott 1988). Occupations are, however, unequal in getting their voice heard. The questions raised in the section are about the social structure (recruitment, occupational ranking and organisational positions), the cognitive structure (education and knowledge basis), as well as culture (care ethos) in Finland. These issues are here empirically examined from different angles. The chapters firstly highlight the profound institutional and cultural reshaping faced by care workers of different ranks and educational backgrounds. Secondly, the chapters provide insights into the perspectives reclaiming social justice and shared responsibility. What is at issue is not only securing comprehensive access to services for care recipients, but acknowledging social innovations related to care work and securing sustainable occupational development and work-related social rights for care workers.

References

Abbott, A. (1988) *The System of Professions. An Essay on the Division of Expert Labor.* Chicago and London: The University of Chicago Press.

Davies, C. (2003) Introduction: a new workforce in the making. In Davies, C. (Ed.) *The Future Health Workforce* (pp. 1–13) Hampshire: Palgrave Macmillan.

EK (2004) *Skenaariot ja strategiat palvelujärjestelmän turvaamiseksi. Esiselvitys.* Eduskunnan kanslian julkaisu 8/2004. Helsinki: Tulevaisuusvaliokunta.

Eräsaari, L.(2002) *Julkinen tila ja valtion yhtiöittäminen.* Helsinki: Gaudeamus.

HeSa (2007) Tuottavuus hoitajien palkkaperusteena saa kannatusta mutta toteutus epäilyttää. *Helsingin Sanomat* 24.11.2007, A 4.

Heikkilä, M. (2005) Julkinen vastuu eräissä sosiaalipalveluissa. In *Julkinen hyvinvointivastuu sosiaali- ja terveydenhuollossa,* pp. 35–39. Helsinki: Valtioneuvoston kanslian julkaisusarja 2/2005.

Heikkilä, M. (2007) Julkinen ja yksityinen hyvinvointivastuu— Näkökohtia valtion, perheen ja markkinoiden rooliin ihmisten hyvinvoinnissa. In Tiihonen P. & Harisalo, R. (Eds) *Monen monta demokratiaa.* Kauko Sipposen juhlaseminaari eduskunnassa 25.4.2007 (pp. 53–57). Helsinki: Eduskunnan tulevaisuusvaliokunnan julkaisu 3/2007.

ILO (2007) *Decent work for a fair globalization.* Overview Paper. Retrieved 2008-4-22. http://www.ilo.org/global/What_we_do/Events/ Symposiaseminarsandworkshops/lang--en/WCMS_084179/index. htm

Julkunen, R. (2004) Hyvinvointipalvelujen uusi politiikka. In
    Henriksson, L. & Wrede, S. (Eds) *Hyvinvointityön ammatit* (pp.
    168–209). Helsinki: Gaudeamus.
Kailo, K. (2007) Naisalojen oletetaan uhrautuvan yhä kansakunnan
    puolesta. *Helsingin Sanomat* 12.10.2007, A 2.
Kettunen, P. (2006) The power of international comparisons. A
    perspective on the making and challenging of the Nordic welfare
    state. In Christiansen, N.F., Petersen, K., Edling, K. & Haave, P. (Eds)
    The Nordic Model of Welfare. A Historical Reappraisal, pp. 31–65.
    Copenhagen: Museum Tusculanum Press.
Lehto, J., Moss, N. & Rostgaard, T. (1999) Universal public social care and
    health services. In Kautto, M. et al. (Eds) *Nordic Social Policy. Changing
    welfare states* (pp.104–132). London and New York: Routledge.
Lehtonen, M. & Löytty, O. (2007) Suomiko toista maata? In Kuortti,
    I., M. Lehtonen, M. & Löytty, O. (Eds) *Kolonialismin jäljet* (pp.
    105–118). Tampere: Vastapaino.
MSHA 2001(a) *Sosiaali- ja terveydenhuollon työvoimatarpeen
    ennakointitoimikunnan mietintö.* Komiteamietintö 7/2001. Helsinki:
    Sosiaali- ja terveysministeriö.
MSHA 2001(b) *Government Resolution on the Health 2015 public health
    programme.* Publications of the Ministry of Social Affairs and Health
    6/2001. Helsinki: Ministry of Social Affairs and Health.
MSHA 2002 *Kansallinen projekti terveydenhuollon tulevaisuuden
    turvaamiseksi. Työvoiman tarve ja keskinäinen työnjako.* 15.1.2002.
    Helsinki: Sosiaali- ja terveysministeriö.
MSHA 2007 *Hyvinvointi 2015-ohjelma. Sosiaalialan pitkän aikavälin
    tavoitteita.* Sosiaali- ja terveysministeriön julkaisuja 3/2007. Helsinki:
    Sosiaali- ja terveysministeriö.
Nieminen, S. (2007) Negotiating Skilled Migration: Professional
    Membership of Nurse Immigrants in Finland. In Wahlbeck, Ö. (Ed.)
    Ny migration och etnicitet I Norden (pp. 99–120). Åbo: Meddelanden
    från ekonimisk-statsvetenskapliga fakulteten vid Åbo Akademi.
    Sociologi Ser. A:554.
Niiranen-Linkama, P. (2005) *Sosiaalisen transformaatio sosiaalialan
    asiantuntijuuden diskurssissa.* Jyväskylä Studies in education,
    psychology and social research 272.
Patomäki, H. (2007) *Uusliberalismi Suomessa.* Helsinki: WSOY.
Sipilä, J. (2005) Minkä instituutioiden varaan uskallamme turvamme
    rakentaa? *Sosiaaliturva* 93(9), 14–16.
Tedre, S. (1999) *Hoivan sanattomat sopimukset. Tutkimus vanhusten
    kotipalvelun työntekijöiden työstä.* Joensuu: Joensuun yliopiston
    yhteiskuntatieteellisiä julkaisuja 40.
Tuomioja, E. (2006) *Remarks presented at a discussion on The Future of
    the European Social Model in a panel with Anthony Giddens and Pekka
    Himanen,* Helsinki 5.6.2006. Retrieved 2008-1-18. http://
    www.tuomioja.org/index.php

Tuomioja, E. (2008) *Northern Dimension and Nordic Cooperation'* -konferenssi, Espoo: Hanasaari 17.1.2007. Retrieved 2008-1-18. http://www.tuomioja.org/index.php?

VATT (2007) *Hyvinvointipalvelujen tuottavuus: Tuloksia opintien varrelta*. Kangasharju, A. (Ed.) VATT-julkaisuja 46. Helsinki: Valtion taloudellinen tutkimuslaitos.

Wrede, S. & Henriksson, L. (2005) The changing terms of welfare service work: Finnish home care in transition. In Dahl, H.M. & Eriksen, T. (Eds) *Dilemmas of care in the Nordic welfare state. Continuity and change* (pp. 62–79). Aldershot: Ashgate.

FOUR

The Making of Medico-Managerial Care Work Culture in Public Home Care for the Elderly

Lea Henriksson and Sirpa Wrede

Municipal home care for the elderly provides a good example of the recent welfare policy shift and its implications for care work cultures and professional agency. Since the 1990s, the scope of public services aimed at the elderly has been narrowed down through policies formulated under the influence of neoliberal ideologies and the deepest recession in the Finnish economy since the 1930s. The restructuring of public sector services has been aimed at breaking down institutional care and limiting elderly care to the so-called basic services and reallocating them to the frailest elderly (Julkunen 2001, Paasivaara 2002, Wrede & Henriksson 2005). The logic guiding the narrowing down of the public services is economic and technocratic. The production of public services relies on cost-effectiveness as well as medical and managerial criteria and expertise.

Since the early 1970's different groups of professionals working in or contributing to public home care, including primary health centre doctors, have been employed by municipalities (Henriksson & Wrede 2004). Until the 1980s, state regulation underpinned the democratisation of professionalism and supported the agency of frontline care workers, both in terms of their employment rights and control over their work (Henriksson et al. 2006). When the institutional matrix of elderly care in the welfare-mix era was demarcated, the expertise of socially defined care was devalued and excluded and the agency of care workers started to disintegrate (Wrede & Henriksson 2004).

The exclusion of socially defined care from municipal home care for the elderly in Finland (1.) is here recognised as a crisis in terms of the erosion of skill and competence of frontline care workers. Instead of valuing the expertise in socially defined care, the reorganisation cut down the frontline care workers' room for self-steered work and their license is defined through the expertise of others, primarily managers, doctors or nurses. Parallel to these changes, the terms and conditions of the turbulent public sector labour market created unsafe employment. Furthermore, the rapid aging of the

Finnish population is expected to create an overwhelming workload to the welfare state that is made worse by the impending shortage of labour in care work.

This chapter examines the institutional matrix of public care services. By 'institutional matrix' we refer to the institutions—the organisations, rules, routines, procedures and assumptions—that shape the public care services and the division of labour in care work (Freeman 1999, 91). We consider how the changes have reframed the care work culture and redefined the frontline care workers' agency. By 'care work culture', we refer to the welfare state ethos structuring the services, i.e. what kinds of services are provided, who are eligible for them and what kinds of skills and competence the provision of these services relies on.

In the following, we first consider institutional shifts in the development of municipal home care for the elderly (2.), paying particular attention to how the universalist welfare state reformed the Finnish care work culture and the position of frontline carers. The second section examines the impact of neoliberal policy reforms at the national-level on the scope of public elderly-home care. The third section draws attention to the implementation of these reforms, from the perspective of the meso-level of the municipality, of which the City of Helsinki is used as an example. Furthermore, we highlight the collective agency of care workers and consider how the trade unions representing the different groups of care workers—public health nurses, nurses, practical nurses—with a stake in public elderly home care have responded to the reforms. In the conclusions we consider the described changes in the institutional matrix as a dynamic process that has impoverished the care work culture in public elderly home care in Finland. It has removed the mandate for care workers to provide comprehensive socially defined care. Instead, public elderly home care now only entails services that are defined as 'basic'.

The rise of socially defined care: from home help to home care

Before the 1960s, it was difficult to talk about an elderly care system or even formal occupations in the provision of care to the Finnish elderly. The situation changed when public home help services specifically directed to the elderly were created in 1966 through the Municipal Home Help Act (Simonen 1990). The new service offered assistance in daily routines, enabling the elderly to continue living in their homes as long as possible. At the same time, home help services created a basis for the gradual formalisation of occupations that provided socially defined care.

The legislation was a sign of a new way of thinking, responding to the pressures caused by urbanisation and women's increased involvement in the labour market. In cultural terms, the home helpers represented a traditional view on how care for the elderly was to be organised. Home help workers were typically former housewives who had a short training course on housekeeping tasks. Thus their formal qualifications were strikingly modest if compared with more regulated health care occupations (Rauhala 1996). The occupation was eventually shaped by the policy into a *homemaking culture* (c.f., Wærness 1992), in which the home helpers occupied what could be identified as a boundary role in the municipal administration. The homemaking service provided by the helpers enabled the elderly to continue their everyday lives largely in the way to which they were accustomed, without becoming dependent on relatives or friends (Wærness 1984, Simonen 1990). Some clients held onto traditional ideas of private service, trying to treat them as 'municipal maids'. However, the legislation underpinning the institutional position of the municipal home helpers as public service employees provided them protection from this attitude by making them, first and foremost, responsible to the municipality (Tedre 1999, 2004).

In the 1980s, policy makers and researchers sought to academise socially defined care as a specific expertise in 'social care'. The new expertise was supported by a knowledge base deriving from social gerontology (Koskinen et al. 1988, Tedre 1999, Paasivaara 2002). While the traditional home-help service emphasised household chores such as cleaning, cooking and shopping, the new social care treated these tasks as secondary. In the social care perspective, instead of caring for the home, the focus was to be on interaction and the needs of the elderly person (Borgman 1998, Tedre 1999). Many scholars have criticised this reformulation of the knowledge base as underpinning a professionalist hierarchy of so-called dirty work (e.g., Tedre 2004, see Chapter 3). On the positive side, however, the redefinition of home help as social care was part of the rise of elderly care as a policy frame. In this framework the elderly person was recognised as a citizen, entitled to care in her/his own right. Elderly care policy promoted individualism and humanism as the ideals that were to form the core of the ethos of elderly care. This was the foundation for the reframing of home help into home care (Paasivaara 2002). Thus, the scientific formulation of the knowledge base was part and parcel of the professional projects of the universalist welfare state (Julkunen 1994). From the point of view of care workers, the state support for professionalising socially defined care also contributed to more egalitarian working conditions and employment safety (Henriksson & Wrede 2004, Henriksson et al. 2006).

In 1988, 46.2 % of the Finnish population aged 75 or older received home help services. Of the same age group, that year 17.6 % received long-term residential care of some type (Vaarama & Noro 2005). Reflecting the expansion of elderly home help in the 1980s, the number of care workers in home care service increased to approximately 13,000 people (Vaarama et al. 2001). This group was one of the largest in the care sector and most care workers worked full-time. Even though the home care personnel consisted of almost equal shares of the lower-grade home helpers and the higher-grade homemakers, their work roles and positions as public sector employees had become increasingly similar (Simonen 1990, Rauhala 1996).

The institutional matrix of the welfare state expansion era made public services readily available on the basis of broadly defined needs. At the same time, however, the figures reflect the long-term Finnish tradition of investing in institutional care rather than in ambulatory services. Elderly home care and residential housing services for the elderly remained only secondary in the elderly care policy despite their positive connotations as more 'humane' forms of care (Paasivaara 2002). Thus, despite the efforts to develop the knowledge base of municipal home help, the most valued forms of expertise were associated with institutional care. Furthermore, if compared with other forms of socially defined care, particularly child day care, Finnish elderly home care was always based on weak universalism that in recent years has eroded (Kröger et al. 2003). Although the public responsibility for elderly care is still extensive; the expectation is that the informal networks would complement the formal service.

Neoliberal policies boosting the medical culture in elderly home care

The institutional restructuring of the Finnish welfare state in the direction dictated by the neoliberal ideology kicked off in the early 1990s with the decentralisation of the responsibility for welfare budgets, planning and organising welfare services to the autonomous municipalities. (3.) The new welfare-mix matrix, implemented through legislation in 1993, encouraged municipalities to purchase health and social services from other service providers rather than providing them directly. The reorganisation of service production was accompanied by education policy aiming at shaping a flexible workforce for the diverse settings of service provision.

Four important ideological starting points directed the neoliberal reforms of Finnish elderly home care. Firstly, the care provided by a family member was defined as the favoured solution in elderly care. Accordingly, from the year 1988 to the year 2002 the volume of family-based care assistance did, indeed, increase by 49 % (Vaarama & Noro 2005). Secondly, the idea of a welfare mix was to be implemented with the aim of achieving cost-efficiency for the municipality and availability of choice for the elderly. Reflecting this idea, the role of the public sector was to a large extent reorganised corresponding to the so-called purchaser-provider model (Kovalainen 2004, Vaarama & Noro 2005).

Thirdly, in search of efficiency in the use of municipal resources, national policy makers promoted trans-sectoral home care services, merging socially defined care with medical care, as the favoured solution to the challenge of dismantling institutional care. Home nursing was assigned the central role in making home care capable of taking over clients that previously would have been cared for by institutions. Furthermore, instead of recognising comprehensive responsibility, the role of the public sector was restricted to producing 'basic services' that were ideally provided through a welfare mix. Our earlier study indicates that policy makers privileged medical needs when defining which services were recognised as 'basic' (Wrede & Henriksson 2004). Accordingly, the re-framed elderly home care was underpinned by an ethos that Wærness (1992) defines as *professional medical culture* (see also Chapter 5).

The fourth starting point for the neoliberal reforms in home care was promoting the deinstitutionalisation of care. Home care was assumed to combine the goals of providing both more affordable as well as a more humane and client-centred form of elderly care than institutional care. However, contrary to the goal of developing home care into a well-built service that readily replaces other more expensive forms of care, municipalities did not in the 1990s generally invest in this service. Instead many municipalities shifted resources from both municipal home care and residential homes to service housing (Vaarama & Noro 2005). The establishment of service housing units was expedited through state sponsorship and great ideological expectations were directed toward this service. Service housing was to provide a choice for the client, thus promoting the emphasis on service quality. However, under the severe financial pressures, municipalities grasped the opportunity to use the service housing concept to shift a substantial part of the costs of residential care to the clients and to the state (through sickness insurance). The municipalities also reorganised residential homes as service housing units (Suoniemi et al. 2005).

It has been calculated that during the 1990s municipalities relocated nearly 4000 municipal home-help workers from home-based services to service housing units (Vaarama et al. 2001, MHSA 2004, 25). This implied a major change in the use of personnel resources. This restructuring, together with the fact that the clients who presently are covered by municipal home care need a bigger number of visits than was the case earlier, has meant that the municipalities cater to a much smaller proportion of the elderly than was the previously. By 2003, the percentage of over 75-year-olds receiving regular home help had gone down to 18.7 %, from 31.5 % in 1988. The decline for the period 1988–2002 was 40.6 % (MHSA 2006, 176), providing evidence of the rapid narrowing down of public responsibility for elderly home care. In 2004, the Finnish government adopted a rather modest goal according to which elderly home care should cover at least 25 % of the elderly over 75 years old (MHSA 2006, 178).

In contrast to the problems of enhancing elderly home care produced by the municipality, the goal of creating a private market was successfully implemented. The number of private providers of home care increased by 70 % in the period 1997–2001 and in 2001, raising the number of private providers to 376, of which 70 % were firms and 30 % voluntary organisations (Finnish Government 2003). This creation of a welfare mix in home care involves care workers both as employees in different kinds of care organisations and as small-scale entrepreneurs (Kovalainen 2004). In 2002, already more than 20 % of the care personnel in Finland worked in the private sector, in contrast to less than 13 % in the late 1980s (MHSA 2003). This suggests that profound changes have occurred also in the structure of the care work labour market and in employment relations.

The narrowing down of the public responsibility for elderly care was carried out by limiting access to services. A popular way to carry out this task was by classifying clients, using indexes based on primarily geriatric knowledge on aging. When previously elderly people with what were identified as 'medium heavy needs' would mainly have been cared for in residential homes or inpatient primary health care, in the new classification they were to be provided home care, with emphasis on basic care, i.e., help with personal bodily care, nutrition or mobility. Those identified as requiring specialised and continuous nursing care where classified as clients with 'heavy needs'. For this group, the policies continued to secure publicly produced care, either in the form of so-called intensified home care or, as a last resort, as residential care. The policies expressed a keen interest in hindering the elderly from turning into clients with 'heavy' needs. Considering this, it is perhaps surprising that after the neoliberal reforms, the elderly who were considered to have 'light needs', and who would earlier have been eligible for home help, were no longer in any way a public concern (Vaarama et al. 2001).

In contrast to the universalist era, the policy documents of the early 2000s thus emphasise the last-resort nature of the public services. The role of publicly provided care is often referred to as the provision of temporary solutions, filling in when family-based care for is not adequate or if the care recipient is unable to buy the substitute services from the market (MHSA 2001, 14). The policy rhetoric continued to reduce the traditional homemaking culture by stating that the person, not the home, was to be the focus. The new element is that household chores are not only excluded from the definition of care but reframed as essentially a private concern.

Even though the scope of public elderly care has diminished and the public sector in important ways has withdrawn from responsibility, the municipalities still have considerable power to regulate the services that they produce. According to the legislation that is currently being implemented, the personnel employed by the private service providers are expected to fulfil qualification criteria corresponding to those required by municipal employees. Additionally, the service providers themselves need to acquire formal approval for their practice from the local authorities. Acquiring such approval presumes that the service provider has not been subject to disciplinary actions for malpractice, or had serious financial difficulties (MHSA 2005, 29–31). The legislation on the supervision of service provision places municipal and other service providers in unequal positions, as the municipality has the authority to issue other service providers permits to operate. Thus it not only controls the market but regulates the activities of the other service providers. By way of contrast, the municipalities themselves are only subjected to retroactive supervision through complaints that citizens can make to the county government. This is an important issue from the point of view of monitoring the adequacy of the personnel resources and divisions of labour.

The national restructuring of the public sector in the 1990s also concerned the vocational education and qualification for elderly care. Most importantly, new occupations were created in the 1990s, reflecting the belief in flexible, trans-sectoral solutions also inspired by life-long learning agendas of education policy. At the core of the reform was the creation of the *vocational qualification in social and health care*, for which the occupational title is officially translated into English with the term *practical nurse*. Practical nurses are frontline care workers, who as a member of a multi-professional team were supposed to provide both socially defined care and general nursing in elderly home care. (4.)

The new occupation disrupted the previous division of labour in elderly home care, at least at the level of credentials. Two previously separate educational orientations preparing for care work, the one for the social-sector homemakers and the other for the health-sector practical nurses (or auxiliary nurses), were merged. The new care worker was included in

the legislation on the registration of health care professionals as one of the groups authorised to nursing care at a level
defined by their formal skill and competence. (5.) The rhetoric of education policy was to broaden the scope of practice
and to reach a better match between education and the labour market (Vuorensyrjä et al. 2006). The policy was aimed
at implanting the idea of flexible professionals into the care
sector (Wrede 2008). However, at the workplace, the occupational roles of the newcomers have remained turbulent (see
Chapter 6).

Though the practical nurse was established as a new care-
worker category more than a decade ago, it is still difficult to
recruit young people to elderly care. The high levels of dropouts reflect the mismatch between educational policies and
working life practices. The problems of front-line care work
have been raised as a national policy concern (MHSA 2001,
MHSA 2006). The relatively easy access and the shortness of
the education, its practical emphasis, and the varying opportunities to obtain partial credentials tempt policy makers to
use the education programme also as a social policy instru-
ment. Long-term unemployed and other groups, particularly
the young and ethnic minorities, who for some reason are
threatened by marginalisation are directed to the occupation
by officials. Research indicates, however, that particularly the
young view the occupation of the practical nurse mainly as a
temporary, low-paid job that competes poorly with a permanent one with a better salary (Pitkänen 2005).

The rise of the medico-managerial culture

In this section, we draw attention to the implementation
of the neoliberal reforms, from two meso-level perspectives.
Firstly, we examine the 'rationalisation' of municipal home
care through policymaking, of which the City of Helsinki is
used as an example. Secondly, we study how the trade unions
representing health care professionals defend the agency of
the care worker.

IMPLEMENTATION OF TRANS-SECTORAL HOME CARE

The national-level institutional restructuring of the welfare state in Finland has implied a profound change in the content and scope of elderly home care, speeded up by the lack of resources. We argue that this institutional restructuring at the municipal level is equally profound. In the late 1990s and early 2000s, most municipalities reorganised public home care. Especially the larger cities implemented some 'trans-sectoral' model of elderly home care. This meant that what was earlier known as 'home nursing' emerged as the key element in the new institutional matrix for home care. The emphasis on health care reflects the aim of replacing rather than postponing expensive residential care with the means of elderly home care.

Our previous examination of the home care reform implemented by the City of Helsinki showed concretely how difficult it is to both save money and to carry out a merger of social and health care into one integrated form of service (Wrede & Henriksson 2004). The experiences gained from this cost-effective restructuring show that home care in some cases is more expensive than residential care (also Ala-Nikkola 2003). Such observations did not, however, disrupt the overall direction of change towards the increasing medicalisation of home-based services. In the model that is currently being implemented the City of Helsinki has gathered different forms of home care for the elderly into one service under the city health authority. The service is, however, still divided into three separate streams: home help, home nursing and the intensive home care unit. This three-fold structure also appears as a hierarchy of expertise, as the home care units are expected to function as a part of the so-called care chain in health services.

The changes resulted in severe organisational and cultural constraints for the employees. The new medicalised and managerialist ethos undermined the expertise of frontline carers, even though it is they who encounter the client directly. One of the key reasons for this development was the implementation of the hospital-like hierarchic division of labour in municipal home care. The frontline care worker, in turn, was assigned the task to only provide 'basic care', which generally referred to the care of the client's body. The service was reorganised according to the medico-managerial logic that approaches home care from the perspective of how to develop its logistics. This approach resulted in the omission of socially defined care and the related skill and competence. Consequently, the social needs of the client were neglected. Practical care work was to be based on general and specialised nursing (Wrede & Henriksson 2004).

UNIONIST ATTEMPTS TO RECLAIM PROFESSIONAL MANDATES IN
ELDERLY CARE

In the face of the managerialist pressures to reorganise welfare services and lower and disrupt occupational boundaries, the trade unions representing care workers appear to share the goal of trying to 'bring the state back' into welfare service policy. The return of the state would imply that the autonomy of the municipality as a employer and a local service producer would be narrowed down as a result of the increasing state regulation. In their statements, the unions representing chiefly health care occupations have argued that the impending shortage of labour cannot be solved with what is referred to as local task displacements in national policy agendas. Instead the unions demand national regulation to guarantee the quality of the services and to steer an 'adequate' division of labour among care professionals, i.e. one that respects traditional occupational boundaries and credentials. Furthermore, the unions attack the municipalities for their 'unethical' employment policies.

The introduction of the 'trans-sectoral' practical nurse has challenged organisational and professional boundaries in many senses. In its response to the new policies, *Tehy*, the union mainly representing nurses, repeatedly argued for the need to 'respect occupational boundaries'. Apparently, however, an even greater threat than the trans-sectoral occupation for

Tehy was the practice of allowing personnel lacking health care qualifications to perform nursing tasks on the basis of workplace level permits. '[The old style] home helpers out of nursing' (Tehy 2003) was a slogan used by the union in the local campaign when trying to defend the mandate of nurses.

The trans-sectoral model for organising elderly home care has, however, also been perceived as a threat by nurses. The loudest reaction against integrated home care came from public health nurses. The union feared that public health nurses would be forced to accept supervision from managers external to their profession, i.e., from either nurses or social care professionals. The union further claimed that public health nurse vacancies were abolished and replaced with nurse vacancies, reflecting the marginal role of preventive care in Finnish health policy since the 1990s. Instead of challenging that policy, the union stated that the elderly needed support in the form of health education if they were to be 'active senior citizens'. In addition to what can be characterised as their traditional strategy of referring to their role as experts in health promotion, the union sought to safeguard the jobs and the competence of the group. The change in their mandates was legalised after 'prolonged negotiations' (Terveydenhoitaja 2002). In 2002, the publication jubilantly announced that a new double credential now qualified them both as nurses and as public health nurses, which also followed the EU standards.

Our analysis of the views and claims of the public health nurses' union shows that policy making concerning the public sector workforce often has an indirect impact on the organisation of elderly home care. When considering, for instance, recent personnel policy, it is evident that the main attention in the national elderly care policy has focused on nurses and medical doctors. Frontline care workers, like practical nurses, have hardly been mentioned, except in terms of recruitment problems. The union that represents the majority of practical nurses (*SuPer*) has frequently tried to draw attention to the mismatch between social policy, labour market policy and education policy and to the conflicting pressures these policies create when combined with the realities of working life. The major threats to their occupational mandate have derived both from below and from above the occupational hierarchy. Even though the union publication of *SuPer* constantly raised the problem of inadequate staffing as an important policy concern, its first and foremost interest appeared to be to uphold strict boundaries towards the uneducated care workers. In the early 2000s, *SuPer* repeatedly claimed that, due to staffing pressures, practical nurses had a hard time in establishing their positions in the labour market, and in getting recognition in the workplace. From *SuPer*'s point of view, when 'tasks [were] taken from the hands [of practical nurses]' (SuPer 2002) the problem was that the new trans-sectoral occupation was unknown and the skill and competence undervalued. The pressures from above were related to nurses. Particularly in the late 1990s, public-sector vacancies at this level were replaced with nurse vacancies.

SuPer has tried to improve the position and esteem of the practical nurses. There have been, however, severe obstacles to those pursuits. Firstly, the new vocational qualification was truly non-uniform and, in many cases, uneven. The standardisation of education has not been a priority for policy-makers. Secondly, *SuPer* itself has faced internal pressures that have forced its leaders to mediate between, for instance, the former and the new types of practical nurses. *SuPer* that was established around one occupation has faced new challenges to create a united front with the traditional members based in health care and hospital work and the newcomers working in diverse care settings (Henriksson 2008). To succeed, the policy claims of the union need to reflect this diversity; at the same time it is likely that the internal power relations within the union play a major role in its strategies. This balancing act is probably reflected in the fact that the union has constantly focused more on opposing the devaluation of practical nurses in hospitals than on defending them as providers of socially defined care.

Impoverishment of care work culture in elderly home care

The institutional restructuring of service provision and the narrowing down of the scope of public responsibility have contributed towards a welfare mix in home care for the elderly. The strategic role municipal home care now plays differs from the comprehensive responsibility it previously held. The curtailed municipal home care caters for those elderly who have the most severe care needs. The elderly whose care needs are less severe or of the 'wrong kind' are no concern of the public sector. Public services aim at providing a last resort scheme, basic service for the sickest elderly, rather than universal service available to all citizens on the basis of care needs. Regulatory changes reflect a new definition of the division of labour among the state, the market and the family. What has resulted is an increasingly medicalised public service along with a non-uniform mix of diverse service settings and care work cultures.

In the resulting institutional matrix, the frontline care workers in public elderly care have lost their license to provide socially defined care. The power to organise the everyday care has been transferred to the managerial elite and the politicians in the municipalities. The care workers who provide socially defined care appear to be the biggest losers when their room to define and to control their work is considered.

The discussion about the views and strategies of the unions of care workers illustrates the disconnectedness of their responses to the restructuring of elderly care. The wave of neoliberal policies that is here characterised as the introduction of a medico-managerialist care culture in public elderly home care appears to have contributed to the polarisation and fragmentation of care workers. As a result of the deregulation, the diverse groups who carry out socially defined care in non-public organisational settings have disintegrated. A new distribution of employment opportunities can be discerned between those who work in the regulated outsourced services and those who work in services that clients purchase directly from the market.

The emerging social order in the Finnish public home care for the elderly has become reorganised along the cultural order of 'upstairs and downstairs' in which only the upstairs is entitled to professionalism (Wrede & Henriksson 2004). Thus the implementation of the neoliberal elderly care reforms created inequalities in the division of labour, evoking traditional professionalism with its divisive, conservative and individualistic tones (Henriksson et al. 2006). Implementation of the medico-managerial care culture in the public elderly home care has strengthened the position of the key experts, the medical doctors and nurses, whereas the competence in socially defined care that practical nurses partly represent is not recognised. To be sure, practical nurses are registered health care professionals authorised to provide general nursing care, but their skill and competence in *social care* are challenged, excluded and devalued.

By reconfiguring the skill and competence in public home care for the elderly, policy makers have set up a hierarchical and task-oriented care work culture. The restructuring of home care has resulted in an *institutional* devaluation of socially defined care. Despite the educational ideals and the policy rhetoric, career opportunities have appeared only for the more educated professionals, for instance, as managers or specialised experts. In contrast, the autonomy available for the frontline workers in their practical work is curtailed. The organisation further blurs their work role through an unclear system of task transferrals. The lack of recognition of the occupational or organisational license to perform nursing tasks appears to be a constant cause for conflicts in the workplace.

A further structural hindrance to stable work roles for practical nurses has been the high prevalence of temporary contracts. Benefiting from the high unemployment rates of the recession years in the 1990s, municipalities created a buffer of the temporary workforce in the public sector. The large group of temporary care workers had poor employment rights and few opportunities to develop their skill and competence. These terms and conditions restricted the autonomy and agency of the frontline workers. In turn, these processes also seemed to generate other pressures, including recruitment problems and boundary struggles for unions. Probably the most severe threat caused by this lack of recognition from the perspective of the frontline care workers is the related crisis of professional commitment and identity that increasingly seems to frighten away potential recruits, especially young people.

As discussed above, *geriatrics* rather than gerontology has emerged as the new core expertise in municipal home care, both at the municipal level and in the national planning of cost-effective elderly care policy. Policymakers are prone to look for answers to the problems identified in elderly care in health care expertise in general and geriatrics in particular. This is demonstrated by one of the most recent policy documents that focused on the need to intensify the medical contribution in elderly care (MHSA 2006). Not surprisingly, the rapporteur recommends the promotion of education and knowledge formation in the subspecialties of geriatrics, such as geriatric psychiatry and pharmaceutical medicine.

In this chapter, we have shown how the care-friendly and the care worker-friendly universalist welfare state became questioned and dismantled through the neoliberal policies implemented since the 1990s. In the reformed institutional matrix, care and economic efficiency are constantly juxtaposed, giving superiority to the latter. When analysing the developments resulting from this austere neoliberal ethos, we have come to underline the ideological chasm between the care-friendly welfare state and its democratic professionalism and the cost-controlling state with its elitist professionalism. In the face of the emerging inequalities in relation to the eligibility for public services and in occupational and employment opportunities for care workers evident in the Finnish society as well as globally, we suggest that researchers, policy makers and citizens once again become concerned about social justice and the equal distribution of resources. Such concerns entail posing questions similar to those once so potently posed by feminist scholars of the 1970s and the 1980s, at the same time taking into consideration the increasing complexity of our societies.

Notes

1 This chapter develops empirical analysis earlier reported in Henriksson & Wrede 2004, Wrede & Henriksson 2004, 2005 and Henriksson et al. 2006. These publications include a more detailed empirical analysis of the documents used.

2 The set of documents was mainly collected for the Academy of Finland project *Service Professions in Transition* (2001–2004). The documents had three foci, national policy, local policy in the city of Helsinki and a discussion of home care in the trade union journals of occupations in the health care sector. At the national level, we privileged policy documents originating from state policy actors. At the local level, our materials originated from one central project of elderly care reform. It was governed by the social authority in the local context, but the central experts in the project group were primarily health care professionals. Our choice of trade union publications excluded trade unions that exclusively represent social care occupations. The systematic review of the union publications covered the years 2000–2004 and the review of the Helsinki policy documents the period 2002–2004. We have since continued to collect diverse materials on elderly home care in two Academy of Finland projects: *The Politics of Recruitment* (Henriksson) and *The New Dynamics of Professionalism within Caring Occupations* (Wrede).

3 In Finland there are more than 400 municipalities, which vary greatly in size, economic capacity, demographic structure and the service needs of the population. Currently, a major structural reform is being carried out that will substantially cut the number of municipalities.

4 A trans-sectoral occupation was also created for the administration of elderly care. In English, the programme is called a 'Degree Programme in Human Ageing and Elderly Service' (occupational title in Swedish *geronom*). This degree corresponds to the nursing and social work programmes which all are offered at the polytechnics. 'Geronoms' remain rare in elderly care administration. Apparently, many of them work in tasks below their educational level, for instance, as practical nurses (Kuntalehti 2007). They are not, however, registered as health care professionals and therefore lack the formal qualification required for nursing tasks (Supreme Administrative Court 2006).

5 Health care professionals are described in the Act (559/1994) and Decree (564/1994) on Health Care Professionals. Health care professionals include a) licensed professionals, b) professionals having a permit c) professionals with a protected occupational title. Registration as a health care professional is the basic requirement for many nursing tasks and for the provision of medical care.

References

Ala-Nikkola, M. (2003) *Sairaalassa, kotona vai vanhainkodissa?* Acta Universitatis Tamperensis 972. Tampere: University of Tampere.

Borgman, M. (1998) *Miten sosiaalialan työntekijöiden ammatilliset tulkinnat rakentuvat?* Tutkimuksia 95. Helsinki: Stakes.

Finnish Government (2003) Hallituksen esitys Eduskunnalle laeiksi sosiaali- ja terveydenhuollon suunnittelusta ja valtionosuudesta annetun lain 4 §:n, sosiaalihuoltolain sekä sosiaali- ja terveydenhuollon asiakasmaksuista annetun lain 12 §:n muuttamisesta. *HE 74/2003.*

Freeman, R. (1999) Institutions, states and cultures: health policy and politics in Europe. In J. Clasen (Ed.) *Comparative Social Policy. Concepts, Theories and Methods* (pp. 80–94). Oxford: Blackwell Publishers.

Henriksson, L. (2008) Reconfiguring Finnish welfare service workforce: inequalities and identity. *Equal Opportunities International* 27(1), 49–63.

Henriksson, L. & Wrede, S. (Eds) (2004) *Hyvinvointityön ammatit.* Tampere: Vastapaino.

Henriksson, L., Wrede, S. & Burau, V. (2006) Understanding professional projects in welfare service work: Revival of old professionalism? *Gender, Work and Organization* 13(2): 174–92.

Julkunen, R. (1994) Hyvinvointivaltiollisten professioprojektin katkos. *Tiede & Edistys* 19(3), 200–13.

Julkunen, R. (2001) *Suunnanmuutos.* Tampere: Vastapaino.

Koskinen, S., Ahonen, S., Jylhä, M., Korhonen, A-L. & Paunonen, M. (1988) *Vanhustyö.* Helsinki: Vanhustyön keskusliitto.

Kovalainen, A. (2004) Hyvinvointipalvelujen markkinoituminen ja sukupuolisopimuksen muutos. In L. Henriksson & S. Wrede (Eds) *Hyvinvointityön ammatit* (pp. 187–209). Tampere: Vastapaino.

Kröger, T., Anttonen, A. & Sipilä, J. (2003) Social care in Finland: stronger and weaker forms of universalism. In A. Anttonen, J. Baldock & J. Sipilä, (Eds) *The Young, the Old and the State. Social Care Systems in Five Industrial Nations* (pp. 25- 54). Cheltenham: Edward Elgar.

Kuntalehti (2007) Geronomi on vanhustyön ammattilainen. *Kuntalehti* 15(3), 47.

MHSA (2001) *Sosiaali- ja terveydenhuollon työvoimatarpeen ennakointitoimikunnan mietintö.* Komiteamietintö 2001:7. Helsinki: Ministry of Health and Social Affairs.

MHSA (2003) Ailasmaa, R. Sosiaali- ja terveydenhuollon työvoiman ja koulutuksen ennakoinnin työryhmä. *Kuntien sosiaali- ja terveydenhuollon henkilöstö 1990–2001.* (Retrieved 2003-10-15.) www.stm.fi/Resource.phx/hankk/hankt/ennakointi/tyovoima.htx.i1535.ppt

MHSA (2004) *Valtakunnallinen omaishoidon uudistaminen.* Selvityshenkilö Elli Aaltosen ehdotukset. Working group reports 2004:3. Helsinki: Ministry of Health and Social Affairs.

MHSA (2005) *Palveluseteli. Käyttöopas kotipalveluun.* Sosiaali- ja terveysministeriön oppaita 2005:1. Helsinki: Ministry of Health and Social Affairs.

MHSA (2006) *Geriatrisen hoidon ja vanhustyön kehittäminen.* Selvityshenkilö Sirkka-Liisa Kivelä. Sosiaali- ja terveysministeriön selvityksiä 30/2006. Helsinki: Ministry of Health and Social Affairs.

Paasivaara, L. (2002) *Tavoitteet ja tosiasiallinen toiminta. Suomalaisen vanhusten hoitotyön muotoutuminen monitasotarkastelussa 1930-luvulta 2000-luvulle.* Acta Universitatis Ouluensis D Medica 707. Oulu: Oulun yliopisto.

Pitkänen, M. (2005) *Raskasta mutta antoisaa. Työvoimapoliittiseen vanhustyön koulutukseen osallistuneiden käsityksiä vanhustyöstä.* Unpublished master's thesis. Tampere: University of Tampere, Department of social policy and social work.

Rauhala, P-L. (1996) Sosiaalipalvelut käytäntönä. In J. Sipilä, O. Ketola, T. Kröger & P-L. Rauhala (Eds) *Sosiaalipalvelujen Suomi* (pp. 121–55). Juva: WSOY.

Simonen, L. (1990) *Contradictions of the Welfare State, Women and Caring. Municipal Home Making in Finland.* Tampere: Acta Universitatis Tamperensis ser A vol 2. 95.

SuPer (2002) Välittäminen on elämän perusvoima. Juhani Palomäki asiaa johtamisesta. *SuPer* 49(2), 7.

Supreme Administrative Court (2006) Kunnallisasia—Työsopimussuhteinen toimi—Toimen täyttäminen—Kelpoisuus—Lähihoitaja—Hallintolainkäyttöasia. *KHO: 2006:28.* Helsinki: Korkein hallinto-oikeus.

Suoniemi, I., Syrjä, V. & Taimio, H. (2005) *Vanhusten asumispalvelujen kilpailuttaminen.* Tutkimuksia 97. Helsinki: Palkansaajien tutkimuslaitos.

Tedre, S. (1999) *Hoivan sanattomat sopimukset. Tutkimus vanhusten kotipalvelun työntekijöiden työstä.* Joensuu: Joensuun yliopiston yhteiskuntatieteellisiä julkaisuja 40.

Tedre, S. (2004) Likainen työ ja virallinen hoiva. In L. Henriksson & S. Wrede (Eds) *Hyvinvointityön ammatit* (pp. 63–83). Tampere: Vastapaino.

Tehy (2003) Kotiavustajat pois sairaanhoidosta. *Tehy* 22(11), 29.

Terveydenhoitaja (2002) Terveydenhoitajat laillistetaan nyt myös sairaanhoitajina. *Terveydenhoitaja* 28(8), 6.

Vaarama, M., Luomahaara, J., Peiponen, A. & Voutilainen, P. (2001) *Koko kunta ikääntyneiden asialle.* Raportteja 259. Helsinki: Stakes.

Vaarama, M. & Noro, A. (2005) Vanhusten palvelut. *Duodecim Terveyskirjasto.* Retrieved 2007-09-28. http://www.terveysportti.fi/terveyskirjasto/tk.koti?p_artikkeli=suo00058

Vuorensyrjä, M., Borgman, M., Kemppainen, T., Mäntysaari, M. & Pohjala, A. (2006) *Sosiaalialan osaajat 2015. Sosiaalialan osaamis-, työvoima- ja koulutustarpeiden ennakointihanke (SOTENNA): loppuraportti.* Jyväskylä: Opetusministeriö, Euroopan Sosiaalirahasto, Sosiaali- ja terveysministeriö, Suomen Kuntaliitto.

Wærness, K. (1984) Caring as women's work in the welfare state. In H. Holter (Ed.) *Patriarchy in a Welfare Society* (pp. 67–87). Oslo: Universitetsforlaget.

Wærness, K. (1992) Bettering the public care services—the only realistic alternative for strengthening the welfare of ordinary people in need of care. In J. Sipilä (Ed.) *Sosiaalipalvelujen kehitystrendejä eri maissa* (pp. 176–202). Tampere: University of Tampere.

Wrede, S. (2008) Educating generalists: flexibility and identity in auxiliary nursing in Finland. In E. Kuhlmann & M. Saks (Eds) *Rethinking Professional Governance. International Directions in Health Care* (pp. 127–40). Bristol: Policy Press.

Wrede, S. & Henriksson, L. (2004) Kahden kerroksen väkeä: Kotihoidon ammatillinen uusjako. In L. Henriksson & S. Wrede (Eds) *Hyvinvointityön ammatit* (pp. 210–34). Tampere: Vastapaino.

Wrede, S. & Henriksson, L. (2005) The changing terms of welfare service work: Finnish home care in transition. In H.M. Dahl & T. Rask Eriksen (Eds) *Dilemmas of Care in the Nordic Welfare State. Continuity and Change* (pp. 62–79). Aldershot: Ashgate.

FIVE

Staffing Levels and Well-being of the Residents with Dementia

Päivi Topo and Saila Sormunen

In Finland regulations define in what situations a person has the right to residential care but the content of residential care as such is not defined. However, the Finnish constitution defines privacy and autonomy as basic rights. As a consequence, physical restrictions in residential care should not be used without good reason and only temporarily. The right to privacy is understood as the resident's right to a home-like environment when living in a residential care institution and that sharing a bedroom with others is acceptable only if it is seen to support the well-being of the resident. A third relevant basic human right defined in the constitution is that of human dignity. This right means that the mental needs of a person in residential care should be met (Pajukoski 2006).

As legislation gives only very general rules for practices in residential care more specific criteria for good care are under continuous discussion and are based on wide consensus (for example STM 2001). When looking at services and care for people with dementia the criteria for good care are even more complex to define because clients have limited abilities to be involved in assessing services due to their problems in cognition. People with problems in cognitive functioning use 80 %–90 % of beds in long-term residential care in Finland (Noro et al. 2005). In order to understand the current state of residential care, we need to pay attention to how the needs of people with cognitive problems such as dementia are met and what is their well-being when living in care institutions.

Dementia syndrome affects the person broadly, with deterioration in abilities to remember, to learn and to act logically, to express oneself, to behave socially, to orientate, and to show initiative. As the syndrome progresses the person affected becomes fully dependent on the help of others.

As people with dementia have difficulties in speaking for themselves, they are one of the most vulnerable groups in society. Several researchers have argued that dementia is a deeply social issue and that the psychosocial environment has a strong impact on the well-being of people with dementia. Some researchers have raised questions about the negative attitudes of society towards people with dementia, demanding alternative ways to assess the situation related to people with dementia, their caregivers, and the content and quality of services (e.g., Gilliard et al. 2005, Bond et al. 2002).

We can already see in Finland that some residential care institutions have difficulties in recruiting enough care workers for short-term tasks and also for permanent positions. Ageing of the population has happened more rapidly in rural areas than in urban areas and has been speeded up by migration of the younger generations to towns. As a consequence the need for elderly services in rural areas has increased at the same time as the number of potential care workers has been decreasing.

Already at the end of the 1990s it was found that the quality of care varied significantly between residential care institutions and even between units in the same institution (Vaarama et al. 1999). Since the 1990's, the debate has been on-going about the quality of elderly care and several improvements have been demanded. The main concern has been an insufficient number of care staff but more recently the treatment of clients has received attention. The Ministry of Social Affairs and Health has reacted to this debate by naming a large expert group that compiled recommendations for quality assurance in elderly care (STM 2001). Later, the Ministry launched programmes for the municipalities for developing elderly care services. An updated version of the recommendations was published in 2008.

In this chapter we will first make an overview of the recent developments of elderly care in Finland and present the challenges involved. The care of people with dementia is one of the main challenges for the care system and dementia care is in the frontline if a care system faces a crisis such as lack of suitably trained care workers. Second, we present our empirical study in two dementia care units. Our goal was to assess the quality of care from the point of view of the residents and to focus on psychosocial issues. We studied two care units: one with a low level of staffing and the other with staffing level in accordance with the national guidelines. At the end of the chapter we discuss the question of possible care crises in the near future from the point of view of residential care services for people with dementia.

Elderly care policy and institutional conditions of care provision in Finland

In the policy documents concerning residential care, the general aims have been to strengthen the patient-centered approach, to support the functioning of residents, to ensure that there are enough care workers available, and to improve the skills of the care workers (STM 2001). The overriding goal in policy documents has been to decrease the need for residential care and to improve community care. The municipalities in Finland have succeeded in decreasing the proportion of older people living in residential care. In practice, those living in residential care have more severe care needs than before, are older and live in institutions for shorter periods of time. The main responsibility for providing residential care to older people has shifted from health care to social care (Vaarama et al. 2004, see Chapter 4)

The cost of elderly care has fallen and its efficiency has been improved in the 1990s and the beginning of the 2000s (Laine 2005). The number of care workers in health care hospitals dropped rapidly between 1991 and 1995 but has slowly increased since that (Voutilainen 2004). In nursing homes the number of care staff has slowly increased since 1993 but the total number of care staff working in residential care was still lower in 2003 than in the beginning of the 1990s. Räty et al. (2003) have estimated that to meet the recommendations of an expert group concerning an adequate staff–patient ratio in residential care, the costs of care would increase 2.6 % annually until year 2030.

Voutilainen (2004) has concluded that the patient to care staff ratio is so low that leads to additional sick leave because of the high workloads experienced by staff. According to her study carried out in Helsinki area in 2001, the ratio was even as low as 0.09 in the evening shift, which meant that there were over ten clients needing extensive help per single care worker (Voutilainen et al. 2001). A linear trend between sick leave and work overload among nurses working in Finnish hospitals has been identified (Rauhala et al. 2007). Low care-giver–patient ratios in nursing homes are also associated with more frequent use of physical restraints and psychotropics and greater frequency of pressure sores (Pekkarinen 2007, Pekkarinen et al. 2006).

Voutilainen (2004) has argued that the low staff–patient ratio in residential care in the evenings follows the practices of acute hospital care even if the needs of the residents are very different than patients in acute care. This comment indicates that the needs of people in residential care are perceived by the organisation mainly as a need for physical care or other health-related needs. Currently the social care sector is orga-nising most of the residential care and for them this medica-lised view is a challenge.

In her analysis Rintala (2003) found that the medicalisa-tion of services for the elderly people started already in the 1950s. By medicalisation she means practices based on a medical approach even if dealing with non-medical or non-health-related issues (see Chapter 4). Based on her analyses she argued that the history of service providers adopting prac-tices for controlling the life of older people has even longer history than medicalisation. By controlling Rintala refers to regulations for behaviour in institutions in order to rule older clients' habits and lifestyle. Rintala further concluded that in contemporary residential care these two approaches are still dominating and shaping practices.

The social construction and reconstruction of the features of 'total institutions' should be given more attention in stud-ies concerning residential care. Research on care workers have shown that the features and routines of a total institution are neither in the control of the care auxiliaries nor the nurses (Lee-Treweek 1997, Paasivaara 2002). Custodial care based on routinisation, surveillance, mortification and ignorance of personhood are aspects of the total institution as described by Goffman in 1969 (see Goffman 1997). The concept of the total institution has correspondences with the concept of 'otherness', which in a care setting can be described as all practices constructing dichotomy and distance between the care workers and the residents. If otherness is taken as being at one end of the dimension describing institutional practices, then the other can be named as communion, meaning practices which are confirming personhood, inclusion and the dignity of both the residents and the personnel. How these features and routines in the institutions are shaped and reshaped need far more research to help in understanding the challenges for developing care. The high rates of health problems reported by the personnel of residential care (Sinervo 2000) in addition to reports showing low quality of care in some units (Vaarama et al. 1999) indicate that improvements in residential care are urgently needed.

Because a person with dementia becomes gradually fully dependent on others, the quality of care and the quality of life of a person are intertwined. There are several factors affecting quality of care and only some of them are under the control of the care workers, those being attitudes towards the clients, treatment of the clients, the quality of interaction, or the updating of professional skills. Other issues affecting the quality of care—such as staff-patient ratio, physical care environment, distribution of tasks in the whole institution, culture of the care unit—can only be impacted to a lesser degree by the individual care workers.

Research design

In this chapter we describe the well-being, behaviour, and activities of people with dementia in two dementia care units: one with a high staff–client ratio and one with a low staff-client ratio. The examination focuses on the resident rather than the care workers. We ask: what is the well-being of the residents in these two units? How are their needs for action and activities met? What features of daily life are important for their psychosocial well-being? We aim to increase understanding about how the resources of the unit are associated with the quality of life of the residents.

Our data was collected through the Dementia Care Mapping (DCM) observational tool which focuses on the psychosocial well-being and the activities and behaviour. (1.) In DCM the situation of people with dementia is looked at as a social and psychosocial issue and as an issue of person centred care. The ultimate starting point of person-centred care is that dementia does not change the human value of the person affected, but because dementia decreases his/her abilities to act, it is the duty of society and service providers to ensure that her/his needs are met and that he/she is treated in a fair way (Kitwood 1997).

In DCM the main focus of interest is on observing the well-being/ill-being of the person and in observing how his/her needs are met, including the need for social engagement, the need to use one's skills, and the need for recreation. The well-being/ill-being is assessed by the use of a scale –5, –3, –1, +1, +3, +5. Value +1 is given if the person does not show signs of ill-being or signs of increased well-being. The assessment is based on what can be observed. Behaviour/activity is described by the use of categorisation around 24 categories, such as eating and looking around. The observer is also recording particularly positive and negative events. There is detailed guidance on how to assess well-being and behaviour (Bradford Dementia Group 1997).

The whole project included eight care units and two data collection points, but here we report only the findings of two dementia care units in the first year of study. (2.) After analysing the data on the unit level, we analysed the background data of each client in order to make pairs of similar residents living in these two units. The criteria for matching the pairs were similarities in cognitive and physical functioning and in diagnoses. These criteria were chosen because several diseases can cause dementia though symptoms may vary by disease and because our analyses of the larger data has shown that both well-being, activities, and behaviour and risk to be treated inappropriately are associated with the severity of dementia and problems in physical functioning. (Topo et al. 2007, Sormunen et al. 2007). Through matched pairs, we aim to control the impact of individual factors of the participants and to be able to focus more on the factors associated with the two units studied.

The care units and the residents

The two units studied were both part of a larger institution and they both utilised the services of the whole institution, but they differed from each other in many ways. Unit A is situated in one of the largest nursing homes in the country. The institution provides services also for those living in service flats and older people living nearby. There is a restaurant, a hairdresser, a fitness centre and several possibilities for hobbies available. The buildings were built before 1960. Unit A has a balcony but no easy barrier-free access to the outdoors or to the park surrounding the buildings. A long corridor divides Unit A and at one end there are large windows. Meals are brought into the unit in metal containers but coffee and tea are made in the unit. The dining room is also used as a sitting room and it has a television, armchairs and a sofa. At the other end of the large room there are tables and chairs, cupboards, a sink, a fridge and a cooker. A big, noisy service lift is situated next to the kitchen corner. There is also room for breaks for the staff and for their meetings, an office for the head nurse and a room for medicines and patient files. The doors to the balcony and to the staircase are locked and at the main entrance of the unit there is a small open space with a television. The balcony is used as a storage area for walking aids and extra furniture. Most residents live in double rooms where they have some personal items such as paintings, photographs and clothes.

In Unit A there are 12 residents in long-term care and occasionally one client in respite care. The staff–client ratio is 0.54 which is somewhat higher than in other units of the same institution, which also have residents other than those with dementia, but is lower than the average across the whole country. The national mean staff–client ratio in nursing homes is 0.61–0.69 (STM 2001). In the morning and night shifts there is at least one nurse working but most staff members are practical nurses and care assistants. The nursing home is run by the municipality and there were several staff members whose position was not permanent. Most residents had severe dementia and difficulties in all activities of daily living (Table 5.1) and the behaviour in Unit A of some residents was very challenging. Most residents could not move independently and only one was clearly orientated in time and place. Many residents used clothes provided by the nursing home together with their own clothes.

Table 5.1 Information on the residents in the two units

	UNIT A	UNIT B
Total number of the residents	13	10
Staff-resident ratio*	0.54	0.75
Observed residents		
Age		
Range	68–104 years	68–92 years
Mean	88 years	84 years
Sex		
Women	90 % (n=9)	86 % (n=6)
Men	10 % (n=1)	14 % (n=1)
Severity of dementia		
Mild	10 % (n=1)	57 % (n=4)
Moderate	20 % (n=2)	14 % (n=1)
Severe	70 % (n=7)	29 % (n=2)
Physical dependence, mean		
(ADL score, to 1–4)	1.8**	2.4**

* Includes whole staff: nurses, auxiliaries of the care, and auxiliary workers
** The lower the score the higher the dependence of the resident (1=fully dependent, 4=independent). The ADL score consists of six items: eating, toileting, transferring from bed to chair, urinary and bowel continence

Unit B was located in a new building which was designed for people living in service flats and for older community members to visit the restaurant or other services (hairdresser, physiotherapy, massage, fitness centre) or activities in the building (for example, ballroom dances). The design of Unit B was done according to the needs of people with dementia: in the middle there was an island with a kitchenette and a tiny office; at one end there was a dining room and at the other a sitting room. The residents were able to walk around the island. The single bedrooms were situated adjacent to the sitting room and the dining room. There were also three rooms used for respite care. The windows were large and located low enough to be accessible by a wheelchair user. There were magazines, newspapers, TV and soft toys in the living room. The unit was located on the ground floor and there was access to a terrace and to a small garden from the dining room. The residents had their own rooms furnished with their own items. Doors to the unit, terrace, and the outdoors were locked. Food was brought from a kitchen that served the whole institution but coffee and tea were made in the unit.

During the observations there were 10 long term residents and two respite care clients and the staff/resident ratio was 0.75 which is higher than the average staff–client ratio of nursing homes in the whole country. The care workers were employed in permanent positions. As in Unit A, during the day and evening shifts, there is at least one nurse working but most are practical nurses and care assistants. All residents except two were able to move themselves but none was orientated in place. Most residents had mild or moderate dementia but two were severely demented (Table 5.1). The unit was run by a third sector service provider and the local municipalities purchased nearly all the services. Altogether we can say that the residents in Unit B were more independent than those in Unit A, while the staff–client ratio was lower in Unit A than in Unit B.

Well-being, behaviour and activities of the residents

Table 5.2 shows different profiles of the well-being of the residents in Unit A and Unit B. The results are more positive in Unit B (group well-being score +2.0) compared to Unit A (+1.1). In Unit B the residents expressed more often increased well-being (values +3 and +5) whereas in Unit A they expressed more often ill-being (values –1 and –3, Table 5.2).

Table 5.2 Well-being of the three residents in Unit A and B, and well-being score of the whole unit based on all observations done in the units, %

	CONSIDERABLE ILLBEING		COPING ADEQUATELY IN THE SITUATION	EXCEPTIONAL WELLBEING		TOTAL, %	MEAN
Unit A,							
group score	0	2	8	73	16	0	100	+1.1
Mrs Koski	0	0	7	58	35	0	100	+1.6
Mrs Joki	0	7	16	47	30	0	100	+1.0
Mrs Lampi	0	0	2	85	13	0	100	+1.2
Unit B,							
group score	0	0	5	44	46	5	100	+2.0
Mr Paju	0	0	6	46	48	0	100	+1.9
Mrs Mänty	0	1	8	39	42	11	100	+2.1
Mrs Haapa	0	2	12	54	30	1	100	+1.3

The profiles of behaviour of the residents in these two units (Table 5.3) are also quite different, with clients in Unit A spending most of the time fulfilling basic physical needs, such as eating, receiving physical care and sleeping. The rest of the time the residents watched television, walked and those who were able to socialise did; the rest of the time was spent in sitting alone with nothing to do (code B in Table 5.3). There was also repetitive behaviour (code W). In Unit B eating and receiving care also took time but several activities were available in addition to watching TV: sing-alongs (code E), reminiscing (code I), playing games and painting (code H). When participating in these organised activities, the well-being of residents

Table 5.3 Profiles of behaviour of the three residents in Unit A and B, and profile of behaviour of the whole unit based on all observations done in the units, %

BEHAVIOUR CATEGORY CODING	UNIT A	MRS KOSKI	MRS JOKI	MRS LAMPI	UNIT B	MR PAJU	MRS MÄNTY	MRS HAAPA
Interaction, A	14	35	23	2	11	13	9	15
Socially involved but passively, B	18	23	3	8	9	9	16	10
Socially withdrawn, C	0	1	0	0	0	0	1	0
Expressive activities, E	0	0	0	0	9	0	5	4
Food, F	20	25	11	38	15	17	7	16
Games, G	0	0	0	0	2	0	0	0
Handicraft, H	0	0	0	0	4	0	0	0
Intellectual activities, I	0	0	0	0	4	0	9	0
Moving independently, K	6	3	15	0	9	22	8	1
Worklike activities, L	2	3	2	0	2	4	1	0
Media, M	8	0	29	0	13	24	31	2
Sleeping, N	5	0	1	25	1	0	0	2
Own care, O	3	0	9	0	3	0	0	15
Physical care, P	13	10	4	25	13	11	12	25
Stimulation of senses, T	1	0	0	2	1	0	0	5
Unresponded communication U	2	0	2	0	0	0	0	0
Repetitive behavior, W	5	0	0	0	1	0	0	1
Toilet, X	1	0	2	0	1	0	2	1
Talking to yourself, Y	1	0	1	0	2	0	0	1

mainly increased or was even exceptionally high (values +3 and +5), showing the importance of involvement in such activities for all residents despite their severity of dementia. But sitting and showing few signs of involvement in the environment (code B) was often associated with being bored (see Topo et al. 2007 for more details).

In Unit B the residents on the whole had better cognitive skills and better physical functioning than in Unit A, and so we paired residents of similar cognitive performance and ADL skills in order to do remove confounding. Three pairs are presented here.[3] First we have **Mrs Koski** and **Mr Paju,** who are among the most able of the residents.

Mrs Koski lives in Unit A. She has mild dementia, is well-orientated, walks with a walking aid and is socially active. She tries to help the other residents and is very supportive towards them. Her well-being was better (mean +1.6, Table 5.2) than the score of the whole unit and it was the highest during lunch, dinner or coffee when she was communicating with other residents. Mrs Koski's good social skills and cognitive abilities are recorded in the field notes:

> Mrs Järvnen's behaviour is very challenging: she grabs the hand of anyone passing her, bites, and pinches the others. She is able to say some words but because of her behavioural problems she is mainly sitting alone. Mrs Koski comes to sit next to her and Mrs Järvinen gives her own teddy bear to her. Mrs Koski shows the teddy bear to her and asks 'What is this?' Mrs Järvinen answers 'A tail'. Mrs Koski goes through all the parts of the toy and Mrs Järvinen answers her questions. At the end Mrs Koski says 'You are a precise girl'!

Even if Mrs Koski is so able the results over two days of observations with her show that the unit did not provide any activities for her (Table 5.3). The following citation reveals that she was hoping for more activities:

> Mrs Koski asks the nurse if she could go out alone and sit on a bench for a while. It is a late sunny afternoon early in the spring. There are two care workers in the shift. The care worker: 'If you do go, you might fall. Can we go tomorrow?' Mrs Koski: 'It is always

tomorrow'. They confirmed that tomorrow afternoon they'll go out together. The care worker opens the door to the shady balcony to Mrs Koski. She goes there for a short moment.

Mr Paju had lived in Unit B for only a couple of weeks. The care workers were not sure about his real cognitive skills because he had so many health problems and strong medication. He was able to walk and is used to be being outdoors on a daily basis. His well-being score was +1.9 and nearly half of the time he showed signs of increased well-being (involvement, engagement, smile) (Table 5.2).

Mr Paju spent most of his time in reading newspapers, watching television and walking around the unit (Table 5.3). During the two days of observations, the care workers acknowledged his preferences and ensured that he had newspapers available and when there were sports programmes on the television he was informed and encouraged to watch the programme. When Mr Paju needed to go to a local doctor a care worker walked him there. During the days observed, Mr Paju's family visited him and when they entered the unit, coffee was served to them in Mr Paju's room and later when Mr Paju was confused about the situation he was encouraged to be with his family.

We can conclude that in Unit B it was easier to take Mr Paju outdoors because of the barrier free design of Unit and care workers had more time to do it than was the case in Unit A. In addition, in Unit B there were activities available to Mr Paju and they were also utilised, and finally, his need for social inclusion was acknowledged. In Unit A the staff was busy with helping the bedridden or very dependent residents and they had less time to be present in the common space, to provide organised activities to those few more able residents, or to take them outdoors. Mrs Koski's well-being improved when she herself found other residents to talk or whom she could help.

The second matched pair is **Mrs Joki** and **Mrs Mänty**. They both have moderate/severe dementia, symptoms of depression and show a lack of initiative. **Mrs Joki** from Unit A wanted to eat constantly and was asking for food all the time. At lunchtime she finished her meal in a couple of minutes. When she repeatedly asked for food, some of the care workers tried to find her some activities such as watching television or doing crosswords. There were also episodes when she was miserable because she was sure that her husband would not ever find her. She wanted to call him but the care workers had understood that her husband did not want to be contacted too often. Mrs Joki spent much time in walking around in the unit to find someone to give her a telephone. Some care workers were obviously uneasy when denying her a phone and they gave her all sorts of reasons for why it was not possible (telephone was broken, no one was at home etc.). In the end they promised to give her sedatives to make her feel better. The care workers were busy with helping another resident and no one seemed to have time to comfort Mrs Joki. Once she was lying on a sofa and crying loudly. The obvious problems were that only some care workers had knowledge and skills to handle Mrs Joki's confusion and anxiety and no one stopped to be with her. Table 5.2 shows her well-being scale (mean score +1.0) and from Table 5.3 we can see that even if she showed a need for care (code P) and comfort she received care less than five percent of time.

Mrs Mänty lived in Unit B. She was confused about the place and was sometimes looking for her relatives, as she was definite that they were waiting for her outside. As she did not find them she became anxious. Mrs Mänty was not easy to engage in any activities but was involved in sing-alongs and in reminiscing. She also liked to watch domestic films when they were provided for her. As can be seen in Table 5.2, Mrs Mänty's well-being score was quite high (mean score +2.1) and she had had several moments when her well-being was exceptionally high (+5). Those were moments when she was sitting on a sofa with a care worker and reminiscing about her childhood, when she proposed songs for a sing-along, and when she was strongly engaged in singing hymns. Two care workers were involved in the sing-alongs.

Compared to Mrs Joki in Unit A, Mrs Mänty received far more time from the care workers (see Table 5.3) and her needs for comfort were taken into account before she became very anxious. The fact that there were enough care workers and especially enough of those with training in dementia care can be seen in the citation below:

> Mrs Mänty is complaining about a headache. She had not wanted to participate in painting but had followed when the others were drawing and painting. Later, after having a painkiller, a care worker sat down next to her and Mrs Mänty told her how the laundry was made when she was a child. The situation was very peaceful and the care worker was able to give full attention to Mrs Mänty for some time. Later other residents got involved when traditional butter-making was discussed.

The third matched pair is two very frail women, **Mrs Lampi** and **Mrs Haapa**. They both had severe dementia and were immobile and fully dependent on the help of others. Mrs Haapa was the only resident with such intensive need for help and care in Unit B, while there were seven fully dependent residents in Unit A.

Mrs Lampi had lived in Unit A for more than ten years. She spent her days either in a geriatric chair or in bed. She had problems in hearing and had incontinence and according to care workers was negative towards the care. She had a pressure sore. She was observed only during the meal times because that was the only time when she was taken to a common space. She was fed and because she was very slow in swallowing the feeding was stopped for several times and several care workers fed her during each meal. In the meantime she was left alone with the bib to be ready for the next spoonful. When the care workers were feeding Mrs Lampi she was always informed about the food and what she will be given next. At the end of the meals she drank from the mug herself.

Mrs Lampi's well-being scale showed quite low values but hardly any experiences of ill-being (Mean score +1.2, Table

5.2). Table 5.3 shows that during the observations only her basic needs were recognised (eating, sleeping, receiving physical care). For example no sensory stimulation was provided and only once did a care worker talk to her about something else except food or care. In both units the care workers sometimes talked in about the very dependent residents as if they were not present. For example when Mrs Lampi was being fed, care workers talked about size of nappies needed for other residents for the night.

Mrs Haapa was living in Unit B. She had pains because of several chronic diseases. She spoke only a few words. She had poor balance and when seated in a geriatric chair she was restrained to stop her falling down from the chair or from getting up. When she was restrained, it was explained to her what was happening and she was monitored.

The care workers constantly recognised Mrs Haapa's problems and tried to comfort her. She was taken to a sing-along session and a care worker held her hand and tried to involve her in the activity. Care workers also encouraged Mrs Haapa to communicate and they stopped to listen when she answered slowly. During meals, she needed help but ate bread herself. Care workers helped her sensitively when eating and gave her sufficient time for the task. She got anxious when left alone restrained in the chair. She wanted to move and cried out that she was freezing. When a care worker took her for a walk she felt better.

When looking at her well-being score it can be seen that even if she had moments of ill-being, a quarter of the time she showed increased well-being (Table 5.2). Those were moments when a care worker was next to her helping and comforting her or communicating with her. She also received plenty of care and was given sufficient time to eat. When restrained in the chair she tried to find a better position to warm her legs, which is marked in Table 5.3 with the code O = own care.

The results of this last pair show how extensively people with severe dementia may need help, comfort and care and how difficult it is to meet this need if the care workers do not have time and/or the intention to slow down to the client's own speed. The fact that Unit B was providing organised activities such as sing-along sessions also served the needs of the most severely demented resident in the unit, while this kind of an opportunity was lacking for the severely demented patients in Unit A. In addition, meals have a very important role in the every life of people living in residential care. The quality of these moments for especially the most dependent residents relies very much on the time the care workers are able to invest in helping them, as well as on their attitudes towards the residents.

Conclusion

Our findings show that on the one hand there is residential living provided for people with dementia that includes mainly waiting for something to happen and remaining with nothing to do other than eating and receiving physical care. Similar findings have been reported in several previous studies (e.g., Gubrium 1997, Karvinen 2000). But on the other hand there is a type of residential care that also meets the psychosocial needs of residents. This diversity needs to be studied in more detail to identify how the social rights of people with dementia are recognised in services. Their own abilities to demand justice in the society are very limited and thus, any unjust treatment of them is an alarming signal for the welfare state. Our findings are based on only two units but they are in accord with a larger study by Pekkarinen et al. (2006) that showed that there is inequity related to resource distribution and the quality of residential care.

This inequity in residential care raises several questions. Will the lack of care workers in the near future increase this inequity and what can be done to prevent this kind of change? An important part of the care is the care culture, which reflects the attitudes among care workers but also reflects the social values of society. These values are seen in the level of financial investments in care but also in respecting the human dignity of those people who need care and in valuing care work. It is very likely that the future care crises will challenge the development of person-centred dementia care. Much can be done to prevent a retardation of dementia care, but it requires political and social will at all levels of society.

How does the care culture and perception of dementia impact on the quality of everyday life of resident living in dementia care units? Our descriptive results imply that if the main focus is on dementia and physical needs, this may cause custodial care practices. But if the focus is on the person, then it is more likely that in the daily life of a care unit the individual psychosocial needs would also be taken into account. There is a risk that residential care will change towards custodial care if the level of resources is allowed to deteriorate to such a low level that the time of the care workers is spent only on meeting basic physical needs. But this is not only a question of staffing levels: the fact that the number of staff is at such a lower level in Finland than in other Nordic countries also implies that there are cultural issues which are not favourable for people with dementia that need residential care. It is accepted by policy makers at different levels that even if in policy documents and in political rhetoric the aim is to promote person-centred care, not enough resources are allocated for this. This cultural climate is also shaping the care culture and the care practices in the institutions.

In both units studied we find some features of total institution (e.g., locked doors without independent access for the residents) as described by Goffman (1997). But in Unit A more such features can be identified (use of clothing provided by the institution, time the resident used for eating defined by routines of the institution). In Unit B, the practices and care culture strengthened the communion of the residents rather than otherness (through encouragement of social contacts and interaction, hospitality towards visitors, well-prepared group activities, respecting individual preferences). Unit B was established quite recently and the ideology has been from the very beginning to provide person-centred care and to integrate the unit into the local community. Unit A also has the aim of providing person-centred care, but in the practice the lower staff–client ratio—taking into account the more demanding residents, the physically challenging environment, and maybe even the long history of the unit—all shaped the daily life towards practices that were mainly meeting the physical needs of the residents.

Unit A was established at a time when most residents were able to move independently and were more independent in their daily activities than residents nowadays. The buildings were designed according to the needs of the first users. The ideology and practice in Finnish elderly care followed the model of hospital care since the 1950s up to the 1980s and the practices were based on tight routines that guided the daily life of the institutions (see Paasivaara 2002, Rintala 2003). Since then the philosophy of elderly care and the care of dying people has changed towards person-centred care, though older layers in current practices can still be recognised (Paasivaara 2002). When Paasivaara (2002) investigated the history of elderly care in Finland, she found that the first documents mentioning individual needs were written in the 1970s and that this was challenged in the 1990s when cost-effectiveness became the main goal in elderly care. Our results suggest that the physical premises can either improve person-centred care, as in Unit B, or they can be barriers for care workers to act according to a person-centred way and to meet the individual needs of the residents. Physical premises are a cultural issue and they should be assessed as such.

The average current staff–client ratios in residential care are lower in Finland than in other Nordic countries. This may reflect a history of more able residents living in institutional care settings and the dominance of the medical view and acute hospital care practices in the decision making related to resource allocation in residential care. The existence of pressure sores in some residents of Unit A is also a signal of the low quality of care. Similar findings have been reported by Pekkarinen et al. (2004) in a large study that included 91 inpatient units: in the units were care staff felt increased time pressures, the risk for residents not receiving all the necessary care was increased. If the reason for the low quality of care is related to a low staff–resident ratio, the only solution is to invest more in these services.

But Pekkarinen et al. (2004) concluded that the stress experienced by personnel may not be directly a matter of staffing levels; it is an issue about how the work is organised, the size of the unit, how much control the personnel have over their job and if they can make their work less schedule-orientated. Our results also suggest that the well-being of the residents may be associated with the care workers' knowledge and understanding about dementia and its consequences on behaviour and way of being. Residential care institutions should provide this training for their employees. Training in dementia care can also improve the well-being of the personnel (Elovainio & Sinervo 1997, Sinervo 2000).

Our case study is in accord with some previous studies showing discrepancies in the quality of residential care (see Vaarama et al. 1999). Careful analysis is needed of which units are more successful in providing good quality of care and ensuring good quality of life for the residents. We need to ask what is required from the head of the unit and the head of the institute. What can we learn about the dynamics between staff members? How do the physical premises shape the practices? What kind of training and counseling is provided? How are the relatives of the residents involved? And finally how do these care institutions relate to the local community and to policy makers?

Investigating residential care as a psychosocial issue can help in inscribing the context of the quality of life of the residents and the quality of care and in increasing understanding about how these two are intertwined. We conclude that there is a need for more respect for the social needs of people with dementia. These rights are already stated in the Finnish law and even in the constitution. This change of ethos of care in society is needed to ensure that also in the near future those people living with dementia will receive adequate services according to their needs. This change will also help those working in elderly care in getting work conditions, salary, and training that ensures they are able and motivated to provide person-centred care.

Notes

1 The study is part of the project 'Assessment of the quality of dementia care from the client's perspective' (Sormunen et al. 2007, Topo et al. 2007). During the observations, field notes were made. Background data was gathered in beforehand through two types of questionnaires that were filled by the care workers: one about the unit and one on each person to be observed.
2 The two units were chosen because they both are specialised for residential and respite care for people with dementia. All units were sourced via contacts to municipalities and via the network of the dementia care professionals. Ethical approval was received from the Ministry of Social Affairs and Health and from the municipalities that either provided or purchased the services. Informed consent was asked from the family members and mutual consent from the people observed. The observations were done by two trained DCM users (Sormunen & Topo) in common spaces such as dining rooms and corridors. The two researchers observed the same client only occasionally but the field notes of both the researchers often described the same events and were both added in the data. We observed six hours per day in total over two sequential days: one day the work was started early in the morning and in one day just prior to lunch time (see Sormunen et al. 2007, Topo et al. 2007 for more details).
3 Personal information and other details are changed to ensure that the participants cannot be identified.

References

Bond, J., Corner, L., Lilley, A. & Ellwood, C. (2002) Medicalization of insight and caregivers' responses to risk in dementia. *Dementia* 1(3), 313–28.

Bradford Dementia Group. (1997) *Evaluating dementia care: The DCM method*, 7th edition. University of Bradford.

Elovainio M, Sinervo T. (1997) Psychosocial stressors at work, psychological stress and musculusketal symptoms in the care for the elderly. *Work & Stress* 11(4), 351–61.

Gilliard, J., Means, R., Beattie, A. & Daker-White, G. (2005) Dementia care in England and the social model of disability: Lessons and issues. *Dementia* 4(4), 571–586.

Goffman, E. (1997) *Minuuden riistäjät. Tutkielma totaalisista laitoksista.* (Original: *Asylums.* First published by Anchor Books, 1961, Doubleday: New York). 2. painos. Lohja: Mielenterveyden Keskusliitto ry, Marraskuun liike.

Gubrium, J. F. (1997) *Living and Dying at Murray Manor.* Expanded pbk ed. Charlottesville: University Press of Virginia.

Karvinen, E. (2000) *'Tulee friski ja hyvä olla'. Toimintatutkimus fyysisen aktiivisuuden edistämisestä Kontulan vanhainkodissa.* Gerontologian ja kansanterveyden lisensiaattitutkimus. Jyväskylän yliopisto: Terveystieteiden laitos. http://selene.lib.jyu.fi:8080/gradu/f/ elkarvinen.pdf (Retrieved 14.2.2007)

Kitwood, T. (1997) *Dementia Reconsidered—the Person Comes First.* Buckingham: Open University Press.

Lee-Treweek, G. (1997) Women, resistance and care: An ethnographic study of nursing auxiliary work. *Work, Employment & Society* 11(1), 47–63.

Laine, J. (2005) *Laatua ja tuotannollista tehokkuutta? Taloustieteellinen tutkimus vanhusten laitoshoidosta.* Tutkimuksia 151. Helsinki: Stakes.

Noro, A., Finne-Soveri, H., Björkgren, M. & Vähäkangas, P. (Eds) (2005) *Ikääntyneiden laitoshoidon laatu ja tuottavuus—RAI-järjestelmä vertailukehittämisessä.* Helsinki: Stakes.

Paasivaara, L. (2002) *Tavoitteet ja tosiasiallinen toiminta. Suomalaisen vanhusten hoitotyön muotoutuminen monitasotarkastelussa 1930-luvulta 2000-luvulle.* Acta Universitatis Ouluensis D Medica 707. Oulu: Oulun yliopisto.

Pajukoski, M. (2006) Oikeudenmukaisuus lainsäädännön näkökulmasta. In J. Teperi, L. Vuorenkoski, K. Manderbacka, E. Ollila & I. Keskimäki (Eds) *Riittävät palvelut jokaiselle. Näkökulmia yhdenvertaisuuteen sosiaali- ja terveydenhuollossa* (pp. 28–34). Hyvinvointivaltion rajat -hanke. Helsinki: Stakes.

Pekkarinen, L. (2007) *The relationship between work stressors and organizational performance in long-term care for elderly residents.* Research Reports 171. Helsinki: Stakes.

Pekkarinen, L., Elovainio, M., Sinervo, T., Finne-Soveri, H. & Noro, A. (2006) Nursing working conditions in relation to restrain practices in long-term care units. *Medical Care* 44(12), 1114–20.

Pekkarinen, L., Sinervo, T., Perälä, M-L. & Elovainio, M. (2004) Work stressors and the quality of life in long-term care units. *The Gerontologist* 44(5), 633–43.

Rauhala, A., Kivimäki, M., Fagerström, L., Elovainio, M., Virtanen, M., Vahtera, J., Rainio A-K, Ojaniemi, K. & Kinnunen J. (2007) What degree of work overload is likely to cause increased sickness absebteeism among nurses? Evidence from the RAFAELA patient classification system. *Journal of Advanced Nursing* 57(3), 286–95.

Rintala, T. (2003) *Vanhuskuvat ja vanhustenhuollon muotoutuminen 1850-luvulta 1990-luvulle.* Tutkimuksia 132. Helsinki: Stakes.

Räty, T., Luoma, K., Mäkinen, E. & Vaarama, M. (2003) *The factors affecting the use of elderly care and the need for resources by 2030 in Finland*. VATT-tutkimuksia 99. Helsinki: Valtion taloudellinen tutkimuskeskus.

Sinervo, T. (2000) *Work in care for the elderly. Combining theories of job design, stress, information processing and organizational cultures*. Research Reports 109. Helsinki: Stakes.

Sormunen, S., Topo, P., Eloniemi-Sulkava, U., Räikkönen, O. & Sarvimäki, A. (2007) Inappropriate treatment of people with dementia in residential and day care. *Aging and Mental Health* 11(3), 246–55

STM (2001) *Ikäihmisten hoitoa ja palveluja koskeva laatusuositus*. Oppaita 4. Helsinki: Sosiaali- ja terveysministeriö, Suomen kuntaliitto.

Topo, P., Sormunen, S., Saarikalle, K., Räikkönen, O. & Eloniemi-Sulkava, U. (2007) *Kohtaamisia dementiahoidon arjessa—havainnointitutkimus hoidon laadusta asiakkaan näkökulmasta*. Research Reports 162. Helsinki: Stakes.

Vaarama, M., Kainulainen, S., Perälä, M-L. & Sinervo, T. (1999) *Vanhusten laitoshoidon tila. Voimavarat, henkilöstön hyvinvointi ja hoidon laatu*. Aiheita 46. Helsinki: Stakes.

Vaarama, M., Voutilainen, P. & Kauppinen, S. (2004) Ikääntyneiden hoivapalvelut. In M. Heikkilä & M. Roos (Eds) *Sosiaali- ja terveydenhuollon palvelukatsaus 2005* (pp. 36–59). Helsinki: Stakes.

Voutilainen, P. (2004) *Hoitotyön laatu ikääntyneiden pitkäaikaisessa laitoshoidossa*. Tutkimuksia 142. Helsinki: Stakes.

Voutilainen, P., Muurinen, S., Vaarama, M. & Isola, A. (2001) *Vanhusten hoitotyön nykytila Helsingin kaupungin vanhainkodeissa*. Tutkimuksia 1. Helsinki: Helsingin kaupungin sosiaalivirasto.

SIX

Practical Nurses' Work Role and Workplace Ethos in an Era of Austerity

Laura Tainio and Sirpa Wrede

This chapter examines the work role of the most numerous care workers in Finnish elderly care, i.e. the practical nurses for social and health care (närvårdare/lähihoitaja).[1] Practical nurses are the rank and file in Finnish elderly care in that they are the ones working on the wards and doing home visits. We consider here the shaping of the work role that practical nurses occupy at the workplace. What limitations in their prospects of providing good quality care does their work role impose from the carers' own perspective? We define the work role in a wide, sociological sense, as an institutional position evolving in the negotiated order of the workplace. From a sociological perspective, the social, cultural and moral aspects of the work role are revealed as products of social construction (Hughes 1984). In this perspective, the institutional matrix of the work place becomes understood as a realm of symbolic representations and constitutive rules that constructs the care worker and frames her actions (Scott 1993). The consideration of the workplace as a social arena gives depth to the often-stated slogan that true competence is developed in the workplace. The demarcation of the work role of the practical nurse can thus be seen as an ongoing process in which multiple actors both inside and outside the workplace participate. In comparison with educators, policy makers and administrators, as well as with nurses and doctors, practical nurses emerge as a relatively weak party in the making of their work role (Wrede 2008).

The ongoing restructuring of Finnish elderly care has led to changes in the expectations of staff competency. Reflecting the pursuit of making the elderly care sector more effective, care organisations have commonly gone through consecutive organisational changes (e.g., Wrede & Henriksson 2005). The practical nurse occupation itself represents perhaps the most deep-going reform. It was aimed at introducing flexibility in the division of labour within the public sector, which with its many specialised job titles was considered rigid (Rintala & Elovainio 1997). The training reform has received mixed reactions among other groups of care workers such as nurses. The widely discussed distrust in the abilities of practical nurses has also been reflected in recruitment patterns, as the occupation has not been favourably met by the hospital sector (Vuorensyrjä 2006). Reflecting the multiple pressures described above, the challenges practical nurses are facing in their work role are substantial. The present chapter illustrates those pressures as seen from their own perspective. The aim is not to offer a mapping of the overall trends or to make estimates of the prevalence of the different problems. Instead, the qualitative study is aimed at highlighting what kind of work role practical nurses encounter at the workplaces.

The chapter is based on an analysis of 15 theme interviews conducted with practical nurses from Helsinki region in the spring of 2004.[2] At the time of the interviews, all of the informants had received their degree in practical nursing. Most of the informants were middle-aged and several of them had prior work experience from elderly care. All had some kind of working-life experience, if not in care then in some other line of work, commonly in the private service sector. Eleven informants were recruited by contacting one cohort of carers that graduated in 2002 from one vocational school in Helsinki area and four with the so-called 'snowball method'[3]. The thematic analysis on which this article is based focused on the barriers to quality care the way these emerged in the talk of the informants (Tainio 2006). This chapter develops further the analysis of these barriers by paying attention to the work role that practical nurses describe in their accounts. Accordingly, we apply an institutional approach (Scott 1993) aimed at examining what we identify as the institutionally embedded work role that shapes the workplace experiences of the care worker. In the final analysis, we are concerned with what kind of workplace ethos the work role expresses and how that ethos impacts on the quality of care[4]. Thus our main concern is not with the individual perspectives of the care workers themselves. We have therefore chosen not to emphasise the person of the carer.

In the following, we first examine how and why the educational goal of flexibility translates into a vague work role. In the second section we consider how task-centred work organisations and insufficient resources structure the work role of the practical nurse. We conclude with a discussion of the implications of what can be identified as an ethos of austerity in welfare policy on practical nursing.

The dynamics of vagueness

When newly qualified practical nurses discuss their work, they often talk about several different contexts, contrasting different employers and different types of work settings. On the basis of a qualitative interview material like ours it is, however, impossible to systematically analyse the organisation of work with reference to concrete workplaces. Instead, we have paid attention to the way symbolic dimensions of workplace organisation are expressed in the way informants discuss various features of their work. Interestingly, hospital-type provision of long-term care was often used as a sort of general point of reference by the informants when they were discussing the workplace. All of our informants had experiences of working in an institutional setting, at least during their training. Other forms to organise elderly care were often either explicitly or implicitly compared with this 'hegemonic' type of organising care. Apparently, working in a hospital-like organisation is a powerful experience for practical nurses, some of which had come to the conclusion that they would 'never again' work in a hospital. Institutional settings were frequently discussed as 'bad' workplaces, even though there were also accounts describing 'good' institutional care. Home-based care, on the other hand, was often considered as basically a 'good' way to organise care, but its recent changes were identified by some informants as leading to poor quality of care. Underneath the relatively common and at surface simplistic characterisation of the workplaces as 'good' or 'bad' lie fundamental issues about the workplace ethos. In our material the experience of a good or a bad workplace was associated with social relations with co-workers and others, i.e., 'our team'. Such social relations are important for supporting and legitimising the worker's definition of work and self. In a good workplace, worker's definition of work and of herself is supported and respected while in bad workplaces these conceptions are contradicted (Ghidina 1992, 76).

In the following we consider the expectations Finnish practical nurses identify in the workplace. Previous research that relies on this same material argues that the work role of practical nurses has turned out as vague rather than flexible, like the policy makers initially intended (Wrede 2008). Here we further develop the analysis of how care workers encounter a vague work role. Furthermore, we consider how the concerns of the shortcomings of practical nurse competence, widely discussed since the training programmes were established (Vuorensyrjä 2006), become visible in the workplace experiences of practical nurses. This section further considers the impact of unclear and diverse work-role boundaries and responsibilities.

QUESTIONED COMPETENCE

Practical nursing as an occupation has been subjected to widespread criticism, which has a variety of causes but has mainly concerned their claimed lack of adequate competence and skills. The first practical nurses were not favourably received by other care workers (Rintala & Elovainio 1997). Many of our informants had experienced some level of distrust, which is rooted in the notion that practical nurse training does not 'go below the surface'. The interviewees were often surprised by the negative attitudes and the distrust that for instance nurses felt towards them when they came to workplaces as newly employed. During their training, thinking ahead to their future positions, practical nurses expected to be able to use the care methods and to perform the tasks they were learning, but, having entered working life, they realise that the competence acquired at school does not inspire trust. The interviews contain many references to their having to prove their expertise and competence, sometimes repeatedly, in order to be allowed to perform tasks they had been trained for. This example is from home-based care.

> Even in quite simple jobs, say administering eye drops, we all had to show the public health nurse several times that we could do it. She then gave her permission, but we still had to talk to the doctor, who asked a lot of questions. Only after that were we allowed to do those tasks. (Kristiina)

In an institutional context, the fact that the newly graduated practical nurses are evaluated by nurses as well as by clients and their family members becomes perhaps most tangible. No doubt the practice of 'testing' the newcomers is a common routine, which all who have recently passed their examination are faced with, regardless of the field, but there are also signs of a lacking recognition for the practical nurse competence. One of our informants commented 'there are certain things I could do as a trainee and I had my tutor there, but now that I'm a practical nurse I can't do them' (Amran).

Several informants were, however, willing to recognise that the practical nurse training has shortcomings and many described a feeling of inadequacy and uncertainty due to the short period of training. However, given that the criticism of the competence of practical nurses may at times be justified, it also needs to be recognised that the critical statements at times may be strategic claims, made in relation to allocation of personnel resources or other similar concerns. Indeed, especially in home-based elderly care, the practical nurses' formal competency actually represents an improvement, as the level of training in elderly care and in home help in particular traditionally was lower than in other sectors (e.g., Paasivaara 2002).

A potential source of both the insecurity among practical nurses themselves and of the questioning of their competence among other parties in the workplace is the disparity of the different training programmes in practical nursing. Kristiina, for instance, who had worked in home-help services prior to her practical nurse training and had a formal qualification for that work, felt that despite of her practical experience the shorter adapted programme that she attended was inadequate: 'You know, quite often we were just scratching the surface.' In addition to the various adaptations of the training, another source of disparity in practical nurse competences was the element of practical training. Several informants were critical about the organisation of practical training, claiming that its focus was not always adequate. Also the quality of the guidance received in connection to practical training at workplaces varied greatly.

One of the informants pointed out that to require a proper competence as a practical nurse one would actually need to complement the programme through independent study in one's own time. Her interpretation of the situation is confirmed by a recent study on practical nursing. At least to a certain extent, educators do expect practical nurses to be willing to commit themselves to 'continuous self-development', even in their free time (Vuorensyrjä 2006, 105). Such expectations create a pressure for practical nurses to show what others define as professional commitment in the sense of taking responsibility for the quality of care beyond that recognised by the organisation (Wrede 2008). The expectations for this type of commitment to the organisation were also expressed by others. Our informants commented, for instance, that relatives and clients often expected them to bear holistic responsibility for care, for instance, by being able to inform them about all of its aspects. The practical nurses themselves felt, however, that their work role did not support holistic responsibility for care. Indeed, they referred to the work role as a barrier against developing an overall understanding of the care of their clients.

Also the vagueness of the boundaries of their work role was a problem. While clients expected a holistic service from the organisation, they at the same time might express doubts about the practical nurses' ability to do certain tasks, as they had an expectation of a traditional division of labour where nurses and doctors control the important knowledge about care. On the basis of our material, practical nurses met the expectation to limit themselves to an auxiliary work role most commonly in home care where recent reforms had changed the tasks of the carers. At the same time as both clients and their relatives might question their competence, practical nurses still felt that they were expected to be much more than wage earners. Practical nurses also sometimes themselves idealised care work. The portrayal of the ideal carer as open, patient, honest and cheerful, as well as reachable at all times by clients and their families contributes to the creation of high expectations that are difficult to meet in practice.

UNCLEAR BOUNDARIES AND RESPONSIBILITIES

Despite the discrepancy between the work roles in training and in working life, there seemed to be some kind of consensus among practical nurses about the core of their work role. The interviewees found it natural that their work was to a large extent concerned with so-called basic care, i.e., taking care of the bodily needs of the clients. They did not expect such duties to be delegated to others. The majority of them did, however, question the expectation that care was to be combined with housekeeping tasks. On the basis of their training they had not expected these duties to be a substantial part of their work role. Particularly for those working in the institutional settings, the toughest bit to accept seemed to be that they were often expected to combine care work with household chores, such as cooking and cleaning, rather than with social contacts. In their view such responsibilities on top of their other care tasks not only make it difficult to devote time to individual clients, the situation on the ward may feel chaotic when the carers constantly have to divide their time between different jobs and several clients.

> I was on shift alone and we had a couple of the demented clients wandering all over the place (...) And then I also had to make

macaroni soup and a couple of clients' relatives were demanding attention all the time, some clients wanting something and then you had to keep an eye on the demented wanderers who, honestly, may relieve themselves wherever they fancy, tear up the plants and knock the radio over. Sort of 'I'll go and pull on that nice flex' and the others shouting 'Keep off that, it's the telly'. And there's my soup burning any moment and I know one of the visitors will eat some of it, and of course it's not nice for the clients either if it's burnt. (Johanna)

Many carers felt that this kind of household work was not compatible with the practical nurses' work role, and that it prevented them from doing what they considered to be their proper job well. In addition to this unclear boundary 'downwards' in the cultural hierarchy of tasks, the practical nurses' accounts suggest a lack of clear definition 'upwards' in the hierarchy. Many practical nurses experienced that there was no clear understanding in the workplaces of what they could and could not do in terms of nursing. Vague boundaries were drawn, but practical nurses often felt that the nurses wanted to restrict their work role to the extent that nursing tasks would be allocated to them only exceptionally or by special authorisation. By contrast, many felt that there on the organisational level was pressure on them to take on more nursing tasks, but without proper institutional support. The transferral of tasks that nurses considered as nursing was also problematic from the point of view of occupational boundaries. Where the so-called basic care of clients is concerned, it is clear that nurses happily pass on less pleasant tasks to practical nurses, but they are less eager to give up valued tasks. As one of our informants put it, 'there are some (nurses) who think that we should just be clearing shit … nothing else.'

Our informants did not express a shared understanding of what kind of work role they should have. However, since their training does not fully correspond to the work role in the workplace, they often pointed at the unclear elements in their duties. Many felt that they were forced to perform tasks that are not a part of their job and that they have too many tasks and too little time:

> I'm not too keen on fiddling with jabs ... some do but I ...and take dressing wounds, not that I think it looks awful or something when you touch them, but it's not my thing ... so more of this other kind of caring (...) I'm not a nurse, and I'm never going to become one... (Susanna)

For others, however, expansion of tasks may be a welcome opportunity to keep up the skill and competence they had acquired at school. One of our informants who at the time of the interview was employed as in a service home for elderly clients, had previously worked in a central unit where the clientele was constantly changing, because the unit served as an intermediate station. She regrets not having more opportunities to make use of her knowledge in her new position. While she herself felt confident and was prepared to assume responsibility for her decisions, her colleagues often reacted strongly to them:

> Sometimes when you start applying antifungal ointment they're upset and how can you do that without the doctor having seen this athlete's foot, so maybe they're very unsure of their own competence (...) yes, in some matters I'm ready to take the responsibility (...) just use some common sense. (Maria)

Distributing medicines is a task that was often mentioned by our informants as one showing a particularly wide variety of practices. Some of our informants had met with total exclusion. In lack of explanation based on formal criteria there was only speculation about the potential reasons for what was interpreted as lack of trust:

> Where I'm working now, none of us has access to the medicine cabinet, the nurse deals with that (...) [I don't know why] maybe something went wrong with the medicines at some point. (Sari)

From the point of view of those who were not allowed to do this task the situation was experienced as a mismatch between training and work role. They felt that too much importance was attached to medicine distribution in their training, as they were not permitted to do it in practice. Their criticism exemplifies practical nurses' frustrations with the conflicting pressures they encounter. They react in different ways: while many practical nurses may criticise their narrow work roles, others feel that they are forced to accept taking on a lot of responsibility, even when they are not comfortable with it, due to the shortage of staff.

Organisation-centred or patient-centred care?

In this section we move on to consider the impact of the macro-organisation of the work on the work role. Janice Gross Stein (2001) argues that in the contemporary welfare service reforms, the overriding concern for efficiency has made it a value rather than a means, turning efficiency into a cult. Our material bears witness to how 'the cult of efficiency' has reshaped the work role of care workers in Finnish elderly care. From the perspective of many practical nurses, the 'effectiveness drive' in the organisation makes the provision of quality care difficult or impossible. Tasks pertaining to clients' basic needs govern day-to-day routines in the workplace, and all of our informants would like to see more time allowed for social contact. In their training practical nurses learn how the elderly can best be stimulated, but in working life there is no room for the social element. For many, contacts with the elderly in the social sphere were a decisive factor in their choice of occupation, and they are deeply disappointed at not having more opportunities to cater for clients' social needs. Under these conditions, the work role does not offer them an agreeable definition of self and the lack of such fulfilment creates serious tensions for the individual (c.f., Ghidina 1992).

THE TYRANNY OF ROUTINES
The allocation of work in care is often justified by the need to organise body care, household duties and nursing in a

'rational' way from an overall perspective: for example, in hospital-type care all the patients on a ward are woken up at the same time or in home-based care the meals of the elderly are taken care of by a separate organisation. In a hierarchical organisational model this often means that care tasks are split up according to the degree of expertise they are assumed to require. Those at the bottom of the ladder are regarded as mechanical routines and require only limited knowledge (Eriksson-Piela 2003). This interpretation of the professional role undermines the carers' own understanding of what their work should consist of. In this type of organisation individual requests and emotions are disregarded. The fact that the organisation of Finnish elderly care currently emphasises basic-care routines was reflected in our material (see Chapter 5). When describing what a typical working day was like, many started by listing the most mechanical tasks. Social contacts with clients seem to feature among the daily routines only in passing, and there are indications that instrumental work methods tend to minimise them. In addition to the routines related to the care of the patients' bodily needs, there are others that are determined by the needs of the organisation, such as paperwork.

> There's always something to do: write a care plan, phone a relative, do somebody's hair here, cut nails there, look after your own patient (...) You must check [the body all over], that everything's OK. Those who can't get out of bed need their position changed, to avoid bedsores. (Amran)

One of our informants pointed out that when there was an instrumental system that other carers and clients were used to, it was easier to act instrumentally and just to rely on routines rather than to 'work against the system'.

> You feel that the older clients and you yourself fall into the same pattern, I was a little disappointed in myself, how very quickly you get the feeling that 'sod it, I'll turn that one round now, and that one, that one, that one'. The routines just take over, some days when we're short-staffed. (Kaarina)

The scope of the practical nurses' work role is formed and re-formed by organisational decisions. In most workplaces they have the opportunity to influence for example the order of work tasks or allocation of clients, but on the policy level these opportunities are limited. Many home-care tasks that used to be performed by practical nurses are nowadays organised on a centralised basis as so-called support services, and the carers concentrate on caring tasks. The reorganisation has changed both the contents and the rhythm of the work. Traditionally, it included shopping, cleaning and washing up, which gave it the character of household work rather than care. Interviewees with work experience in home care stressed that it generally was less hierarchical. However, the differences between practical nurse work in home care and in institutions narrow at the same rate as home care is streamlined. Informants with experience from home care talked about the frustration not to be able to manage work in a satisfactory way in the allocated working hours:

> You get so many who are in a bad way these days, and you know we're not allowed to do overtime (…) it's precisely this lack of time, so you feel stressed when you know you should take these old people out and that's what they'd like, summer is coming and all, and wouldn't it be smashing to sit out there for an hour or two with everyone, but we, we just can't manage that. (Susanna)

THE WORKPLACE AS A HARSH REALITY

Many interviewees talked about how they, when coming to work as new employees, reacted negatively to the care work culture they encountered. Many opposed the uncaring nature of work practices, but were met with pressure from colleagues not to cause problems: 'They were saying just you wait, when you've been here two or three years you'll be like us.' One of the interviewees laconically identified a process through which care workers 'learn' to put up with what they feel is bad care: 'That sort of thing makes you cynical.' As new carers settle in, drawbacks do not stand out so clearly to them.

You lose your detached perspective on your workplace as you get to know your colleagues and begin to identify with them (Twigg 2000). The workplace itself and the colleagues' example, rather than their words, socialise carers to treat emotions evoked by their work, including reactions to poor quality care, in the 'right' way (Molander 2003).

It seems that practical nurses fresh out of school are not prepared for how heavy the work they are taking up really is, even though our informants typically had other working life experience prior to entering care work. According to their accounts, their training conveys an idealised picture of what care should be like, but in many workplaces staff shortages and insufficient funding restrict the facilities for care, and the carers' own possibilities of exerting influence are limited. The workload appears too big in most workplaces where elderly people are being cared for, regardless of whether it is an old people's residence, a hospital or the client's home. Some pointed out that this would have negative effects on the general standard of the care given, despite efforts to maintain the level. At the same time as working as efficiently and as quickly as possible, you are conscious of neglecting somebody, which triggers constant stress.

The work may be heavy on several levels. When asked to describe what they felt that was heavy in their work, the interviewees mentioned the working hours, the physically demanding tasks (lifting, showering) and the mentally stressful duties (the care of demented or mentally ill old people). The care of the demented is taxing because the relationships with clients become monotonous, and the contacts may feel unsatisfactory (see Chapter 5). Exhaustion may result in indifference: 'When they're demented, they get forgetful and keep asking you lots of things, the same questions again and again ... 20–25 times a day (...) you get fed up with it.'

Several informants identified the task of caring for mentally ill clients as particularly difficult and sometimes unsafe. One of our informants told about the anxiety involved in caring for a particularly threatening client:

> She used to dig out all sorts of belts and knives and she sat down near you and clearly wanted to show you that now ... scare you a little, I think. I haven't got her out of my mind, because she was always so threatening. I used to wonder where I could go when she's sitting ... if she really did something. (Helena)

There are demented old people in most workplaces, and some-times mentally ill, too. The informants who commented on the pressure created by the presence of such clients identified working alone as the major concern. Facing aggressive behav-iour when working alone made the carers feel uncertain and powerless. Other aspects of working solo also made them feel unsafe. Several interviewees pointed out that working night shift on their own felt unpleasant for them as well as for the old people.

> Doing the round at night is a bit spooky. If there were an accident ... I remember somebody had had a fall and there was blood all over the place when I went there ... it was pretty awful. You open the door and see just blood. Then there's somebody sitting there in the dark. (Samira)

Situations where carers are overburdened appear highly prob-lematic from the point of view of good care as there were hints that unethical actions could occur in circumstances beyond the carers' control, such as in cases of undermanning, stress and possibly exhaustion. Our informants discussed such oc-currences as shortcomings of the system, when carers faced unreasonable working conditions.

> They didn't have enough staff and there were older carers suffer-ing from stress (...) they were unpleasant to the clients (...) If I'd been in charge there, and had seen how those carers ... I'd have sent them on sick leave. (Jamila)

Another informant had worked in care units where she saw the standard of care going down, although she herself felt that she was trying her best all the time. She pondered on how work pressure necessarily resulted in a changed attitude towards the clients that she could not have imagined earlier. Instead of providing holistic care, she was focusing on specific tasks.

> At the time (on a long-term ward) I was thinking there's no sense in this and no point in me here slaving my butt off twisting and turning these people without any sort of break, so that's how it was (...) when [I was] studying and thinking about these things I thought I'd never take that kind of an attitude towards patients, but there you are ... (Kaarina)

The organisational drive for efficiency thus became visible in her work as an orientation towards specific tasks that she described as 'twisting and turning'. The same expression was used also by another informant who reflected how alienating these practices must feel from the point of view of the client:

> The carers seemed to be there for their own sake and to get their job done somehow. As long as you can have your coffee break soon, then some turning and twisting and that's your job done. I was thinking is that how they lie there all day, nobody talking to them, now and then they get some food stuffed down their throats and that's maybe the only contact when they see a carer at all. (Maria)

One of our informants, who herself was currently unemployed and considered elderly care workplaces in the public sector as generally inhospitable and poorly run, pointed out that the carers themselves also needed some stimulus to be able to provide good care. Otherwise machines could do it just as well.

> I felt that everything human and all charity had gone out of it, it was just a matter of doing your job (...) with the demented I suppose it's hard, it's terribly hard, but then there should be something offered to the staff to offset this and then they'd cope again and not be like robots... (Anneli)

Many of our informants, newly qualified carers, found the prospect of becoming so cynical that they could live with providing bad care daunting, and many interviewees emphatically distanced themselves from this kind of workplace ethos. One said she would rather quit before she became like that: 'I'll quit the very day I start showing such a sour face.'

Conclusion

In this chapter we have examined the work role of the practical nurse in elderly care the way it is described by practical nurses when they talk about their work. Our analysis has been guided by an idea of the division of labour in the workplace as a negotiated order. In other words, the work role is not stable and constant, but embedded and subject to frequent definitions and redefinitions in negotiations and conflicts between different actors at different levels. The work role can therefore be given widely disparate meanings in different contexts, such as in training and working life. The occupation in focus in this chapter is one that is found at the lower levels of the occupational hierarchies, so the practical nurses themselves are not powerful parties in the negotiations on their work role. Instead, their work roles depend on the attitudes, values and politics of others with more power in the shaping of the workplace and its ethos.

In our analysis, we have explored what we in the beginning of the chapter identified as a crisis concerning the quality of elderly care in Finland, paying attention to how practical nurses describe their work role. Our central conclusion is that the work role in many respects functions as a barrier to quality care in that it does not offer a stable source of self-definition in the workplace (c.f., Ghidina 1992). On the basis of our study, at least some of the problems of the work role appear to be related to the questioning of the competence of practical nurses. The vagueness of the work role, in its turn, appears to be a constant source of unmet expectations for all of the parties involved, i.e. care organisers, other professionals, clients, relatives and practical nurses themselves.

From the perspective of practical nurses themselves the unclear occupational boundaries of practical nursing are related to organisational structures and practices and, in part, to organisational non-action. There are no signs in our material that organisations would be taking effective measures to tackle the distrust nurses and others show to practical nurses. Instead, a motley set of workplace-level control measures are practiced to monitor their competence and regulate their practice. The organisational neglect of attending to the vagueness of the work role is further made worse by the emphasis on effectiveness, constituting a problematic foundation for workplace ethos in elderly care. From the point of view of our informants, it is not the quality of care or the needs of clients or care workers that are prioritised. Instead, the overriding emphasis on austerity in the politics shaping elderly care suggests to practical nurses that decision makers do not care about fulfilment of other than the most basic needs of the clients. There is also a sense that the wellbeing of the care workers themselves is not valued. The lack of consideration for their perspective creates from their point of view a crisis of commitment, fuelled by a sense of powerlessness that many care workers feel in the face of increasing pressure at the workplace.

The present austerity of resources felt by our informants in many workplaces seems to put their commitment under test rather than supporting it, as it seems that carers are more patient-oriented when they take up their first jobs after qualifying, and the more work experience they have, the less sympathetic they become. Thus our examination of the experiences of practical nurses in the workplace indicates that the practical nurse's work role often may restrict patient-orientation. Accordingly we maintain that the differences between workplaces, which mostly appear to be about work organisation and the ethos it supports, are more important for the delivery of the quality of care than differences in carer performance.

Deficient work organisation produces poor care, which in turn may trigger processes in the carers that may result in their becoming accustomed to providing insufficient and unsatisfactory care.

The care work practical nurses do is all about working with people, and thus involves a constant quest for the right choices (Hughes 1984). Carers make decisions with an immediate bearing on other people, and promoting the welfare of another human being is, ideally, the ultimate goal of their actions. Given the present pressure to ration care, practical nurses are also expected to be able to prioritise. Although care work is not particularly rewarding in terms of pay or status, and most of those employed in that sector find their opportunities restricted and experience difficulties and stress, the work in itself offers certain rewards. Since practical nurses work with people, they often receive direct feedback. The feeling of being appreciated by their clients and being important to them is very gratifying (Twigg 2000). If the care is not good, negative feedback from the clients can be taxing and may trigger self-defence, particularly as practical nurses commonly share the cultural image of the ideal care worker as self-effacingly and boundlessly caring.

Daniel F. Chambliss (1996) calls care work a noble and at the same time terrible profession, a view shared by many who study care work (see Chapters 3 and 13). Helping other people is indeed noble work that may feel rewarding, but at the same time carers are potentially exposed to exploitation. Because of this exposure of carers to organisational neglect, instead of emphasising the distinction between patient-oriented versus instrumentally oriented carers, we prefer to highlight the conflict between theory and practice as the decisive element. No carer is exclusively one type or the other, every one is a bit of both. Under the conflicting pressures of working life, some may find patient-orientation mentally very hard and many may end up 'working like a robot'. In the emerging literature on the linkage between job satisfaction and ethics-related work factors, this phenomenon is recognised as ethics stress and related to the ethical climate of the workplace (Ulrich et al. 2007). When inquiring where to place the responsibility for the present crisis of the quality of care it is, however, also important to go beyond the workplace and consider current elderly care policy (see, e.g., Chapter 4). There is reason to believe that the austere ethos of welfare policy transmits to the workplace and to the culture of care.

Notes

1 The current form of Finnish certification for the regulated carers and auxiliaries was introduced in 1993 on the basis of a new joint curriculum for health and social care, replacing seven earlier occupations in health care and three in social care. The new occupational title *närvårdare/lähihoitaja* emphasises the idea of the carer being close to the client. Legislation only protects their occupational title, the tasks they do in workplaces can generally also be done by non-trained workers. The secondary-level education for practical nurses was first 2, 5 years of which the last six months were dedicated to studies in one of the several alternative orientations. In 1999, as a response to critique from the field, the training was extended to 3 years that include one year of specialisation in one of the study programmes. A national system of skills tests was included in the curriculum in 2006 to control the quality of the practical nurse training (Wrede 2008).

2 The interviews were conducted by Malin Grönholm, Laura Tainio and Sirpa Wrede in spring 2004 using an interview guide developed in collaboration with Lea Henriksson and her research project 'The Politics of Recruitment'. The interviews lasted from 50 minutes to 1, 5 hours. The interviews were taped and transcribed in verbatim.

3 We wanted to secure that our materials would reflect the emerging ethnic diversity of care workers and therefore four informants with foreign origins were interviewed. In this chapter we chose not emphasise the origins of the informants as this analysis that focuses on work place experiences has not taken ethnicity into account (see Chapter 7).

4 One alternative would have been to emphasise more how the work role impacts on the care workers themselves and their experience of working in the care sector. The same material has, however, been used to another study with that emphasis (Wrede 2008).

References

Chambliss, D., (1996) *Beyond Caring. Hospitals, Nurses, and the Social Organization of Ethics.* Chicago: The University of Chicago Press.

Eriksson-Piela, S. (2003) *Tunnetta, tietoa vai hierarkiaa? Sairaanhoidon moninainen ammatillisuus.* Tampere: Tampere University Press.

Ghidina, M. (1992) Social relations and the defition of work: identity management in a low-status occupation. *Qualitative Sociology* 15(1), 73–85.

Hughes, E.C. (1984) *The Sociological Eye. Selected Papers.* New Brunswick: Transaction Books.

Molander, G. (2003) *Työtunteet—esimerkkinä vanhustyö.* Helsinki: Työterveyslaitos.

Paasivaara, L. (2002) *Tavoitteet ja tosiasiallinen toiminta. Suomalaisten vanhusten hoitotyön muotoutuminen 1930-luvulta 2000-luvulle.* Acta Universitatis Ouluensis D Medica 707. Oulu: Oulun Yliopisto.

Rintala, T. & Elovainio, M. (1997) *Lähihoitajien työ, ammatti-identiteetti ja hyvinvointi.* Tutkimuksia 86. Helsinki: Stakes.

Scott, W.R. (1993) The organization of medical care services: Toward and integrated theoretical model. *Medical Care Research and Review* 50(3), 271–303.

Stein, J.G. (2001) *The Cult of Efficiency.* Toronto: Anansi.

Tainio, L. (2006) *'Man vänjer sig'—En studie av närvårdare inom åldringsvården.* Unpublished Master's Thesis in sociology. Åbo Akademi University.

Twigg, J. (2000) *Bathing—The Body and Community Care.* London: Routledge.

Ulrich, C., O'Donnell, P., Taylor, C., Farrar, A., Danis, M. & Grady, C. (2007) Ethical climate, ethics stress, and the job satisfaction of nurses and social workers in the United States. *Social Science & Medicine* 65(8), 1708–1719.

Vuorensyrjä, L. (2006) Lähihoitajat 2015. In M. Vuorensyrjä, M. Borgman, T. Kemppainen, M. Mäntysaari & A. Pohjola (Eds) *Sosiaalialan osaajat 2015. Sosiaalialan osaamis-, työvoima- ja koulutustarpeiden ennakointihanke (SOTENNA): loppuraportti* (pp. 90–156). Jyväskylä: Jyväskylän yliopisto.

Wrede, S. (2008) Educating generalists: the flexibilisation of Finnish auxiliary nursing and the dilemma of professional identity. In E. Kuhlmann & M. Saks (Eds) *Rethinking Governance, Remaking Professions: International Directions in Health Care* (pp. 127–140). Bristol: The Polity Press.

Wrede, S. & Henrisson, L. (2005) Finnish home care in transition: the changing terms of welfare service work. In H.M. Dahl & T.R. Eriksen (Eds) *Dilemmas of Care in the Nordic Welfare State. Continuity and Change* (pp. 62–79). Aldershot: Ashgate.

SEVEN

Immigrant Nurses in Finland: Political Negotiations on Occupational Membership

Suvi Nieminen and
Lea Henriksson

Globalisation has had a tremendous influence on the terms and conditions of care work during the past few decades. The recruitment of care work professionals, most importantly nurses (Buchan & Calman 2004), presents a dynamic and challenging situation worldwide. In cases of a severe shortage of labour force, migrant care workers have become an increasingly significant part of the health care labour force in many Western countries. The labour-based migration of care workers is not a new phenomenon as such; many Western countries have depended on migrants for decades in meeting the demands for health care labour force (e.g., Buchan & Calman 2004). However, for some countries—like Finland—there is a new urgency to such migration as they try to cope with increasing demands for nurses that they are not able to meet nationally.

The international migration of care workers shows up in a rather specific context in Finland. Finland is a distinctive combination of a welfare state with a recent history of emigration in the international nursing workforce market and a very small immigrant population—which is practically non-existent among practicing nursing professionals. However, since the end of the 1990's the situation has been changing little by little and now, it can be argued, the national situation is in transition. The unemployment among nurses in the 1990's is expected to turn into an extensive fight for new nurse recruits by the first decades of the 2000's.

In the situation of a rapidly changing labour market and labour shortage, various political agencies are challenged into debates and action in order to manage the looming recruitment crisis in national health care. In this context, also various marginal groups, like immigrant professionals, attain a new kind of political interest: Many nation states have put into action changes in professional regulation and paid special attention to discriminatory practices along with new immigration policies (Kofman 2004, Iredale 2001). At the same time the cultural, occupational and juridical borders and regulations of different occupational groups become targets for redefinitions (see Henriksson 1998, Henriksson & Wrede 2004). In this redefinition, it is the gender and migration status that play significant roles in structuring the occupational opportunities of skilled migrants (c.f., Raghuram 2004, Iredale 2005).

As the terminology used in migration studies is somewhat mixed, a clarification about the terms used in this chapter is needed. The term *immigrant* is used here to refer to such persons who are of foreign origin and who have migrated to the destination country with an intention to settle down there permanently—whatever the reason for the migration may be. Instead, the term *migrant* is used to refer to a person who may migrate also on a short-term basis, often so for work. The difference between these terms is in places subtle and the meaning of the terms may overlap, but the differences are nonetheless relevant in some respects. In the research data there is no difference drawn between the terms; the term used is *maahanmuuttaja* in Finnish, correctly translated as immigrant, but in practice referring also to a migrant.

In this chapter the aim is to examine primarily the position of immigrant nurses in the context of the current transition in the Finnish health care labour market. The interest in this inquiry is, what kind of a membership is constructed for immigrant nurses as a labour force resource and as health care professionals in the multiculturalising welfare state of Finland? Firstly we introduce the analytical perspective of an occupational group. The argument is that the focal question about immigrant professionals not only concerns their possible exclusion from the membership of an occupational group; the question is also about the specific ways of inclusion. Secondly we describe the significant role that national policy agencies play in shaping the societal terms and conditions for immigrant nurses' occupational membership in the regulated health care labour market. Thirdly we explore empirically the ways in which different policy agencies configure the position of immigrant nurses in the country context of Finland. This analysis focuses on the intersections that migration status, occupation and gender play in the political negotiations over immigrant nurses' occupational membership. In focus are the questions:[1] What is said about immigrant nurses as a national labour force resource and as professionals?[2] What kinds of categorisations are in-built in these accounts? and[3] How do migration status, occupation and gender intersect in these accounts? We conclude by arguing that the exclusion of other than labour-based skilled migration makes current research frameworks inadequate in analysing immigrant nurses as part of and from a perspective of an occupational group.

The empirical data consists of national policy documents produced by focal agencies at the state and the labour market organisations. These agencies take part in defining the policy needs regarding the nursing workforce in Finland, i.e: The Ministry of Labour (*MOL*), the Ministry of Social Affairs and Health (*MSAH*), The Association of Finnish Local and Regional Authorities (*Kuntaliitto*) and the Union of Health and Social Care Professionals (*Tehy*). For a detailed analysis we have chosen one key document from each actor. Other relevant documents of the selected actors are used as complementary data. The time period is from 2000 to 2005. The documents are read and interpreted as entities from the perspective of immigrant nurses. By adopting a discursive way of reading and interpreting the data, a special attention is paid to the functional nature of the speech (e.g., Wetherell & Potter 1992, Jokinen et al. 1993, Potter & Wetherell 2001). The functions are produced in language both explicitly and implicitly; thus also silences are significant. When reading the data, the modes of speaking are important alongside with the contents. We look for the contexts and the ways through which immigrant professionals are discussed, assessed and argued.

The perspective of migrant care workers in European welfare states

Many of the occupational groups in care work can be categorised under the vast concept of skilled workers. Skilled migration in care work is becoming a more significant part of the overall migration flow than ever before (Raghuram 2004), as migrants are expected to bring relief for the severe shortage of labour force driven by demographic challenges in many Western societies. For many countries, one of the most problematic human resource challenges is currently a shortage of nurses (e.g., Buchan & Calman 2004). However, the shortage of nursing professionals is not a new phenomenon as such, but has prevailed in many countries in cyclical periods also in previous decades. Furthermore, the concept of a shortage as such is relative and not easily quantifiable. Buchan and Calman (2004) remind that it should rather be understood as a shortage of professionals who are willing to work as nurses in present conditions; and thus it is primarily a crisis of recruitment. Migrants are used to do the marginal or otherwise less popular work in health care.

The theoretical frameworks of migration studies highlight many social, cultural and political aspects associated with international skilled migration (see Iredale 2001). There have also been a growing number of gendered analyses of such flows, acknowledging the importance that gender plays in shaping the conditions and experiences related to migration. As many occupational groups are strongly gendered, gender plays an important role in explaining migration flows. Men dominate movements within transnational corporations, information and communication technology and science, whereas women circulate through welfare service work such as education, health and social work (Kofman 2004). In health care the state usually plays a crucial role in regulating the labour market for higher skilled professionals. Thus skilled women migrants tend to be more at the mercy of the power of the state than men (Kofman 2004, Raghuram 2004).

The contemporary theoretical frameworks focus on the less skilled fields of productive and reproductive labour such as domestic work, entertainment and prostitution (Kofman 2004). The vast majority of international (nurse) migration research is also based on the premise that migration is intentional, planned and takes place primarily for work-related reasons (e.g., Yeates 2004). They are therefore inadequate in analysing migrant nurses from a perspective of an occupational group, which is comprised of members with various migrational backgrounds. Sociology of professions is helpful here to widen the view on the reconfiguration of occupations and professions. It pays attention, for example, to the transformation of occupations through cultural segmentation and segregation, which shape the conditions of professionalism and play a role in inter- and intraprofessional relationships (e.g., Davies 1996, 2003, Henriksson & Wrede 2004). The focal question about migrant professionals not only concerns their possible exclusion from membership in an occupational group; the question is also about the specific ways of inclusion. The interest lies especially in how this inclusion is rhetorically constructed and cloaked into gendered and ethnocentric discourses which are rooted in the core understanding of professionalism and which are further interconnected to larger socio-political interests (c.f., Davies 1996).

The need to enlarge the perspective beyond the traditional labour-driven frameworks of migration studies is evident especially in a context in which migrant nurses have arrived mainly through other routes than labour migration and mostly on a permanent basis—as is the case in Finland. Finland has not attracted as a country nor has there been a strong demand for migrant nurses or other migrant health care professionals for work-related reasons until very recently, and thus most of the immigrants who are working in health care have come here for reasons other than work. Finland had a significant surplus of nurses throughout the 1990's and the beginning of the 2000's (see Santamäki 2004), and for example other Nordic countries have been able to fill part of their recruitment deficit by recruiting Finnish nurses. Furthermore, the policies related to the accreditation of nursing degrees taken outside of the EU or EEA countries have been rather strict and unorganised, preventing effectively migrant nurses from entering the Finnish health care labour market.

According to the statistics of the National Authority for Medicolegal Affairs, there were only about 140 foreign nurses and 1000 physicians who had been trained outside the EU or EEA countries and who had been granted a permit to practice their occupation in Finland by May 2005 (L. Kinnunen, TEO, personal notification 26.8.2005). In 2005, there were no new permits granted to nurses trained outside the EU or EEA countries and 56 new permits were granted to nurses trained in other EU or EEA countries. For physicians the numbers were 146 and 311 respectively. (TEO 2005.) In comparison, in Ireland 69 per cent of the nurses recruited in 2001 were international recruits, in the UK 52 per cent and in Norway 28 per cent (Buchan et al. 2003).

Thus, according to statistics, immigrant nurses do appear as a very marginal group in Finland, whether in relation to the total number of nurses or to the proportion of immigrant workers in other occupational groups like physicians. However, the statistics presented above do not describe the whole phenomenon of immigrant nurses in Finland in 'reality', but rather the interests of the various institutional actors who regulate the accreditation of foreign professional degrees and compile the statistics (cf. Ronkainen 2004). There are no statistics available concerning the numbers of such immigrant nurses who have not been granted a permit to practice nursing in Finnish health care. Numbers have the status of 'factual knowledge' and they are used as a method of factual rhetorics (see Ronkainen 2004). Indeed, in policy making arenas it is the statistics that count.

Political agencies: regulating the entry to the occupational fields

The research on immigrants' position in the labour market has proven that there is overt racism in the labour market that appears in personal forms and on organisational levels (e.g., Paananen 1999, Ahmad 2002, Forsander 2002, Kyhä 2006, also Hugman 1991, 147–173). However, the conditions for

acquiring formal accreditation, and thus fulfilling the precon-
ditions for achieving occupational membership in the receiving society and its labour market, are defined beyond the personal and organisational levels. Obtaining entry to care work
can be prevented already on the policy level. Policy frameworks have significant, but still little considered and documented, implications for the migrant professionals' position
in the labour market (Hugman 1991).

The extent of internationalisation varies between occupational groups and a unique situation pertains to each of these
arenas. The interactions between the market, the state and
the occupation play significant roles in explaining the status
and positions available to migrant health care workers (see
Iredale 2001, Bach 2006). Health care professionals have been
traditionally closely tied to state and corporatist regulation,
and the skill and competence have so far been less readily
transferable (Iredale 2001, Kofman 2004). The requirements
for qualification in health care are thoroughly defined in the
EU directives and in national legislation. The national legislation and the process of qualification assessment in regard to
the degrees taken abroad differ between countries (Wickett &
McCutcheon 2002). Thus, in the context of the migration of
health care professionals and the experiences of migrant professionals, the state operates through complex intersections
of the regulation of vocational training, accreditation, ethics
and standards, besides defining broader migration regulations
(Iredale 2001, 2005, Yeates 2004, Bach 2006).

In Finland the areas of responsibilities related to the governance of migrant health professionals are fragmented, the
two most central agencies being the Ministry of Social Affairs
and Health (MSAH) and the Ministry of Labour (MOL). The
Ministry of Social Affairs and Health is responsible for national health and social policies, covering the overall functioning
of the country's health care, including ensuring the appropriate workforce in quality and quantity (MSAH 2006). As a key
document presenting MSAH's visions concerning the health
care labour force, we examined *the Report of the Commission on*

Anticipating the Need for Labour in Social and Health Care (MSAH 2001, authors' translation). It assesses the need for social care and health care labour, the scale of professional education and other questions related to the recruitment of the workforce for the time period 2001–2010 (MSAH 2001). The field of the Ministry of Labour covers national labour and immigration policies as well as immigrants' integration into the society and the promotion of ethnic equality in the society (MOL 2006). It is also responsible for arranging complementary vocational education for unemployed adult immigrants. The key document representing the governmental employment administration is *Labour Policy Strategy for 2003 to 2007 to 2010* (MOL 2003a), authors' translation, which presents the vision, challenges and aims of the national labour policies.

Also various meso-level actors like labour market organisations and professional bodies intervene actively with a variety of instruments in migrant professionals' position in the labour market (Iredale 2001, Raghuram 2004, Bach 2006). Professional associations and trade unions are not the authors of rules like the state, but they mediate governmental regulations in many ways (Bach 2006) and are important cooperation partners with the state's different administrative branches. Hugman (1991, 156–157), for instance, suggests that the trade unions may strengthen racism 'by pursuing policies which have the unintended consequence of perpetuating racist divisions of access to the labour market.' Iredale (2001) brings up the significance and power of professional bodies in the regulation of the labour market in regard to migrant professionals. However, it should be acknowledged that there are fundamental variations in regard to the power that different occupational groups possess. Hence different professional bodies are not actors of the same weight. In health politics it is the medical profession—and thus the medical professional bodies—that have traditionally possessed the power (e.g., Julkunen 2004).

Meso-level actors are represented in the empirical data of this study by two agencies. The Union of Health and Social

Care Professionals (*Tehy*) is explored as a guardian of the professional interests of nurses. The rate of unionisation is high among nurses in Finland, almost 90 per cent of the employees, and *Tehy* is the biggest trade union of nursing professionals with its 124 000 members, a majority of whom are nurses (Tehy 2005a). The data is based primarily on a short report titled *the Account of Multiculturality*, published in two parts (Tehy 2005a, b, authors' translation). The issues discussed include immigrant nurses' position in work organisations, the employment situation and immigrant professionals' expectations regarding the trade union's activities. The Association of Finnish Local and Regional Authorities (*Kuntaliitto*) is explored as a representative of the most significant employers of nurses, the municipalities. In Finland around 80–85 percent of nurses are employed in the public sector by the municipalities (MSAH 2001, 60). It is thus the municipal sector that is going to be hit hardest by the shortage of nursing personnel. The key report *The Workforce and Personnel of Municipalities 2010* (Kuntaliitto 2002, authors' translation) focuses on the preparations for the looming recruitment crisis.

Political agencies set formal regulations on the membership of migrant professionals in receiving countries by elaborating and promoting definitions of migrant professionals as well as allocating resources for authorities. However, they also reconstruct more broadly immigrant professionals' modes of belonging to the nation state. Policy makers conduct their activities based on certain representations, on image construction and the labelling of migrants; thus also the regulations draw on and rearticulate different kinds of gendered, racialised and nationalised hierarchies and categorisations. Political language and stands have significant roles and implications in constructing national and cultural meaning-making and categorisations of different groups of people. (Carling 2005, 15, Huttunen et al. 2005, 25)

Choosing from the margins: are immigrant nurses needed?

The shortage of the labour force in health care, the factors affecting it and the means for coping with it form central topics in the research data. Indeed, there seems to be a shared political consensus about the need to take active measures in order to battle the looming recruitment crisis. The need for new nurse employees is estimated to range between 32 000–50 000 persons in the years 2000–2010 (MSAH 2001, 112, MOL 2003a, 32) and 40 000 persons during 2010–2030 (MSAH 2001, 112). The growing multiculturality in Finnish society and its health care services is recognised in the data all down the line. It is acknowledged that a growing number of immigrants need diverse backup services (MSAH 2001, 99) and that multicultural work generates the need for special know-how (MSAH 2001, 107).

One of the five strategies lined up in the Ministry of Labour's labour policy strategy is an active, work-based immigration policy. Migrants are thus considered as an essential labour force resource in the future. Geographical areas possible for recruitment are targeted outside the EU and EEA countries, especially Russia, but also the population-rich Asian countries (MOL 2003a, 90, 94). Estonia is also regarded as one possibility (MOL 2003b, 37). However, Estonia is particularly vulnerable to the out-migration of nurses; its reserve of nurses is very small, with less than 7000 nurses and midwives altogether, and there is also a prevailing lack of nursing staff (Järvinen 2004). Thus Estonia can hardly be considered as a substantial source of nurses for Finland.

The Association of Finnish Local and Regional Authorities also regards the migrant labour force as an essential resource for future social care and health care and expresses the need to promote more active immigration policies than the current one (Kuntaliitto 2002, 16). The Union of Health and Social Care Professionals takes a rather moderate stance by regarding migrant nurses as one of the possible resources on a small scale but not solving the recruitment problem (Tehy 2005a, b).

This is in contrast to the Ministry of Social Affairs and Health's pragmatic view according to which 'the migrant workforce will enter social and health sectors in the same volumes as in other sectors' (MSAH 2001, 112–113), and no special measures are needed to promote this recruitment. It is noted though that the vocational education of the immigrants is an issue to be taken care of (MSAH 2001, 124). This viewpoint is in contrast with the statement of the equivalent Swedish Report of the Commission on Anticipating the Need for Labour force in Social and Health Care made in 1999, stating that the young and the immigrants are clearly underrepresented in the health sector in Sweden (MSAH 2001, 33). The Swedish report, which is introduced by the MSAH in detail as an example (MSAH 2001, 32–34), features the importance of immigrant labour throughout its agenda. Against this background it is even more interesting to note that the questions related to the immigrant labour force are rather thoroughly silenced in the Finnish proposals.

The Ministry of Social Affairs and Health takes a rather ambiguous stand in positioning migrant professionals in relation to Finnish health care. On the one hand, the ministry states that the national reserves are adequate in meeting the need for new recruits (MSAH 2001, 112–113). Policy addresses various *domestic* marginal groups—the aged, the young and the people in 'various ways not fully fit for work'—as potential sources of labour and thus in need of special measures. Immigrants are not mentioned as a part of these national reservoirs, as one of the diverse domestic marginal groups. On the other hand, however, it is stated that 'the growth in the need for services, the working conditions and the development of the personnel and pay policies in regard to the other sectors affect the matter if the Finnish social and health sectors are able to get labour from other sectors in our own country or if we follow the model of other Nordic countries and acquire workforce beyond our borders' (MSAH 2001, 85). It is also worth noting that the model of the other Nordic countries in 'acquiring labour' has relied rather substantially on Finnish recruits and has partially been based on collaboration with the governments (e.g., Piippola 2003).

Categories of the respectable nurses

In the policy accounts there can be seen different kinds of discourses that segregate between the 'potential' migrant professionals on various bases. Although the Ministry of Labour considers migrant professionals as an essential labour force resource in the future, the distinction can be seen made on the basis of the form of migration. Labour migrants are labelled as 'well-educated, skilful migrants with good labour market competences' (MOL 2003a, 53), whereas many of those already living in the country, notably refugees, are pointed at as people who face major difficulties in employment (MOL 2003a, 42, 53). Furthermore, cultural differences and language problems are attached especially to refugees (MOL 2003a, 42). Hence, it is not only the skill and competence or the employment opportunities of the migrants that are being defined on the basis of the form of migration, but also the cultural competence and adaptability of the migrants in working life— or rather, in the whole Finnish society indeed. Refugee flows and family reunion are not acknowledged as possible types of skilled (nurse) migration.

This discourse, where the recognition of skills and qualifications is primarily determined by the conditions applicable to different forms of entry (c.f., Iredale 2001, 2005), asserts the view that skilled migrants outside the category of labour-based migration seldom invoke any interest related to a labour market—in spite of the fact that these categories form the major part of international migration and an overwhelming majority in particular in Finland. By ranking the migrants' skills and adaptability in working life as well as in the whole society on the basis of their reason for migration, the overwhelming majority of the current immigrant population and migrant professionals who work in Finnish health care are excluded from the segments of the potential and valued professional labour force. Yet the skills are not dependent on the reason for immigration, though the skills of other than labour-based immigrants are not 'known' beforehand in the same way. For immigrant professionals the segregation conducted through this discourse will bear notable consequences through proposed labour policy activities as well as through the process of cultural meaning-making.

Despite the subtle discrepancy within the Ministry of Social Affairs and Health's account of the need for migrant labour in health care, we argue that the statements can be interpreted to draw on and reconstruct rather congruent discourses on migrant professionals and the immigrant population as whole. In case the national reservoirs are not adequate, the question of a migrant workforce seems to appear to the Ministry as a rather simple question of *'acquiring'* them, *'like the others have done'*. Immigrant professionals are not taken into account as active actors. One may also see the same discourse on skills recognition and the reason for migration in work here as in the account of the Ministry of Labour: It is the 'invited'—or in this case indeed the acquired—*labour*-based migrant professionals who may be needed. The segmentation occurs also by excluding immigrants from the potential categories of recruitment of the other 'domestic marginal groups'. In this context it is not only the potential occupational competency of immigrants already living in the country that is being pointed to. In addition, segregating immigrants outside the categories of 'domestic' can be interpreted as excluding them from a fully authorised, (occupational) membership in the Finnish society.

We argue that these accounts draw on and rearticulate a discourse of 'clientelisation' that is common in Western societies. There immigrants are—many times unremarkedly—fixed in the position of the objects of care, that of 'recipients' of the services rather than that of possible 'givers' or active professional actors. Despite the fact that the growing meanings of multiculturality in health care settings are acknowledged, immigrant professionals and their know-how may be left invisible.

However, this discourse is not applied alike in regard to different occupational groups; rather they are placed in a hierarchy. While immigrant nurses are practically dealt with as a trivial question, immigrant physicians' position in the Finnish health care labour market is highlighted by paying attention to the facilitation and (re)organisation of their accreditation process (MSAH 2001, 71). This is done despite the fact that the labour shortage is expected to concern most severely the nurses. We interpret this change of discourse to reflect the fundamental power structures that are intertwined in the interoccupational relations, with the domination of the medical profession (see Hugman 1991, Julkunen 2004). It can also be linked to the issue of gender. Nurses represent clearly one of the most women-dominated occupations. While the medical profession is also women-dominated in many countries nowadays (Riska 2001), for physicians the prominent 'idea of a medical doctor' is still male (Löyttyniemi 2004). However, the gender relations are mediated by other socially constructed categories such as class, age, 'race' and ethnicity (Carling 2005). We suggest that the occupational group is one of these mediators: Being a woman means different things for an immigrant nurse than for an immigrant physician.

The Association of Finnish Local and Regional Authorities approaches the issue of the migrant labour force through a discourse in which immigrants' occupational and cultural capital and assets are acknowledged and the focus is primarily placed on other than labour-based skilled migrants:

> Among immigrants there are many of those who have acquired basic education and have graduated in various occupations. But so far immigrants' know-how has not been put to use sufficiently. The municipalities need teachers, nurses, home aids, social workers—thus well-educated personnel, who have personal experience or a background in different cultures. Auxiliary tasks traditionally assigned to immigrants can serve as a route to Finnish labour markets and learning the language, but moving and schooling for

more demanding tasks is important for the municipal labour force supply. (Kuntaliitto 2002, 15)

Also from the perspective of the Union of Health and Social Care Professionals, strengthening the position of those immigrant nurses who are already living in the country is the most vital. Evidently it is also in the interest of the trade union to protect its members' labour markets from a flow of international, possibly cheaper labour force. This union and the Association of Finnish Local and Regional Authorities share a similar kind of discourse by stressing the importance of qualifying vocational education, acknowledgement of the skill and competence obtained abroad and the overall development of foreign professional degree accreditation schemes. Immigrant nurses are constructed as 'experienced professionals', who offer language skills, cultural knowledge, work experience and further undefined 'positive skills' for the benefit of national health care (Kuntaliitto 2002, 15, Tehy 2005b). It is further reminded that 'Without specific measures immigrants' recruitment into vocational education and the labour market will not bring desirable results.' (Tehy 2005b).

Conclusion

The migration of health care professionals is attaining more significance than ever before, as many Western societies have turned to migration and migrants as solutions to demographic challenges and the shortage of labour in health care. In regulated sectors such as health care, various stakeholders in national and professional politics play significant roles in defining and reshaping the juridical, occupational and cultural borders and regulations for migrant health professionals' membership in the labour market of the receiving countries. A detailed analysis of (political) language may reveal discourses with their in-built categorisations that are many times unconscious but important to be made visible, as they can lead to discriminatory policies and misleading accounts of migration. Indeed, expectations related to different kinds of migrant groups may result in downplaying the roles of those who do not fit the stereotypical patterns (Carling 2005). The frameworks for the policies on the occupational groups in care work have significant but still under-acknowledged and examined implications for the migrant professionals and their position in the labour market (Hugman 1991).

This analysis of the political negotiations on immigrant nurses' occupational membership in the Finnish health care labour market illustrates how different discourses construct and define the position of varied kinds of migrant professionals through various categorisations and segmentations. There are divergent views among stakeholders, and so the position of immigrant nurses in the Finnish health care labour market is defined in conflicting ways. These perspectives draw different kinds of cultural and structural borders and conditions for immigrant nurses' occupational membership in the national health care labour market. It is important to reflect on the political debates and negotiations in terms of the broader historical, structural and socio-cultural contexts, which have obvious effects on the discussions. Yet we argue, firstly, that the terms and conditions for immigrant nurses' occupational membership are dependent on the international and national labour market situation. Secondly, we argue that these conditions are mediated through national immigration regimes and occupational rules and regulations. Finally, we argue that the conditions are shaped by discourses and categorisations related to hierarchical notions of (skilled) migrants, occupation and gender.

The exclusion of other than labour-based skilled migrants makes current frameworks inadequate in analysing migrant nurses from the perspective of an occupational group. This applies especially in a context where the nurses have immigrated to the country mainly through other routes than labour migration, like in the case of immigrant nurses in Finland. Skilled migrants tend to be framed only from the perspective of labour-driven migration both in policy making and in the field of research, leaving those immigrants, who move primarily for humanitarian or social reasons, deskilled. Thus a significant number of immigrant nurses are given a powerful shove towards deskilling their occupational competence. Different migrant categories are needed in administration and research (see Portes 1997), but we argue that the meanings and consequences of these categorisations must be reflected on and analysed, both within policy agendas and research. There is a need to question the relegation of other than labour-based skilled migrants to the subordinate circuits of labour-based migrants.

References to the data

Kuntaliitto (Association of Finnish Local and Regional Authorities) (2002) *Kuntien työvoima ja henkilöstö 2010.* (The Workforce and Personnel in Municipalities in 2010.) Helsinki: Kuntaliitto.

MOL (Ministry of Labour) (2003a) *Työpolitiikan strategia 2003–2007–2010.* (Labour Policy Strategy for 2003 to 2007 to 2010.) Helsinki: Työministeriö.

MOL (Ministry of Labour) (2003b) *Osaamisen ja täystyöllisyyden Suomi. Työvoima 2020. Loppuraportti.* (Finland of Competence and Full-employment. Workforce 2020. Final Report.) Helsinki: Työministeriö.

MSAH (Ministry of Social Affairs and Health) (2001) *Sosiaali- ja terveydenhuollon työvoimatarpeen ennakointitoimikunnan mietintö.* (The Report of the Commission of Anticipating the Need of Labour Force in Social and Health Care.) Komiteamietintö 2001:7. Helsinki: Sosiaali- ja terveysministeriö.

Tehy (The Union of Health and Social Care Professionals) (2005a) *Maahanmuuttajien vaikea saada hoitoalan työtä—Rasistiset kokemukset yleisiä.* http://www.tehy.fi/viestinta/tiedotteet/--print?x20983=10490 Retrieved June 2005.

Tehy (The Union of Health and Social Care Professionals) (2005b) *Hoitoala monikulttuuristuu—Maahanmuuttajien tukea ja työpaikkojen vetovoimaa parannettava.* http://www.tehy.fi/viestinta/tiedotteet/--print?x20983=10647 Retrieved December 2005.

References

Ahmad, A. (2002) Yhteisten työmarkkinoiden erottelemia? Maahanmuuttajien työllistymismahdollisuudet suomalaisilla työmarkkinoilla. *Sosiologia* 39(3), 227–241.

Bach, S. (2006) *Going Global? The Regulation of Nurse Migration to the UK.* Paper presented at the British Journal of Industrial Relations Workshop on the Political Economy of Immigration and Migrant Labour, Centre for Economic Performance, London School of Economics, 10–11 March 2006.

Buchan, J. & Calman, L. (2004) *The Global Shortage of Registered Nurses: An Overview of Issues and Actions.* Geneva: International Council of Nurses.

Buchan, J., Parkin, T. & Sochalski, J. (2003) *International Nurse Mobility: Trends and Policy Implications.* http://www.rcn.org.uk/downloads/ InternationalNurseMobility Retrieved August 2007.

Carling, J. (2005) Gender dimensions of international migration. *Global Migration Perspectives* May 2005(35). http://www.gcim.org/mm/File/ GMP%20No%2035.pdf Retrieved December 2006.

Davies, C. (1996) The Sociology of Professions and the Profession of Gender. *Sociology* 4(30), 661–678.

Davies, C. (Ed.) (2003) *The Future of Health Workforce.* London: Macmillan.

Forsander, A. (2002) *Luottamuksen ehdot. Maahanmuuttajat 1990-luvun suomalaisilla työmarkkinoilla.* Helsinki: Väestöntutkimuslaitos, Väestöliitto.

Henriksson, L. (1998) *Naisten terveystyö ja ammatillistumisen politiikka.* Tutkimuksia 88. Helsinki: Stakes.

Henriksson, L. & Wrede, S. (Eds) (2004) *Hyvinvointityön ammatit.* Helsinki: Gaudeamus.

Hugman, R. (1991) *Power in Caring Professions.* Basingstoke: Macmillan.

Huttunen, L., Löytty, O. & Rastas, A. (2005) Suomalainen monikulttuurisuus. In A. Rastas, L. Huttunen & O. Löytty (Eds) *Suomalainen vieraskirja. Kuinka käsitellä monikulttuurisuutta* (pp. 16–40). Tampere: Vastapaino.

Iredale, R. (2001) The Migration of Professionals: Theories and Typologies. *International Migration* 39(5), 7–26.

Iredale, R. (2005) Gender, Immigration Policies and Accreditation: Valuing the Skills of Professional Women Migrants. *Geoforum* 36(2), 155–166.

Jokinen, A., Juhila, K. & Suoninen, E. (1993) *Diskurssianalyysin aakkoset.* Tampere: Vastapaino.

Julkunen, R. (2004) Hyvinvointipalvelujen uusi politiikka. In L. Henriksson & S. Wrede (Eds) *Hyvinvointityön ammatit* (pp. 168–186). Helsinki: Gaudeamus.

Järvinen, A. (2004) Virossa pulaa sairaanhoitajista. *Tehy* 23(9), 32–33.

Kofman, E. (2004) Gendered Global Migrations. Diversity and Stratification. *International Feminist Journal of Politics* 6(4), 643–665.

Kyhä, H. (2006) Miksi lääkäri ei kelpaa lääkäriksi? Korkeakoulutetut maahanmuuttajat Suomen työmarkkinoilla. *Aikuiskasvatus* 26(2), 122–129.

Löyttyniemi, V. (2004) *Auscultatio Medici: Kerrottu identiteetti, neuvoteltu sukupuoli.* Tampere: Tampere University Press.

MOL (2006) *Työministeriö.* http://www.mol.fi/mol/fi/06_tyoministerio/index.jsp Retrieved June 2006.

MSAH (2006). *Tietoa ministeriöstä.* http://www.stm.fi/Resource.phx/orgns/index.htxinternetpages Retrieved July 2006.

Paananen, S. (1999). *Suomalaisuuden armoilla: Ulkomaalaisten työnhakijoiden luokittelu.* Helsinki: Tilastokeskus.

Piippola, S. (2003). *Gränsvandrare Positioner sig på Arbetsmarknaden.* Institutionen för Arbetsvetenskap 2003:22. Luleå: Luleå Tekniska Universitet.

Portes, A. (1997) Immigration Theory for a New Century: Some Problems and Opportunities. *International Migration Review* 31(4), 799–825.

Potter, J. & Wetherell, M. (2001) Unfolding Discourse Analysis. In M. Wetherell, S. Taylor & S.J. Yates: *Discourse Theory and Practice. A Reader* (pp. 198–209). London: Sage.

Raghuram, P. (2004) The Difference That Skills Make: Gender, Family Migration Strategies and Regulated Labour Markets. *Journal of Ethnic and Migration Studies* 30(2), 303–321.

Riska, E. (2001) *Medical Careers and Feminist Agendas.* New York: Aldine de Gruyter.

Ronkainen, S. (2004) Kvantitatiivisuus, tulkinnallisuus ja feministinen tutkimus. In M. Liljeström (Ed.) *Feministinen tietäminen* (pp. 44–69). Tampere: Vastapaino.

Santamäki, K. (2004). Sairaanhoitajatyöttömyys ja ammattikunnan lohkoutuminen. In L. Henriksson & S. Wrede (Eds) *Hyvinvointityön ammatit* (pp. 144–167). Helsinki: Gaudeamus.

TEO (The National Authority for Medicolegal Affairs) (2005) *Annual Report 2005.* http://www.teo.fi/uusi/engl_1.htm Retrieved December 2006.

Wetherell, M. & Potter, J. (1992) *Mapping the Language of Racism. Discourse and the Legitimation of Exploitation.* Cornwall: Harvester Wheatsheaf.

Wickett, D. & McCutcheon, H. (2002) Issues of qualification assessment for nurses in a global market. *Nurse Education Today* 22(1), 44–52.

Yeates, N. (2004) A dialogue with 'global care chain' analysis: Nurse migration in the Irish context. *Feminist Review* 77(1), 79–95.

NORWAY

INTRODUCTION TO PART III

Care Work and Care Work
Education in Norway:
Problems of Modernisation

Håkon Høst

Report 25 (2005–2006) to the Norwegian Storting depicts a dramatic increase in the need for nursing and caretaking staff in forthcoming decades. Despite the uncertainties relating to life expectancy, health, the need for care and nursing among the elderly and the extent to which this will be met by public services, this prognosis is in no way controversial. In an international comparison, Norway and the other Nordic countries represent solutions based on the state assuming the major responsibility for meeting families' obligations for nursing the sick and the elderly. The growth in the number of old people will, with a great deal of certainty, lead to a dramatic increase in the demand for employees in the care and nursing sector. The questions of the division of work, who to recruit, and what educational background these personnel should have, however, are also strategic considerations in planning the further developement of this sector. There are several possible directions in which to go.

Based on what we might call the national qualification structure, the most common is to divide the employees in the public nursing sector into three main cathegories, based on level of education: personnel lacking formal qualifications (home helpers and nursing assistants), skilled (upper secondary level) and professionals (higher education). What we here will call skilled staff (auxilliary nurses and careworkers) have up until now constituted the by far the largest group, followed by the home helpers and nursing assistants, while the higher educated/college trained group has been the smallest. In Report 25 to the Storting there are, however, clear signals of a desire for a dramatic change in this picture, by increasing the proportion of personnel with higher education. In this report, the prognosis is that over time this group will constitute the largest group of employees. The report offers two arguments for this change of direction. The first argument is that the number of students applying for courses in social and health care at the higher level is so significant, that recruitment of employees with higher education is mostly a question of public regulation of the educational capacity—while the recruitment of employees with upper secondary education is limited by low demand. The second argument is that an increased number of personnel with higher education in itself will contribute to a quality improvement within the nursing and caring services.

Such a policy can be said to represent the position that it is possible to assure the quality of the care and nursing sector by recruiting personnel from higher education. From this perspective, recruitment of unskilled staff is seen as a threat to the overall quality of service. This way of thinking is based both on the faith in certain types of competences, and a certain type of educational planning. By increasing the educational capacity it is possible to increase both the quality and the recruitment of personnel at the same time.

As a counter argument, it is possible to adopt another position, that the educational policy does not exert a direct influence on the care and nursing sector, but rather through other mediating conditions such as the labour market and employees' interest organisations (Sakslind 1985). As will be shown in this section, in the care and nursing sector, efforts to modernise recruitment patterns through educational reforms have failed so far. Instead patterns based on recruiting unskilled careworkers and offering them training and education have shown to be crucial. In this way it is possible to achieve both quantitative and qualitative aims. From this position it is possible to argue that a strategy for recruiting personnel from the higher education sector is also likely to fail. It would probably offer less stability. At the same time a larger share of higher educated personnel will tend to strengthen the hierarchy, which in turn will threaten the learning environment and the existing recruitment model, which is based on vertical mobility. This could undermine the potential and resources of individualised care orientations based on what is known as a rationality of caring (Wærness 1984), as practised within home-based care services.

The Norwegian contributions

The two Norwegian contributions both address the process of modernisation of care work and care work education. They also both take as their starting point the situation before care and nursing mainly became a public responsibility. During this early period, voluntary organisations took care of those sick and elderly people who were neither able to pay nor had families to care for them. In the two contributions, this voluntary care and nursing work is described as developing into a Norwegian female culture with important implications. One such implication was that this female dominated voluntary work was an important factor behind the development of state-supported care work. Another implication was that the evolving public care and nursing services recruited their main work forces from this female culture of care. The recruitment patterns soon revealed that adult women were dominating also the paid care work. Due to the connection between formal and informal care, what may be called the first stage of organised modernity, represented a rather smooth transition from privately to publicly organised care and nursing work. Thus, many characteristic features of informal care went into paid care work, preserving the existing position of subordination of the care worker. The role of the housewife was replaced by the role of the publicly funded home carer. Nevertheless, the change gave these women greater independence and provided new opportunities to develop their own interests and their practical skills. However, a dichotomy was established early on between these care workers with a background as housewives and those qualified through formal educational qualifications, as represented by nurses. In home care it was regarded as appropriate and sufficient for care workers to have a background as a housewife. But care and nursing work connected to hospitals and nursing homes was more influenced by the professions and the weight they placed on formal education. Education for auxiliary nurses provided a midway position. This was established in 1963 and came to represent an

attractive opportunity to many women, in particular to nursing assistants working in the care and nursing sector. Through
this education they obtained status as authorised auxiliary
nurses and this opened up the possibility of a position in hospitals, nursing homes and home nursing.

Within care work as well as in care work education, there
has been a continuous and huge expansion in the number of
employees and students, which probably puts Norway in a
rather privileged position compared with other Nordic countries. A perspective of modernisation, implying a look at all
parts and parties in these changes, however, reveals several
problematic issues concerning the way the work is organised
and how the education in this field has been constructed.

Perhaps the rather late modernisation of this field is one of
the reasons for importing solutions from other fields rather
than developing a more sector specific modernisation. Instead
of building upon the resources of experienced home helpers
and the rationality of care (a rationality combining work and
empathy), which many studies have pointed at, home care is
being organised according to private market thinking, including the purchaser and provider model. And instead of taking
the traditional recruitment patterns as a basis, education for
care and nursing has been integrated into the adolescent educational system and directed towards 16–19 year olds.

In Chapter 9, *Karen Christensen* points at the unused potential and resources of individualised care orientations based on
the rationality of care and practised within the home based
care services. By conceptualising these resources as 'social capital' with the potential to strengthen community and democracy, she is able to trace the roots of the care work crises in
political solutions that so far mainly have been inspired by
ideas from outside this field. In parallel to Christensen, *Håkon
Høst* in Chapter 8 comes to the same conclusion, but from the
angle of care education. After having first been modernised
in a rather rigid way where the women were given little individual flexibility, the education is now reorganised according
to a more liberal modernity where collective arrangements

and the set courses in the education are being removed. His conclusion is that the educational policy has resulted in a continuous educational crisis in this field. He further argues, in the same vein as Christensen, that important forces within the care field are ignored in favour of ideas from other fields through which efficiency is sought through bureaucratic means.

To provide the field with adequately skilled labour in sufficient numbers is, by no doubt, an important issue. So far, however, neither the crisis of care work nor the crisis of auxiliary nurse education have been recognised by the politicians as crucial problems. The analyses presented by the two chapters in this section show, however, that these crises cannot be addressed merely by allocating more financial or staff resources, and thereby ignoring perspectives from the field of care and nursing itself.

References

Sakslind, R. (1985) *Arbeid og utdanning: Omriss av et forskningsfelt.* Sosiologisk Institutt. Universitetet i Bergen.

St.meld. nr. 25. (2005–2006). *Mestring, muligheter og mening. Framtidas omsorgsutfordringer.* Oslo: Helse- og omsorgsdepartementet.

Waerness, K. (1984) The Rationality of Caring. In Söder (Ed.): *Economic and Industrial Democracy.* London: Sage Publications.

EIGHT

Reforming Auxiliary Nurse
Education in Norway—A Story
of Failed Modernisation

Håkon Høst

The Norwegian system for auxiliary nurse education was established in 1963 as a child of what is often called organised modernity. It soon became a popular area, attracting women of all ages, and auxiliary nursing became one of the largest occupational groups within the Norwegian welfare state. Through extensive reforms, the education of auxiliary nurses has been gradually integrated into a national upper secondary educational system and directed towards adolescents. The aim has been to develop a more efficient and modern educational system, and at the same time to expand auxiliary nurse recruitment by basing it on the recruitment of adolescents rather than adults. However, younger people do not seem to regard auxiliary nursing as an attractive educational choice, and it is perceived as being low status education. Today, when demand for auxiliary nurses in the care and nursing services is stronger than ever, only marginal numbers of adolescents are recruited through upper secondary school. Instead recruitment continues to be based mainly on the traditional recruitment basis, that is, adult women working as unskilled nurse assistants.

Based on broad empirical work[1], this chapter will discuss this development and the efforts to modernise auxiliary nurse education. It will also make a limited cross-national comparison with the parallel education of SOSU-assistants in Denmark[2].

Theoretical framework

I have chosen to use Peter Wagner's (1994) historically informed analysis of modernity and modernisation as a broad framework for analysing the development in auxiliary nurse education. Wagner defines the core of modernity as human beings striving to control their lives and surroundings, and as a project of liberalisation from traditional ties. According to Wagner, modernity contains a dichotomy which can also be seen as ambivalence between a development towards greater individual autonomy on one hand, and more effective societal control on the other. All modern activity involves striving both for autonomy and mastery, and all modern institutions are characterised by the tension between liberty and discipline.

In the vocational education system, the range of reforms could be seen as the authorities aiming at mastery and efficiency through rationalisation. At the same time, the educational reforms might also be regarded as a modernisation at the individual level if they contribute to increased autonomy. Even though both values characterise modern society and modern institutions as educational arrangements, the interpretations and the weight applied to liberty and mastery will vary through time and space between the institutions and actors. This provides the starting point for my efforts to analyse and understand the establishment and the development of auxiliary nurse education and the occupation. To what extent do the educational reforms contribute to modernisation in the sense of more efficient systems on the one hand, and more options for individual life projects on the other?

There are four distinctive reforms that may be regarded as efforts to modernise auxiliary nursing. Reform 63 introduced auxiliary nurse education; Reform 74 established a common upper secondary education; Reform 94 expanded upper secondary education to include adolescent vocational education; and Reform 2000 introduced systems for evaluating informal education and individual paths to upper secondary education. Each of these reforms can be related to the different historical stages in the development of modernity (as Wagner describes it), characterised by a shifting relationship between mastery and autonomy. These stages in history were:

1 A period of restricted liberal modernity during the 19th century when freedom of the individual predominated, but was limited to societal elites.
2 A period of organised modernity characterised by development of mass institutions and a strong public government from late 19th century until the mid 1960s.

3 A contemporary period of extended liberal modernity in which individual autonomy is given priority, social collectives are weakened and the space for political action is strongly limited.

Care and nursing during restricted, liberal modernity

Having no ambition to recount the history of care work, as a background I will roughly sketch out what the situation was before the introduction of auxiliary nurse education. The increased range of options provided by medical treatment contributed to the development of hospitals during the second half of the 19th century. Also established during this period were homes for the elderly, asylums for psychiatric patients and institutions for persons suffering from mental retardation. To a large extent these institutions employed unskilled persons. Except for the heavy work in psychiatric hospitals and asylums for mentally retarded people that was seen mainly as men's work, the care and nursing work was dominated by women. However, despite the growth of these institutions, most of the care work continued to be carried out in the private sphere and within families, predominantly by women.

The first nurse education programmes were established at the end of the 19th century, directed towards unmarried daughters from the bourgeois class (Martinsen 1989, Melby 1990). The nurses' primary mission was to establish hegemony in care and nursing work in the hospitals by replacing unskilled labour from the 'lower classes'. In addition to this, nurses worked privately for people that could afford to pay.

Even if the number of authorised nurses (1.) expanded rapidly during the first half of the 20th century, this expansion fell short of covering the demand for care and nursing. The majority of employed as nurses did not have an authorised nursing qualification. The situation was also characterised by a mixture of private and public arrangements, as well as paid and unpaid care and nursing work directed at both patients that could afford to pay and those who had be supported by poor relief funds.

Taken together the situation was characterised by many of the features of the restricted, liberal modernity, as described by Wagner. Modernisation during this period was something which to a large extent was still to be found at the discursive level. Modern institutions covered only a small part of the population, and there was a strong bias towards the idea of individual freedom on behalf of the public government. The tradition of enlightenment had presupposed self-regulating individuals who did not need to be governed through state authority. However, an increasing number of people acknowledged that this would not lead to any modernisation for the majority of the population. Such modernity would need to be achieved through social activity. A mobilisation from below took place, both through political demands for better health care, and through a process where women took part in voluntary organisations taking care of those sick and elderly who could neither pay nor had families to care them. Organising voluntary care and nursing work was to become a central part of the Norwegian female culture. At its peak, more than three out of every four women in Norway were members of a voluntary organisation in which care work was the central activity (Bjarnar 1995).

Through the world wars, economic crises and mass unemployment, the idea that the freedom of the individual could not be assured through the efforts of the individual, but required collective action, had grown strong. This had created the basis for political changes that made possible the organised modernity and the welfare societies that characterised Western Europe in the post-war period.

Auxiliary nurse education: a child of organised modernity

The building of a country-wide health care system that could serve the whole population was one of the modernisation projects in the post -war welfare state construction in Norway. It became clear that access to publicly authorised nurses could not cover the demand for care and nursing services. From a governmental point of view, education of many lower-level care and nursing personnel was necessary to assure services of an adequate quality. When the head of the Directorate of Health, Karl Evang, proposed the establishing of auxiliary nurse education, this could also be seen as an expression of another important modernisation project at the time: the expansion of the educational system to include the whole population, and the development of vocational education to include all parts of society.

Auxiliary nurse education can be characterised as a child of organised modernity. It was directed not only towards the many unskilled nursing assistants, but also towards adult women and young girls who wanted to enter the work force. At that time auxiliary nurses required a rather short period of training to qualify to execute nursing tasks under the supervision of authorised nurses. These tasks were previously undertaken by unskilled workers. The subordinate role of auxiliary nurses to fully qualified nurses was clearly stated from the beginning. The range of tasks auxiliary nurses were to be trained for was also stated exactly. This had been sanctioned by the nurses who were also among whom the teachers in the auxiliary nurse education programmes were recruited.

The launching of the education had all signs of modernisation from above (Wagner 1994), meant to secure a work force with the particular set of skills required in health care. On the other hand, this project also met the strong demand from many women. As such, it also became a project from below, consisting of women who wanted paid work but also formal education and an occupation. Auxiliary nurse education soon became very popular, and the number of applicants was huge. Criteria such as age and work experience from care and nursing, combined with characteristics of the applicants, contributed to a pattern where the typical auxiliary nurse was to be an adult woman with long practical experience from paid and unpaid care and nursing work. Nurse education was still exclusive, something which made the auxiliary nurse education programmes popular particularly among women from the lower middle and working classes. Statistics from the Directorate for Health affairs show that more than 15 per cent of the age cohorts born in the mid 1950s have been educated as auxiliary nurses.

Auxiliary nurse education was seen as a contribution to modernisation, both by facilitating a higher quality of health care, and by expanding the options for greater autonomy for a lot of women. It became a catalyst for modernisation of vocational education because it made a decisive contribution to the construction of a new employee category, located between the nurses and the unskilled. That this new occupational category organised its own organisation, and through this established a boundary between it and the union of (unskilled) municipal workers, illustrates that auxiliary nurse education laid the basis for something qualitatively new.

REFORM 74: MODERNISATION OF EDUCATION AS A SYSTEM

The way the auxiliary nurse education was established, as a separate arrangement connected to and formed by a certain field of work, was typical for this period. In the same way as other vocational education programmes at the time, it was organised and administered by the sector authorities, not a common educational authority. From the second half of the 1960s, however, the modernisation of education as a system was to become the dominating project. By establishing a statutory education period of nine years, a new level in the development of the so-called unity school (*enhetsskolen*) was reached. Now a restructuring of the 'mess of educational arrangements' in the vocational field at the upper secondary level seemed to be required by modernisation logic (Telhaug 1979). The 1974 reform represented a first step in the project to integrate and rationalise all the forms of education, both vocational and general, in order to construct the new upper secondary education system under the Ministry of Education.

For several reasons the reform became critical in the development of auxiliary nurse education. Auxiliary nurse education was to find its place in relation to other vocational education and to general education, and the rationalisation and restructuring of these. In addition to this it was to be related vertically to nurse education, and horizontally to what was seen as types of education close to it, in particular home economics education.

Equal access to education independent of social and geographical background, and to an increasing extent independent also of gender were the core arguments for replacing the old divided systems of general and vocational education with a new, integrated and common upper secondary school system. While politicians from the labour movement previously had stated that social equality in the educational question should be achieved through equalising vocational and general education, this position had been left during the 1960s. Integration between the two was now seen as the key. From 1976, a new common upper secondary school system was established, to a large degree on the basis of the general education model.

The Labour government had proposed, however, a vertically integrated education system for providing training for the health sector, but this proposal did not obtain a majority in the parliament. Together with other professional groups, the nurses' union succeeded in winning support for the principle that general education was to be the main admission criterion for this education. Thus this became the new line of demarcation between lower and higher nurse education. Even though further education was not a major objective of most of the women aiming for auxiliary nurse education, the way the upper secondary and tertiary level in the educational system were constructed limited their future options.

For auxiliary nurse education, integration into the common upper secondary school system did not initially mean any change in curriculum or teachers. Even the admissions criteria, based on age and work experience, were retained.

According to data from Statistics Norway on upper secondary education for the period 1980–1989, auxiliary nurse education during these years was one of the fields of education with the most applicants and also with the most stringent selection criteria. As before, most of the students were adults with long work experience in care and nursing. Parallel to the new system, adult courses outside the upper secondary schools were retained. The pattern of recruiting adult women hence was strengthened rather than weakened.

In spite of the processes of rationalisation and coordination to create a common upper secondary school system, at this stage the integrational and unifying measures were not extensive. The traditional fields of education to a large degree kept their original substance. In addition to this, the 1976-proposal reduced the range of general subjects in all upper secondary education compared with the original plans (Lindbekk1992). All though this period is often characterised as the age of standardisation (Slagstad 1998), pluralism can still be said to be the predominant feature of the Norwegian system of upper secondary education.

At this stage one might conclude that the system building in education also contributed to a strengthening of traditional auxiliary nurse education and its characteristics. Seen from a perspective of modernisation, it represents a balance between the authorities' need for control through rationalisation and the maintenance of autonomy for auxiliary nurse education. At the individual level, auxiliary nurse education was still seen as contributing to the empowerment of women.

The second stage of organised modernity

The process of rationalising the various fields of vocational education was given much more strength in the second stage of organised modernity. Upper secondary education experienced a strong increase in the number of applicants and students. While 60 per cent of an age cohort entered upper secondary education in 1976, this had increased to 84 per cent in 1984.

On top of this there was a flow of older applicants, both due to the difficulties they experienced in the labour market and because they saw the new upper secondary school as being attractive. One could also observe a new pattern where a significant number of the students who had finished general education returned to upper secondary for vocational education. This resulted in stronger competition for school places in vocational education, and for places in auxiliary nurse education in particular. The diagnosis of the Blegen Committee (NOU 1991:4) was that these mobility patterns were not rational, and that the structure needed to be changed. The solution the authorities chose was to try to construct standard educational profiles in vocational education in the same way as in general education. Thus, vocational education was to be undertaken by the 16–19 age groups. In order to make a slimmer and more efficient system, applicants who had finished general education or other forms of upper secondary education were to be rejected when applying for a place in a vocational programme such as auxiliary nursing.

During the 1980s, auxiliary nurse education experienced a dramatic change in the educational discourse. From being a well reputed field of education serving modernisation, it was now characterised as one of the most problematic and least modern fields (*Lyftingsmo-utvalget* 1988). The recruitment pattern dominated by adult women working part time was seen as a threat to gender equality. Auxiliary nurse education should instead be based on the recruitment of younger people, both male and female, aiming at full time work and lifelong careers in the vocations. It was thought that by moving this training into the apprenticeship system it would probably improve its status.

Through Reform 94 these discourses materialised through the construction of a new and more integrated upper secondary education system, seen by many as the final integration of general and vocational education (Olsen 1996). All persons in the 16–19 age groups were given a statutory right to upper secondary education. However, someone had to pay the price for the generosity towards younger people, and this had to be the adults. In 1994 there were as many as 9000 adult applicants for the social and health field of studies of whom more than 6000 were rejected. From a perspective of mastery, however, the reform was seen as a success. Younger people were guaranteed a school place, something that contributed to the reduction of unemployment among this group. Efficiency, measured by the extent to which the students complete their upper secondary education, was increasing (Støren, et al. 1998). In the first year of the reform, programmes in both auxiliary nursing and for new care worker education experienced a huge increase in the number of younger applicants. However, as many as 40 per cent of them used a new supplementary option introduced by the reform and re-entered general education (Grøgaard et al. 2002), thereby gaining the opportunity to enter higher education. Only after one year, the demand for both auxiliary nursing and care worker education was severely reduced. The previously popular education in auxiliary nursing was now constructed as low status upper secondary education, a place for those unable to compete for places in more popular courses or those unsure about what they want. New care worker education suffered the same fate. Younger people did not see these programmes as a liberating educational choice leading to strengthened personal autonomy. These fields of education did not fit into their life plans. The reform made visible a structural inferiority that had not manifested itself previously because of other attractive features of auxiliary nurse education. On top of this, young girls did not want to work in care of the elderly, which had by now become the predominant field of work for auxiliary nurses and care workers.

Auxiliary nurse education has never been very popular among younger people. Directing the education towards this group only, changes the clientele completely according to grades required. Comparing the number of applicants and the number admitted for the auxiliary nurse education programme among 17 and 18 years-olds in 1988 and 2000 is indeed illuminating. In both 1988 and 2000, the number of applicants in this group was around 920. In 1988, only about 100 of these were admitted. The rest were rejected because of competition with the adults who filled up most of the available school places. In 2000, all of the 920 adolescent applicants for the auxiliary nurse education programme were admitted, because there were no adults to compete with (Høst 2006).

The disciplinary aspects of Reform 94 were strong. The age flexibility in the educational system was removed. However, the reform turned out to be catastrophic for the recruitment and as an attempt to modernise the field it must be regarded as a failure.

According to Wagner's' division of modernity into stages, Reform 94 took place almost 30 years after organised modernity experienced its crises, in which confidence in public planning, mastery and bureaucracy suffered a set back, in the same way as the confidence in economic progress and stability, and the potentials of knowledge. However, Norwegian educational policy during this period does not fit very well within this description. It still carried strong features of organised modernity during this period. Standardisation is meant to increase efficiency both to the society and the individual. However, the strong efforts to construct profiles where people are presumed to undertake education at both the upper secondary and the tertiary levels during a short period of their life, contradicts the way people live their lives. The patterns of recruitment to auxiliary nurse education are a clear example of this.

Adult reform between organised and liberal modernity

In many respects, Reform 2000 could be regarded as an answer to the criticism against the way Reform 94 rejected adults. The core element of the reform at the upper secondary level was a redistribution of educational resources in the way that adults without an upper secondary education were given the right to education, at the same time as rejecting those applying for a second programme at this level. The reform also introduced assessment of informal competence, which was to be treated equally with formal competence. In addition to this, shorter and flexible courses were to replace all standardised educational programmes for adults.

The reform was directed at all sectors of work life. It was, however, more or less transformed into a female reform, and to a large degree to an auxiliary nurse education reform. Quite unintended, the reform seems to have contributed to a reopening of a reservoir of women who wanted auxiliary nurse education. Thousands of adult women, many of them from outside the target group, applied for entry under the new programme. The reform seems to have found a persistent pattern of recruitment that has served as a recruitment basis for the auxiliary nurse education programme since the beginning in 1963. In spite of the many regulations put in place to restrict the use of the programme to those without an upper secondary education from before, my survey shows this part of the reform has not been very efficient. Amongst those completing auxiliary nurse education in 2002, 50 per cent had already been enrolled in another programme at this educational level, either vocational or general (Høst 2004). While the intention behind the reform was to satisfy the demand for upper secondary education among adults who had 'missed the boat', the applications show that the demand among adults for auxiliary nurse education does not necessarily disappear when the educational level rises. Instead this demand seems to be a lasting phenomenon. Even if this contradicts the dominating thinking in educational planning, it is good for the care and nursing sector, where the adults are a highly valued resource. This might also explain why adults in many places are admitted to the new programmes, even though they do not satisfy the entrance criteria because they already have an upper secondary education. A tentative conclusion is that Reform 2000 paradoxically contributed to a revitalisation of the recruitment patterns the educational authorities wanted to get rid of.

However, not everything is the way it used to be. Some students are given the right to free public education, while others have to pay for it, and still others have their education paid for by their employers. Standardised education has been replaced by short, individually flexible courses, based on competency tests. The recognition of informal competence also includes new options for entrance to higher education. This means that for the first time, individual mobility from auxiliary nurse to nurse education is possible without completing general education at the upper secondary level. This option is exploited by a significant number of auxiliary nurses. Taken as a group, however, auxiliary nursing seems to have been weakened by the reform. Auxiliary nurses are left with an adolescent education in which very few are interested. The education for adults is fragmented and individualised. In this situation, the auxiliary nurses' union chose to disband and merge with the municipal workers' union.

The development can be characterised by using Wagner's description of the new, extended, liberal modernity as a period characterised by more weight on individual freedom, but where social collectives are being eroded.

Even if the educational authorities still have not succeeded in making auxiliary nurse education into young people's education 13 years after the Reform 94, the focus on the young continues to be predominant in the discourse and policy of modernisation in the field. This is illustrated when a new forms of auxiliary nurse education is being discussed; inclusion of the adults is not even a theme. This may be contrasted with the situation in which the average age of those being educated as auxiliary nurses is 33 years, and adults represent 80 per cent of the recruitment (Høst 2004).

A cross-national comparison

On what terms is it possible to compare the auxiliary nurse education in Norway with similar categories in other countries? It is common to differentiate between a strong, variable oriented and systematic comparison (such as Mill's Method of Agreement and Method of Difference), with a more heuristic comparison where the aim is to contrast the studied case with another in order to understand the studied case better (Ågotnes 1989).

The problems and pitfalls connected to a strong, variable oriented approach are many if you try to compare education in different countries. It presupposes that it is possible to break up the whole and isolate those structural variables one finds similar or different in the countries compared. However, the educational system in a country and single programmes as well, are embedded in particular national patterns in relation to the labour marked and other social structures in a way that makes it difficult to select and isolate single elements in order to make systematic comparisons. It is necessary to make so many simplifications that the result can easily become superficial and uninteresting.

A comparison as a contrasting view would seem to be preferable in this context. This comparison will not aim to explain completely differences and similarities, but will aim to shed light on the development of Norwegian auxiliary nurse education.

As a basis for comparison I have chosen Danish social- and health assistant education. This is a field of education and employment category that is similar to the auxiliary nurses in the level of education, the area of work and the position in the division of work.

Denmark: modernisation and autonomy

Even if there are differences between the Norwegian and the Danish welfare states, the many similarities make it common in social science analyses to speak of a Nordic welfare state model. One feature that both countries share is the service-intensive state (Kjølsrød 2003). As in Norway, in Denmark an extensive public care and nursing sector has been developed in the post war period. The establishment of the first programme in auxiliary nursing in Denmark in 1960, called *sygehjælperuddanelsen*, had many similarities with what happened in Norway three years later. It was the health authorities that initiated the new programme. Admission criteria were based on age (above 18), ability, and work experience (preferred). A pattern where adult students dominated was soon established.

In contrast with the situation in Norway and the other Nordic countries, the so-called unity school (*enhetsskole*) principle had problems gaining strong support in Denmark, and the Danish upper secondary level is divided into separate systems of vocational education and general education. To explain this situation, some have pointed to the strong position of the senior secondary teachers on the one hand and the strong traditions of the apprenticeship system on the other (Lindbekk 1992). A lot of effort has been put into trying to modernise the system and also into bringing the two parts of the system closer together. A common school-based basic education has been introduced for the vocational system. Since the late 1970s, there have been several initiatives to integrate auxiliary nurse and other social and health programmes into the common system of vocational education. These efforts have been rejected by the employer side in particular. A core argument has been that these forms of education have a strong background in recruiting mature women, and it would be difficult to preserve this recruitment if these programmes were to be integrated in the common system. In 1991, an autonomous educational system for social and health education, called the SOSU-programmes, was established through a compromise between the educational authorities, the municipal employer organisations, and the employee organisations. This is a vertically integrated system, and the SOSU-assistant can be compared to auxiliary nurse education in Norway. The education is closely linked to the workplace as the municipalities play a central role in the recruitment of the students.

The 1991 Reform, which established a broad education programme based on five old ones, also seems to have succeeded in its ambition to increase the competence level in the old programmes. The SOSU-assistants now have a competence level that is higher than the old occupations, for instance the nurse assistant (sygehjælper). Further vertical mobility is possible through the SOSU-assistants' right to enter nurse education and finish it in a shorter time than students without this background.

The educational authorities have been negotiating with the nurses' organisation to get this accepted through changes in both the educational system and also in the workplace. As a result of their support of the new programme, the nurses gained increased educational capacity and nurse education was made more academic.

A so-called entrance year constructed to recruit young people that had finished lower secondary education has not been a success. The other parts of the SOSU-system, however, have been experiencing an increase in the number of applicants over the past few years.

In 2001 a survey of the students in the SOSU-education (*Danmarks Evalueringsinstitutt*) was carried out. The profile they drew of the recruited students can be summed up in a few points:

- 93 percent were women
- Students' average age has been rising and are at the moment the average is around 35 years
- Most of the students have considerable work experience
- Two out of three have care and nursing work experience from before they entered the programme, but less than half of these have come directly to the education from such a job
- Almost half of the students have been enrolled previously in another vocational education programme
- Many of the students are married with children

Conclusion

To what extent can the efforts to modernise auxiliary nurse education be said to have been a success? There are different ways in which the question could be analysed and answered, but here I will try to stick to a discussion based on a perspective of modernisation, and in particular aspects of control and autonomy.

The auxiliary nurse education has been modernised in the sense that it has been integrated into the overall educational system at the upper secondary level. During the 1970s and 1980s this process of integration was perceived by most actors as necessary and as a way to strengthen the education. Through Reform 94, people aged 16–19 years were given a statutory right to undertake an upper secondary education, including auxiliary nurse education. At the same time adults were no longer to be admitted into the ordinary auxiliary nurse education. Instead they were offered competence assessments and shorter courses outside the upper secondary school sector. This was seen as a contribution to a slimmer, more efficient and modern educational system, and also to a more modern form of auxiliary nurse education. From the perspective of control these changes may appear as part of a successful modernisation. This is also how the educational authorities evaluate it. From the perspective of individual autonomy, however, it looks quite different. To young people, auxiliary nurse education hardly appears as modern. It is not seen as empowering the individual, nor does it fit into their intended life plans. The efforts through the educational system to construct profiles where auxiliary nurse education is completed before the age of 20 have not succeeded. The result has been a drastic reduction in the number of students, and auxiliary nurse education has experienced a decrease in status.

The system for the evaluation of informal competence among adults may be seen as modern in the way that it is efficient and individually flexible. It gives individual, experienced auxiliary nurses the option of entering either nurse education, or higher education in general. This must be regarded as modern in the way that it strengthens individuals' autonomy and social mobility. To the occupational group as a collective, however, this reform does not contribute to an enhancement. Rather the opposite is the case. The majority of applicants for auxiliary nurse education are still adults. However, they are no longer offered a standardised education programme, only short courses through temporary educational arrangements. This must be seen as a backward step. In this way the modernisation of education as a system has contributed to disconnecting auxiliary nurse education from its established recruitment base.

From the perspective of the care and nursing sector, it is neither efficient nor modern that an education programme that recruits woman of all ages has been replaced by a system directed towards young people who only represent only a marginal part of the new auxiliary nurses.

In the educational discourse, women applying for auxiliary nurse education programmes are constructed as backward and traditional. That is, they are seen as not being modern, not aiming at gender equality and not choosing a career on the basis of their own free will. This contributes to a degradation of status for the whole group. In this situation the occupation's position and options for articulating their own interests have been changed, most probably weakened, by the closing down of the auxiliary nurse union as an autonomous organisation.

The comparison with Denmark reminds us of the fact that educational arrangements are not natural but are socially constructed. It is possible to modernise a field of education without destroying traditional recruitment patterns. Contrasting the Danish age-flexible system makes the rigidity and disciplinary aspects of the Norwegian system of upper secondary education very visible. The Danish arrangement is characterised by a higher degree of autonomy for both the field and for the individuals than is the case in the Norway. The Danish arrangement has also kept close links with the work places. In this way it may be seen as more modern, which in turn gives it a higher status than in the Norwegian case.

It is an interesting finding that completely different strategies of modernisation have led to very similar results concerning actual recruitment. In both countries recruitment is dominated by women with an average age in the mid 30s. This outcome can hardly be seen as natural. Rather, it points to inherited and culturally mediated patterns of gendered life courses and choices that are deeply embedded in both countries. They can not be characterised as being very modern. At the moment, it is exactly these patterns that seem to be of critical importance in order to recruit sufficient numbers for education and the care and nursing workforce, which again is necessary to meet the growth in the number of the elderly in both Norway and Denmark.

The comparison with Denmark also demonstrates that it is possible for the state to create vertically integrated systems in education, and to strengthen subordinate groups in the jurisdictional conflicts with fully-qualified nurses. While there still is a strong demand for SOSU-assistants in Danish hospitals, the Norwegian auxiliary nurses have experienced a marginalisation in this field of work. However, the recruitment of younger people continues to be weak in Denmark as well. As in Norway, young Danes know that this form of education will probably lead to a job in care of the elderly. This demographic development makes this the field where the demand for labour is strongest.

Notes

1 The analyses of the Norwegian case are based on studies carried out over a period of more than 10 years. The chapter is also to a large extent based on the trial lecture connected with the public defence of my doctoral dissertation. A large number of previous studies on the topic include, for example, Gran et al. (1994), Høst (1997), Michelsen, Høst og
2 Gitlesen (1998), Høst (2001), Høst (2002), Høst (2004), Høst (2006). The comparison has been based on an investigation of statistics and research undertaken in similar fields of education in Denmark, Finland and Sweden (Høst 2006).
3 Up till 1948, 'authorised nurses' included registered members of the nurses union. Since 1948, they have been authorised by the state

References

Bjarnar, O. (1995) *Veiviser til velferdssamfunnet. Norske Kvinners Sanitetsforening 1946–1996*. NKS: Oslo.

Danmarks Evalueringsinstitut (2001) *Social- og sundhedshjælper. Undersøgelse av en uddannelse i forandring*. København.

Gran, T., Høst, H., Halvorsen, T., Sommervold, W. & Tuntland, E. (1994) *Hjelpepleiernes organisasjonsproblem: i spenningsfeltet mellom myndigheter, organisasjoner og andre yrker*. Bergen/Oslo: Institutt for administrasjon og organisasjonsvitenskap og De Facto.

Grøgaard, J., E. Markussen og N. Sandberg (2002): *Seks år etter. OM kompetanseoppnåelse fra videregående opplæring og overgang til arbeid og høyere utdanning for det første Reform 94-kullet*. Oslo. NIFU STEP.

Høst; H. (1997) *Konstruksjonen av omsorgsarbeideren –i spenningsfeltet mellom utdanningspolitikk, kommunalisering og interesseorganisering*. AHS—gruppe for flerfaglig arbeidslivsforskning, Universitetet i Bergen.

Høst, H.(2001) *Yrkesdanningsprosess i krise? Rapport fra en studie av utdanningene til hjelpepleier og omsorgsarbeider etter Reform 94*. AHS Serie B 2001-1. Universitetet i Bergen.

Høst, H. (2001) *Yrkesdanningsprosess i krise? Rapport fra en studie av utdanningene til hjelpepleier og omsorgsarbeider etter Reform 94*. AHS Serie B 2001-1. Universitetet i Bergen.

Høst, H. (2004) *Kontinuitet og endring i pleie- og omsorgsutdanningene*. Bergen. Rokkan-rapport 4-2004.

Høst, H. (2006) *Utdanningsreformer som moderniseringsoffensiv. En studie av hjelpepleieryrkets rekruttering og dannelseshistorie, 1960 - 2006.'* Avhandling for graden dr.polit. Institutt for samfunnsvitenskap, Universitetet i Bergen.

Høst, H. (2006) *Kunnskapsstatus vedrørende rekruttering og utdanning til pleie- og omsorgstjenestene i nordiske land*. Notat 4–2006. Rokkansenteret. Universitetet i Bergen.

Høst, H. & Michelsen, S. (2003) Hvem skal pleie oss når vi blir gamle? Om forsøket på å modernisere et kulturelle og sosiale grunnlaget for pleie- og omsorgsutdanningene. *Tidsskrift for velferdsforskning*, 6(1), 17–29.

Høst, H., V. Erichsen og T. Halvorsen (1996) *Norsk Helse- og Sosialforbunds alliansevalg: Arbeider-, funksjonær- eller sektororientering*. Institutt for administrasjon og organisasjonsvitenskap. Universitetet i Bergen.

Kjølsrød, L. (2003) En tjenesteintens velferdsstat. In I. Frønes & L Kjølsrød (2003) *Den norske samfunn*. Oslo: Gyldendal akademisk.

Lindbekk, T. (1992) Systemforskjeller i yrkesutdanning og utdanningspolitikk. Vesteuropeiske kontraster. In T. Halvorsen & O. J. Olsen (Eds) *Det kvalifiserte samfunn?* Oslo: Ad Notam Gyldendal.

Lyftingsmo-utvalget (1988) *Jentedominert utdanninger.* Utredning fra en arbeidsgruppe utpekt av Kirke- og undervisningsdepartementet. Oslo.

Martinsen, K. (1989) *Omsorg, sykepleie, medisin.* Oslo: Tano.

Melby, K. (1990) *Kall og kamp—Norsk Sykepleierforbunds historie.* Oslo: Norsk Sykepleierforbund & J.W. Cappelens Forlag A.S.

Michelsen, S., H. Høst og J. P. Gitlesen (1998) *Fagopplæring og organisasjon mellom reform og tradisjon. En evaluering av Reform 94.* Sluttrapport. AHS—gruppe for flerfaglig arbeidslivsforskning. Universitetet i Bergen.

Norges Offentlige Utredninger (1991) *Veien videre til studie- og yrkeskompetanse for alle.* NOU 1991: 4. Oslo.

Olsen, O. J. (1996) Fagopplæring i omforming. In Olsen, O. J. (Ed.) *Yrkesutdanning og fagopplæring under en moderniseringsoffensiv. Opplegg for evaluering av Reform 94.* AHS—Gruppe for flerfaglig arbeidslivsforskning. Universitetet i Bergen.

Slagstad, R. (1998) *De nasjonale strateger.* Oslo. Pax Forlag.

Støren. L. A., Skjersli, S. & Aamodt, P.A. (1998) *Evaluering av Reform 94: Sluttrapport fra NIFUs hovedprosjekt.* Oslo: NIFU.

Telhaug, A. O. (1979) *Vår nye videregående skole : oversikt over og kommentar til reformarbeidet.* Oslo. Didakta Forlag.

Wagner, P. (1994) *A sociology of modernity. Liberty and discipline.* London and New York: Routledge.

Ågotnes, K. 1989: *Komparasjon eller oppdagelsesreise.* AHS- Serie B 1989-8. Universitetet i Bergen.

NINE

Social Capital in Public Home Care Services (1)

Karen Christensen

The direction of recent changes in Norwegian home-based care is a rising concern among care researchers (e.g., Wærness 2003). This concern is associated with the direction of the overall process of modernisation that is perceived as problematic from the perspective of care (Christensen 2005). This chapter continues that analysis, focusing on what I here identify as a *crisis of care values* within home based care, resulting from a reduction of the social capital of care workers to silence. On the one hand, I point out the fact that women's power has been set aside and weakened by the process of modernisation. In other words, it has been silenced. On the other hand, I argue that the silencing of these voices also means that social capital in the form of potential and resources of individualised care orientations and dialogues, which might otherwise strengthen the sense of community and democracy in society, have been overlooked and undermined.

In what follows I take as my starting point a presentation of the concept of social capital followed by a discussion of how to relate power and gender to this phenomenon. The aim of this first section is to provide a theoretical foundation for the subsequent analysis. The remaining discussion is divided into three parts. The first presents a short historical review of the significance of the changes that have taken place in the distribution of the responsibility for the care of the elderly and physically disabled people. Particularly, this is done by applying the different aspects of care defined by Joan Tronto (1993). This examination shows that despite modernisation, public care work continues to depend to a large degree on unpaid care work within the family and—not least importantly in this context—voluntary elements of care in paid work. In the second part a predominantly bottom-up perspective is used to discuss what can be learnt from research into the everyday workings of public care services. This part shows the importance of women's voices and discusses the potential for and barriers to social capital in these services. Finally, I close in on these 'voices' that research has shown to be present, yet often ignored and seldom heard by the forces that determine the power structures in the field.

Social capital, power and gender

Social capital consists of norms and networks that enable people to act collectively, or more precisely, enable people to act relying on the strength of social relations (Putnam 2000, 2002, Coleman 1988). The core idea in the theories on social capital is very simple: social networks matter (Putnam 2002:6). Social capital is based on the individual's voluntary participation in social relations. It is seen as a central characteristic of civil society and the way social capital is accumulated affects the health of democracy, communities and people. While there are other sociological approaches to social capital (e.g., Bourdieu 1986), Putnam's concept is used here as it offers a fruitful starting-point for a discussion of sociability, solidarity and democracy in society. These issues are exactly the wider subjects of this chapter.

In Putnam's approach, the central characteristics of social capital norms are reciprocity, trust and volunteering. Reciprocity means short term altruism and long term self-interest: a current act is expected to be returned at some point in the future but not as a direct response to the first act. Trust implies the willingness to take risks in a social context in the sense that not everything is formalised and based on rules concerning the relationship. As for volunteering, the concept of social capital has primarily been connected with voluntary work and activity in civil society and in some cases social capital has even been seen as equivalent to volunteering. Nevertheless, this does not mean that the potential for volunteering is always recognised (Leonard & Johansson 2008). However, while we can say that all unpaid voluntary work can contribute to social capital, social capital can be based on more than voluntary work. According to Onyx and Leonard (2000:123) 'all activity that builds social capital for the common good is an essential ingredient in the maintenance of a healthy civil society, and should be explicitly recognised as such.' This chapter is aimed at contributing to such recognition. Individualised care orientations, based on what is known as a rationality of caring (Wærness 1984) and named other-orientation (Christensen 1998b), are characterised by features very similar to the elements of social capital. Other-orientation consists of features such as altruism and being prepared for unforeseen wishes and needs. These things are not dictated by the formal conditions and rules for the work, rather they are done in spite of or in defiance of such rules, sometimes even in the borderline between paid and voluntary work. The concept of social capital is fruitful here, as it illuminates the individualised care orientations in the public care services as social capital for society and, simultaneously, it can help identify the barriers to this capital.

Since the nature of the care services is determined by the interaction between structural conditions and forms of social practice, there are two main power spaces involved. The first of these encompasses the *structural power* that determines the economic, ideological, juridical, epistemic and organisational conditions of the services. This space is largely concerned with national strategies and intentions within the field. But it is also concerned with the sector's workaday realities, such as specific forms of organisation.

The second principal power space is what we might call the space of *relational power*. This power manifests itself in the relationship between the caregiver and the care recipient. Care is produced within the relational space through the interaction between the employees of the welfare state and the citizens. Much of the empirical research on the care services is focused on the relational power space as it appears in the light of the structural power conditions. Research is able to assess to what extent intentions become realised and where.

The distance between the structural and relational forms of power is simultaneously both so great and so minimal (due to interaction), yet also so complex, that it becomes necessary to introduce an intermediate power space in order to

understand what is going on. The fundamental aim of introducing such an intermediate space is to remind ourselves of
the significance of actors as human individuals, who negoti-
ate with the structural aspects in the form of conditions, and
with the relational aspects in the form of the specific framework for action.

Gender is, in various ways, an integral aspect of the power
defined by these spaces. This can be clarified by relating these
power spaces to a differentiation of the concept of social capital between *bonding* and *bridging* variants of social capital
(Woolcook & Narayan 2000). While bonding social capital
consists of strong vertical *intracommunity ties* between people, especially in families or close relationships, bridging social capital consists of weak horizontal *intercommunity ties* between people or groups crossing various social divides based
on social class, gender, ethnicity, religion, geography etc.
Although bridging social capital seems to be the most powerful one because it has the potential to reach the wider society and world, bonding social capital is seen as the important
ground for all other networks. Another important point is that
while bonding capital is related to private domains, bridging
social capital is related to public domains. Also, bonding capital is less visible and less valued and it is less likely that participants create personal advantage from this work than from
bridging work. Women have had less access to bridging than
men (Onyx & Leonard 2000). This reveals that social capital
is gendered. If we take this statement back to the discussion of
power spaces of the public services, it becomes clear that the
two discussions can illuminate each other. The bonding vari-
ant of social capital can only be developed within the space
of relational power because it is developed through close relations between people. But if it is limited to this space, which
means that it does not create a ground for wider openness and
bridging, it cannot really empower the people involved. This
is exactly the case with the potential for social capital in public services for elderly and disabled people in Norway today.
The following historical overview shows how this potential is

present in the context of gendered services, characterised by invisibility and reduced power. In consequence, this potential is a force or capital, but if undiscovered and unused as a collective force, it will instead contribute to keeping women in subordinated positions in the labour market.

Modernisation of public home based care services

SHIFTS IN THE RESPONSIBILITY FOR CARE: NEGLECT OF THE CARE DIALOGUE

Up until the 1950s, the elderly and the physically disabled people in Norway were cared for informally, by middle-aged daughters or daughters-in-law, who combined daily care work with the housework and care required to maintain the rest of the family (Wærness 1982a, Wærness 1982b, Danielsen 2002). In practice, women assumed this 'family responsibility'. The post-war welfare state changed this situation by introducing an element of social responsibility to care (see Kitterød 1993). Before formal care services received public financing, however, they were organised and performed by women's organisations as voluntary work. With the introduction of public support, the responsibility for care was partially taken over by the welfare state. This tended to encourage the attitude— at least by setting a signal—that the duty of offspring to care for their ageing parents had been abolished with the passing of the 1964 Social Services Act.

Many of the women recruited to the care services were middle-aged housewives. With them many of the characteristics of informal care were carried over into paid work, helping to preserve the subjugation of the care worker, as exemplified in the roles of the housewife and the public home carer. On the other hand, the formalisation of care work gave these women greater independence and new opportunities to develop their own interests and practical skills (Wærness 1982a, Christensen 1998a). Following the *Primary Health Care Act* of 1984, a greater part of public responsibility was transferred from the state to the municipalities. The increased decentralisation gradually led to a greater variation in terms of working conditions and the specific frame for care relationships (e.g. Christensen 2001a).

The kinds of responsibility that either were given to women, or which they themselves took on in the above-described process can be clarified with the fourfold division of the phenomenon of care proposed by Tronto (1993):

1 Caring about: The recognition that care is necessary.
2 Taking care of: Assuming some responsibility for the identified need and determining how to respond to it.
3 Care-giving: Carrying out the direct work needed to meet the care requirement.
4 Care-receiving: The subsequent review of the care recipient's situation.

In the 1950s, when society first became involved in taking care of those in need of care, voluntary organisations were already both caring about and taking care of those in need of care. In addition, they were starting to address actual care-giving. When the welfare state later took over care-giving, it was still women who performed the care work. The responsibility they assumed was similar to that earlier taken by the family. To be sure, the roles occupied by care workers vary, since public care work is organised hierarchically. Some groups have more responsibility than others, insofar as they perform leadership functions in addition to or without carrying out practical care work. For most care practitioners, however, the core of their responsibility is performing the actual care work. It is useful to divide the second stage of Tronto's model, taking care of the care needs identified, into two parts. There is an important distinction to be made here between the *responsibility associated with the power to influence the way the work is carried out* or even to determine whether it is carried out at all, and the *responsibility to get the work carried out but without any authority to influence its content*. The majority of female care workers find themselves in the latter of these two situations. Their influence is thus restricted to mere details of the practical care work. This means that care workers are denied a significant part of the power they might otherwise use to shape the care they provide in dialogue with the recipient. In terms of social capital, this serious barrier to developing and maintaining bonding social capital through this work persists, despite the professionalisation that the care sector has undergone since the 1950s, not least in terms of training (Wærness 1982a, Martinsen and Wærness 1991, Christensen 1998a). One aim of this professionalisation was to increase the competence of care workers in making their own work-related decisions, that is, to positively increase their power within the relational space. Female care workers assume responsibility and carry out care work, yet at the same time, that part of the responsibility that concerns power and authority is held by managers or municipal welfare offices, or lies quite simply in the formal arrangements of the work, controlled by ideologies and laws. The fact that decentralisation did not give women more power within the respective organisations can only be explained in terms of this crucial distinction between responsibility as authority and responsibility for the actual performance of care work.

During the 1990s, the welfare state transferred responsibility for care formerly provided by the welfare state to commercial actors that are new to the field. Prior to that period, the responsibility had been shared primarily by female relatives, female volunteers and either the state or local authorities. To be sure, the welfare state also encouraged the participation of these 'old' actors. The entry of the 'market forces' was thus not a simple matter of a liberal-economic division between the municipalities and the private market. One form of the ongoing privatisation of public care services is the so called out-sourcing model. Here the municipalities compete with private actors in the open market to supply specific services, such as, for example, the running of a nursing home. If a private organisation bids the most efficient solution, it wins the contract. These changes do not seem to have any immediate consequences for recruitment of labour force to the home care services. But in the long run they will probably affect the working conditions of the women employed in these organisations, possibly also leading to changes in care interactions and value orientations that motivate the work.

In the abovementioned division of care responsibility into stages (Tronto 1993), the fourth element consisted of the care recipient's situation. In order to throw some light on this aspect of responsibility, the impact of New Public Management on the organisation of domestic care services needs to be considered (Pedersen 2001, Vabø 2001). The implementation of the new model involves documentation, quality control, competition and an emphasis on legal protection, especially for the care recipient. The model is also concerned with breaking down hierarchies by shifting responsibility closer to the service recipient, so as to make the individual more responsible for the work performed. But as was shown above, greater responsibility does not necessarily imply greater power. Vabø (2001) demonstrates how this model imposes constraints on care sector work by controlling the details of the work by means of contracts. In order to illustrate how this comes about, she examines the so-called purchaser-provider model. The principal feature of this model is that assessments of the kind and amount of work to be performed in the individual household are made by employees who do not themselves provide those services. The legislation on social services requires a requisition, i.e. a legal contract, to be written each time it is decided that a citizen should receive a certain service. The purchaser-provider model represents a further step in the formalisation of this decision, thus distancing the care assessment still further from the actual 'provision' of services. This means that performance is transformed from what should in practice have been a care interaction to the performance of a municipal service task. The market-economic inspiration is evident insofar as care is treated as a commodity that can be ordered at a distance and delivered to the door.

This has clear consequences for the possibility of shaping care services to fit the needs of individual clients in specific situations. If we look at this in the context of the changes that began in the 1980s, it becomes obvious that care recipients are increasingly seen as individuals who receive services. To be an efficient service recipient requires more resources than many of the most needy welfare state clients actually have (Christensen 1998a, Christensen and Næss 1999, Vabø 2001). People who were formerly regarded as patients and clients are now framed as consumers of welfare state services.

In the 2000s, another element of privatisation has been added to the public services through a model known as user's free choice (St.meld.nr.25 2005–2006). This means that when the local authority has allocated a certain amount of help to a person, he or she has the opportunity to choose between caregivers employed by the municipality or caregivers employed by a private company contracted by the municipality. Similar to the purchaser-provider model, it is likely that this arrangement increases job insecurity among care workers because of the direct competition between public and private market based organisations within this model.

In general, the changes in responsibility of care in society have substantially limited the options of developing care dialogues in this field. The care workers have lost influence over their work and both they and care recipients are individualised. Pushed to the extreme, care workers are reduced to service deliverers while care recipients are reduced to purchasers and users of services. Obviously, this is a weak framework for developing future social capital as this depends on interactions. However, as the remaining chapter will show, there still is potential for social capital in this field. Furthermore, this analysis demonstrates that the changes that have taken place in this sector were not rooted in listening to the voices and making use of the resources of the sector itself but instead in ideas and models from outside the sector.

THE POTENTIAL FOR SOCIAL CAPITAL IN CARE

What can we learn about social capital from research into public home based care? Kari Wærness (1984) pointed out early on that care work involves a rationality that is at odds with the dominant instrumental rationality in modern society. In order to clarify that care involves actions based on both reason and feelings, she brings these two aspects together in the concept 'rationality of caring'. The term has since found acceptance as an important analytic tool in empirical studies of modernisation in the field (e.g. Bungum 1994, Szebehely 1995, Christensen 1998a) and resulted in the concept of other-orientation mentioned earlier. As far as everyday care practice is concerned, the rationality of caring implies that care can only take place where there is freedom to develop it by means of interaction, through a process of dialogue. Or, to put it another way, it involves a significant element of the unforeseeable or spontaneous (Christensen 1998b). As shown above, social capital is based on a similar rationality. As the present form of modernisation ignores this capital, it clashes with the modernisation process. Here two such clashes are relevant. The first concerns the concept of knowledge that underlies care service work while the second is related to the organisational changes that affect the recipients.

The knowledge currently underlying the care services is based on general knowledge of the processes of aging, illness, health, environment etc. None of the current systems of care training can justifiably be described as learning a craft, even if craft training has been a source of inspiration for the education system for care workers (see Høst 1997). There is a long-term trend in nursing to shift the emphasis in training to the theory and science of nursing, at the expense of learning through practice. Bedside care has gradually lost its appeal among professional nurses (see Martinsen and Wærness 1991). The fact that greater emphasis on science and theory can lead to an encroachment on the power relationship between the caregiver and the recipient has been documented in several studies, especially concerning the care of the mentally disabled who live in a borderland between constraint and non-constraint and are therefore vulnerable to the misuse of power and constraint (see Sandvin et al. 1998, Erichsen 2001, Folkestad 2003). The new top-down knowledge-based management of care increases the risk of care recipients ending up in exposed situations owing to the superior authority invested in the caregiver. Remoteness from care practice can easily lead to detachment from the rationality of caring—a rationality that might instead have provided the basis for a care dialogue and further social capital, in which the provider's power could be used positively so as also to empower the care recipient. In this case, it would no longer be a matter of caregiver and recipient, but of two partners in a dialogue. The fact that we lack the terms needed to describe what the dialogue participants should be called[2] shows in itself that modernisation in this field has so far taken place based on premises that lie well outside the field itself.

Modernisation has pushed the care sector from a state of integration of the services, characterized by a flexible approach to the amount of time devoted to each recipient, to a state of ever-increasing fragmentation of services specified by means of contracts and the like (Szebeheley 1995, Thorsen 2001, Andersson 2007). In contrast to home care work, the work of home nurses already in the 1980s became focused on specific limited and defined tasks in each home (Christensen 1998a). This work often consisted of concrete and specific nursing activities, while a home carer still took care of the time-consuming aspects of care, generally various kinds of housework. During the 1990s there was an increase in the total number of hours worked by home carers (Sosialt utsyn 2000), while at the same time the number of hours devoted to the individual recipients decreased. The stricter time frames imposed on the work in the homes of individual clients have clearly been detrimental to the care dialogue, dependent on what has been called quality time, which is in turn dependent on a flexible approach to the quantity of time (Christensen 1998b). The central problem is that the more the time is limited and fixed beforehand in terms of content, the more difficult it becomes to give the care recipient a degree of power to shape the care dialogue.

Care activists have developed various new models of care in the attempt to empower the people dependent on help in everyday life. One of the central sources of inspiration has been the *Independent Living* movement, which has protested against the disempowerment of physically disabled people and sought to develop a user-controlled model (Askheim 2001). This model, known as the personal assistance model is specially used in the case of young physically disabled people who live in their own homes. They receive financial support from the welfare state to buy the assistance they require. From a power perspective, this consumer-controlled model can be regarded as an alternative to the traditional welfare state model, whereby the state employees decide what care services should be given on the basis of the available guidelines, and also to the private model, whereby the welfare state entrusts the running of certain care services to private market based organisations. In the consumer-controlled model, the welfare state only finances the care work, but leaves it to the disabled individual to make arrangements with the helpers. Although the consumer-controlled model solves some of the problems of the traditional welfare model of care, it creates its own problems in relation to power: It presupposes care recipients to be relatively clever in showing authority, able to make decisions and organise the work of their employed personal assistants. Many frail elderly people, especially among women, do not have much of such resources. Another problem with this model is that it focuses too closely on the powerlessness of the recipient and thereby fails to protect the care worker (the personal assistant) from the same condition. Wærness draws a distinction between a care relationship and a service relationship where the first is characterised by the caregiver having the power, while in the latter the power is held by the recipient. When expressed using these two terms—care and service (Wærness 1982a)—the power of the caregiver in the welfare model is transformed into the power of the recipient in the consumer-controlled model. From a power perspective, care has thus been converted into a service. Thus only one side of the power problem has been solved.

At present we still have no simple organisational model for the actual care interaction. Perhaps it is the thinking in terms of models that in itself poses the problem, since the application of a model presupposes a possibility of finding a standardised solution rather than individualised solutions. The praiseworthy aspect of the consumer-controlled model is that it gives scope to the voices of people who deserve to be heard when it comes to finding solutions and making decisions. However, this is still a model including asymmetry between the caregiver and the care recipient and therefore, in general, insufficient for developing dialogues of care contributing to collective action. The possibility of care dialogues is in place but the model itself does not frame such symmetry (Christensen 2006).

The unheard voices of the care sector

One of the central problems in the planning of care services is that the voices of those directly involved in the practical work within the sector are not treated as fundamentally important. In research on democracy (see Martinussen 2003) a distinction is made between different types of democracy—and the type of democracy that is relevant for the following analysis of social capital in the care sector is referred to as discursive, or participatory, democracy. The basic idea of this democratic form is that citizens contribute to communal decisions in various areas of society through discussions and shared reflections. Applied to the care sector, it should imply the involvement of the mostly affected citizens in the relevant planning processes. This is not only a matter of including representatives in various planning groups, although this too should not be ignored. Neither is it a matter of producing occasional consumer surveys. It is rather a case of working more systematically on the basis of the voices in the field. In other words, it is a case of discovering social capital within the framework of interactions between caregivers and care recipients and developing the potential for its emergence. Because of the power distinctions evident in this field this has to be done more systematically—and it is here that care research might have an important intermediary function. So far research that has given voice to care workers and clients has had rather little influence in the planning process. With the intention of identifying the aspects of welfare state organisation that can be problematic from a discursive democratic perspective, research could start with uncovering resistant voices. This means documenting where there is a mismatch between the implemented structural power and the needs and wishes found in the domain of the relational power of practical care. These voices thus have a place in the intermediate power domain.

Two such mismatches are discussed in the following. The first one, concerning the mismatch between the organisation of the public home care services as brief, temporally limited services of predefined content, with a high turnover among care workers and the wishes expressed by the elderly people themselves regarding this organisation, has been well documented. A number of studies show continuity of service to be a widespread wish among elderly people (Kähler 1992, Szebehely 1995, Christensen 1998a, Helset 1998). This practical wish concerns not having to repeat again and again for different helpers where things are to be found, it is, furthermore, the wish to know who is coming, and simply to feel safe in the relationship. For many elderly and physically disabled people, home care employees are their most important contact with the outside world, and this makes the choice of organisational structure of vital importance to them. The fact that loneliness is an acknowledged phenomenon not least among the elderly (Thorsen 1990) ought to be a reason for emphasising continuity in care. Several studies have documented that care cannot be realised with a lot of different people as each of them carries out just one limited task. But despite this research knowledge, the modern organisation of the services is based on principles that have far more to do with formalisation, standardisation and rotation of personnel than with principles of continuity and consideration of individual differences.

A second mismatch concerns the relation between the recipient and the caregiver, as framed by the purchaser-provider model that separates the responsibility that goes with authority and the responsibility associated with the performance of the work. Research into and assessments of this model (see Vabø 2001, Nygård 2001) have shown that home carers who are asked to carry out instructions that they themselves have not helped to define do not always comply with those instructions. They also make their own decisions, for example because they find that the recipient's situation has changed from the time when the instructions were drawn up, or because the work schedule that was determined in advance does not match the needs that are most felt in the actual situation of the helper's visit. This is a very concrete example of bonding social capital developed in spite of its mismatch with the work rules. In order to do the work properly, that means creating a kind of community together with the recipient, it is necessary in this situation for the home carer to break or ignore the rules. Besides, this is also pointing to the importance of the intermediate level in the power spaces mentioned earlier because it shows the importance of reflection and praxis in these services.

Vabø's study (2001) documents that also the providers, who might be a nurse or a superior home carer, are concerned with this mismatch and the latter tend to be critical of what they perceive to be an increased bureaucratisation of care services. They might for example find it uncomfortable to turn up with application forms and write requisitions, when the potential care recipient has just come home from hospital, knowing that these applications and requisitions will determine the kind and amount of help the recipient will be given in the

future. My own study of home care distribution in a number of Norwegian municipalities (Christensen 2001a) supports these findings. The study clearly reveals a discrepancy
between what the nurses consider necessary in terms of home
care, and the requisitions they write for the actual number of
hours of help to be provided. To order less help than seems
necessary evidently causes dilemmas for these women. The
resistant voices of the commissioning authority, the recipients and the home carers—although hardly quantifiable in
terms of extent—show that it ought to be possible to use and
develop the skills that these women have to let them make
independent and flexible decisions concerning the help each
potential care recipient should be given, rather than force this
process into bureaucratically standardised patterns. For such
a change to happen, however, the skills involved would first
have to be regarded as social capital from which the welfare
state can benefit and which it can frame in ways that will encourage its development.

The particular challenge for care research in trying to trace
these voices of resistance is that they are largely silent, a fact
that has to do with the predominance of women in this field
and the symbolic connotations of this work as a female activity, i.e. as something essentially unproductive and subordinate. This means that those voices tend to remain unnoticed
and no effort is made to help them be heard. In addition,
one important thing to note is that in this field we are dealing with some of the weakest groups in our society. None of
these groups are given space in a discursive democracy. The
problem of silence therefore entails that the researcher simply cannot plunge into these voices. They need to be analysed empirically.[3]

Listening to the voices of social capital

In the post war period, basic themes such as responsibility,
community and democracy were focal themes of the ideology of the modern welfare state. Society was to assume much

of the responsibility for the risks that citizens face in life, including those that come with age and sickness that could and still can lead to a loss of income and a dependence on help. Social policy was meant to protect those who became peripheral to the community due to age, sickness and the like. The idea was to give them the chance to be part of the community again by covering their support needs through allowances and services. This was supposed to build upon solidarity among citizens, in terms of, for example, economic redistribution, which would be served by the taxation principle. The idea of ensuring a return into the community was also to safeguard the fundamental requirements for democracy in society. In other words, the community in itself was to provide security for the individual. If we relate these ideas to the purposes and implications of social capital, it becomes obvious that the two general discourses of the welfare state and social capital are aiming for the same thing. In view of the chapter's discussion about social capital, however, the care service sector, due to the type of modernisation it has undergone, is in crisis. This is not a crisis that can be addressed merely by allocating more or sufficient financial or staff resources although this is currently an important issue.[4] Neither is it a crisis that could be addressed simply by acknowledging certain values that have developed against the background of a gender-based division of labour in society. What is needed is that the welfare state finds a new balance between the private and public domains. In order to avoid new forms of power differentiation, the most constructive way to start this work would be by listening to the voices in this field of public care practices.

As shown in this chapter, there is care research documenting what we might call potential for developing social capital in home based care. Researchers, scientists and practitioners should never stop looking for social capital in voluntary work and private informal domains etc. However, this should not hinder the inclusion of public frameworks like the welfare state. It should not hinder the possibility of finding social capital in paid care work, easily developing fluent boundaries between paid and unpaid work. Furthermore, we should not forget that the women's movement brought some of the earlier voluntary work done by women (and occasionally the associated social capital) into the sphere of paid work. The pressure on two-career families is seen as one of the reasons contributing to the decline in social capital (Putnam 2000: 283). The public welfare framework offers options of bridging the private and public domains that can be hard to find otherwise. While the welfare state is responsible for the organising and financing of its home-based care services, these are still mainly taking place in the homes of ordinary people through relations between these people and the workers employed by the municipality, private companies or even the recipients themselves (as in the case with personal assistance). Although the welfare state is not necessarily the employer, it still is the main responsible agency. This gives a fruitful option to cross the borderlines between the private and the public, between bonding and bridging social capital. No further steps should be made without listening to the voices of workers and recipients from this field and developing frameworks that—instead of undermining interactions—strengthen the interactions as care-dialogues, and thereby the potential to strengthen social capital.

Coleman points out two stages of the analysis of social capital. Stage one aims at revealing the values and organisation of social capital. Stage two goes into the components of social organisation that contribute to those values (Coleman 1988:101). In the case of public home-based care-work, this chapter has tried to contribute to both stages: To the first one by revealing the *potential for social capital in this field* and to the second one by pointing out *the welfare state framework as an option for bringing together bonding and social capital*. It is likely that the current welfare state arrangements for home based care would not exist without the earlier bridging of social capital represented by, for example, voluntary women's organisations and currently the 'Independent Living' movement for disabled people. The welfare state maintained and expanded this capital within the public, but also modernised it in the sense mentioned in this chapter. If the welfare state restores its post war ideology of equality, solidarity and community, there is no better way to do this than by listening to the voices in this field and recognising that some of them are voices of social capital. Rather than making the sector dependent on unpaid voluntary work both outside and within the sector, it is time to bring this resource of social capital to the centre of the services and make it visible. This recognition should include paying for it. The voices the welfare state should take into consideration can come from different groups of welfare recipients or from the many, mostly female, care workers who want to build solidarity with the elderly and the disabled, but are denied the opportunity in actual practice. In the final instance, this is not merely a matter of helping dependent people, but rather a much larger matter of developing and maintaining a healthy democracy in society.

Notes

1 This chapter is a revised version of my article 'Silent Voices—on Gender-related Power in Public Care Services.' in the report *Dialogue on care* (edited by Kari Wærness, 2004). Initially, this article was based on a paper for the conference on Dialogue of Care in Bergen 2003. Thanks to Kari Wærness for encouraging me to revise the article, and thanks to Stina Johansson who at a seminar in Denmark gave me the idea of bringing the concept social capital in to my discussion.
2 The word 'recipient' is inadequate in so far as it reduces the role of the person in need of care who also might be a family member, a professional (or ex-professional) etc. But in order to stress the relation to the welfare state in this context, the recipient role becomes central.
3 I consider that a basis for this exists in research networks such as suggested by Kari Wærness in her programme for care research (Wærness 1989).
4 According to the Ministry of Health and Care Services (St.meld.25: 51), the largest future challenge within the care sector is to provide adequate skilled labour to the sector.

Legislation

Social Care Act of 5.6.1964
Primary Health Care Act of 19.11.1982 (passed in 1984 and revised in 1988)
Social Services Act of 13.12.1991

References

Andersson, K. (2007) *Omsorg under förhandling—om tid, behov och kön i en föränderlig hemtjänstverksomhet.* PhD thesis. Umeå University.

Askheim, O.P. (2001) *Personlig assistanse for funksjonshemmede i Norden.* Forskningsrapport (Research report) no.61. Lillehammer: Høgskolen i Lillehammer.

Bourdieu, P. (1986) The Forms of Capital. In J.G.Richardson *Handbook of Theory and Research for the Sociology of Education.* New York: Greenwood.

Bungum, B. (1994) *Effektivisering av omsorg. Kjønnsperspektiv på omstilling av offentlig omsorgsarbeid.* Report from a LOS-project 'Mulighetsstrukturer i offentlige og private foretak.' University of Trondheim: Department of Sociology and Political Science.

Christensen, K. (1998a) *Omsorg og arbejde. En sociologisk studie af ændringer i den hjemmebaserede omsorg.* University of Bergen: Department of Sociology.

Christensen, K.(1998b) Andre-orientering og omsorgsarbejde. *Tidsskrift for velferdsforskning* (Journal of Welfare Research), 1(2), 82–96.

Christensen, K. (2001a) Mellem politikken og folket. De sociale tjenesters græsrodsbureaukrater og deres fordelingspraksis. *Tidsskrift for velferdsforskning* (Journal of Welfare Research), 4(4), 222–238.

Christensen, K. (2005) The Modernisation of Power in Norwegian Home Care Services. In H.M. Dahl & T.R. Eriksen (Eds.) *Dilemmas of Care in the Nordic Welfare State* (pp. 33–46). Aldershot and Burlington: Ashgate.

Christensen, K. (2006) A Stark Choice. *Community Care.* 6–12 July, 32–33.

Christensen, K. & Næss, S. (1999) *Kunnskapsstatus om de offentlige omsorgstjenestene.* Bergen: Senter for samfunnsforskning.

Coleman, J.S. (1988): Social Capital in the Creation of Human Capital. *The American Journal of Sociology,* 94, 95–120.

Danielsen, Hilde (2002) *Husmorhistorier.* Oslo: Spartacus Forlag AS.

Erichsen, V. (2001) Den disiplinerte fagligheten. In *Makt og kjønn i offentlig omsorgsarbeid.* Report, Oslo: Makt- og demokratiutredningen 1998–2003.

Folkestad, H. (2003) *Institusjonalisert hverdagsliv. En studie av samhandling mellom personale og beboere i bofellesskap for personer med utviklingshemning.* University of Bergen: Department of Sociology.

Helset, A. (1998) *En god hjemmehjelpstjeneste for eldre? Brukernes og hjemmehjelpernes syn på kvalitet.* NOVA-report 19/98. Oslo: Norsk institutt for forskning om oppvekst, velferd og aldring.

Høst, H. (1997) *Konstruksjonen av omsorgsarbeideren.* AHS 2/97. Bergen: Arbeidsliv-Historie-Samfunn.

Kitterød, R. H. (1993) Uformell omsorg for eldre og funksjonshemmede. In *Sosialt utsyn 1993.* Oslo: Statistics Norway.

Kähler, M. (1992) *Faste forhold ønskes—om gamle mennesker og deres hjemmehjælpere.* København: SIKON.

Leonard, R. & Johansson, S. (2008) Policy and practices relating to the active engagement of older people in the community: A comparison of Sweden and Australia. *International Journal of Social Welfare* 17(1): 37–45.

Makt og kjønn i offentlig omsorgsarbeid. Report, Oslo: Makt- og demokratiutredningen 1998–2003.

Martinsen, K. & Wærness, K. (1991) *Pleie uten omsorg.* Oslo: Pax Forlag.

Martinussen, W. (2003) *Folkestyre? Politisk medborgerskab i Norge den siste mannsalderen.* Report 34. Oslo: Makt og demokratiutredningen 1998–2003.

Nygård, L. (2001) *Fana bydel, Bergen kommune. Evaluering av bestiller-utfører-organisering av hjemmehjelpstjenestene.* Report. Stjørdal: Ressurssenter for omstilling i kommunene.

Onyx, J. & Leonard, R. (2000) Women, Volunteering and Social Capital. In J. Warburton & M. Oppenheimer (eds.) *Volunteers and Volunteering* (113–123). Sydney: The Federation Press.

Pedersen, A.R. (2001) Fortællinger om hjemmeplejens organisering. In E. Skånning Nielsen & K. Lomborg (eds.) *På arbejde i hjemmet* (84–112). Copenhagen: Gyldendal.

Putnam, R.D. (2000) Bowling Alone. The Collapse and Revival of American Community. New York: Simon & Schuster.

Putnam, R.D. (2002) (Ed.) Democracies in Flux. The Evolution of Social Capital in Contemporary Society. Oxford: Oxford Press.

Sandvin, J. et al. (1998) Normaliseringsarbeid og ambivalens. Bofellesskap som omsorgsarena. Oslo: Universitetsforlaget.

Sosialt utsyn 2000. Oslo, Kongsvinger: Statistics Norway.

Sosialt utsyn 2000. Oslo-Kongsvinger: Statistisk sentralbyrå (Statistics Norway)

St.meld.nr.25 (2005–2006) *Mestring, muligheter og mening. Framtidas omsorgsutfordringer.* Ministry of Health and Care Services, Norway.

Szebehely, M. (1995) *Vardagens organisering. Om vårdbiträden och gamla i Hemtjänsten.* Stockholm: Arkiv.

Thorsen, K. (1990) *Kontakt, ensomhet og helse.* GerArt 9/90. Oslo: Norsk gerontologisk Institutt (Norwegian Institute of Gerontology).

Thorsen, K. (2001) Et kjønnsperspektiv på makt og avmakt hos tjenestemottakerne. In *Makt og kjønn i offentlig omsorgsarbeid.* Report,

Oslo: Makt- og demokratiutredningen ('Power and Democracy' research project) 1998–2003.

Tronto, J.C. (1993) *Moral Boundaries. A Political Argument for an Ethic of Care*. New York: Routledge.

Vabø, M. (2001) '(For)brukerorientering og omsorg' in *Makt og kjønn i offentlig omsorgsarbeid*. Report, Oslo: Makt- og demokratiutredningen ('Power and Democracy' research project) 1998–2003.

Woolcook, M. & Narayan, D. (2000) Social Capital: Implications for Development Theory, Research and Policy. *The World Bank Research Observer*, 15(2), 225–249.

Wærness, K. (1982a) *Kvinneperspektiver på sosialpolitikken*. Oslo: Universitetsforlaget.

Wærness, K. (1982b) Familien. In Dahl & Klausen (Eds.): *Det moderne Norge*, vol. 2: Samliv og nærmiljø. Oslo: Gyldendal Norsk Forlag.

Wærness, K. (1984) The Rationality of Caring. *Economic and Industrial Democracy* 5: 185–211.

Wærness, K. (1989) *Et program for omsorgsforskning*. Skriftserien no.4/89. University of Bergen: Department of Sociology.

Wærness, K. (2003) Noen refleksjoner omkring det velgende individ, feministisk omsorgsetikk og den sosiologiske tradisjonen. *Sosiologisk tidsskrift* 11(1): 12–22.

PART IV
SWEDEN

INTRODUCTION TO PART IV

Focus on Knowledge Formation and Care Work Organisation

Stina Johansson

In the public debate on the crisis of care in Sweden problems concerning recruitment of staff in elderly care are often raised to the foreground. The central concerns deal with sufficiency of potential recruits in the future. There are too few people who choose to work as care workers and even those who are trained for such work often choose jobs unrelated to elderly care. Less attention is paid to the fact that a long period of expansion in Swedish public elderly care has been interrupted and substituted by downsizing and reorganisation. Many tasks have been transferred from the public sector to the market, the family or the voluntary sector (Szebehely 2005). Within a wider circle of changes, we can talk about a transformation from a 'bottom-up' organisation based on experiential knowledge to a 'top-down' organisation based on vocational knowledge and managed by academics.

In July 2002, the government gave nine public authorities, namely The National Board of Health and Welfare, The Swedish Work Environment Authority, The National Authority for Financial Aid for Students, The Swedish Migration Board, The Swedish Integration Board, The Swedish Social Insurance Agency, The National Agency for Higher Education, The Swedish Agency for Advanced Vocational Education and The Swedish Labour Market Administration, the assignment of drawing up a plan for manpower supply to the municipal services for the care of the elderly and disabled.[1]

In the report *Invest now!* (Socialstyrelsen 2004) the crisis was presented in the following way: 'Just over 360,000 people—8 per cent of the population—work in the assigned field of study. In 2002, costs in the field amounted to SEK 104.3 billion, or 4.5 per cent of GDP. The formal level of qualifications among personnel in the field is low. Four out of ten personnel in the care services have no formal professional qualifications for their work.' (p 8) According to the investigators, current problems in care work are caused by factors related to the work environment and to the insufficient formal qualifications of care workers. Employment and working conditions are not good enough to attract professionally qualified personnel in sufficient numbers. Illness-related absence and the number of work-related injuries are at relatively high levels.

The report linked the issue of future manpower supply to the ongoing generation shift. Many employees will be retiring and a large number of professionally qualified personnel must be recruited. The supply of personnel with upper secondary level qualifications in health care does not even begin to meet expected demand. The dimension and orientation of care science courses at universities and colleges must also be reviewed. The work, working conditions and the working environment would have to be made more attractive so that enough people with the right skills choose to work in the care services. Emphasis was further placed on the need to increase the number of personnel with post-upper secondary level training in the health and caring sciences. The authorities' analysis of the prerequisites for manpower supply shows, however, that there are considerable difficulties involved in meeting short-term and, especially, long-term demand for personnel. The National Board of Health and Welfare (*Socialstyrelsen*) found a contradictory recruitment strategy documented in the literature. The situation seems to be alarming. Even if the municipalities have a strategy for recruiting care workers who have undergone the upper-secondary level qualifications in health care, the proportion of care workers recently employed and with a background corresponding to those demands was lower than the percentage in the already existing personnel[2] (Socialstyrelsen 2006).

Even though the report presented the connections between education policy and recruitment as anything but clear-cut, it is evident that the authorities have a strong belief in education as a solution to the recruitment crisis as well as to the crisis of quality of care. A key argument of the report is that investments in higher education constitute a counter-force that strengthens the care workers in their struggle for better work conditions and for better care services. The academisation of the management of social care/elderly care is presented as a success story and the report also discusses far-reaching plans for the vocational training of care workers. Chapter 10, authored by *Stina Johansson*, examines the tensions of the academisation of the management of social care / elderly care, shedding light to the complex tensions shaping the new field.

The public image of care work

Some individual cases where obvious neglect has been shown in the caring situation have been paid much attention to in the Swedish media during the past couple of years. Violent behaviour and/or carelessness from care workers have caused revised directives and general counsels from the National Board of Health and Welfare (Socialstyrelsens författningssamling, SOSFS).

Another theme to receive wide attention in the media is the cut-backs in care services. In comparison with other Nordic countries, fewer old people in Sweden live in residential care arrangements. Sweden is also the Nordic country where the smallest proportion of elderly people receives help from home care services (Szebehely 2005). As a result of the changed perception of care and care work, the conception of social care has become something diffuse, something which the rank and file can not really define any more. Social tasks, especially domestic services, are imbued with low status. Cutbacks aside, social tasks have a tendency to be overshadowed by medically-oriented tasks (especially the distribution of medicine) within the status hierarchy (Franssén 1997, Wreder 2005).

It is difficult to determine, whether the aversion for care work among potential care workers is caused by the neglect scandals in care, but it is evident that care work has a low status in society. So far, the plans issued by national authorities have had little impact on the choices of young people of whom too few enter work with elderly people. A more 'age balanced' workforce that improves future recruitment prospects and creates a more diverse workforce is desirable but difficult to achieve. In Chapter 11, *Petra Ahnlund* describes the complex relation between formal education and psycho-social work environment. The ambiguity to formal education is still there but the arguments have to be adapted to the new organisation of care work.

Tensions in the work place arena

When home care was first offered in Sweden as a public service for old people, it was organised by allocating care recipients specific amounts of time. It was the recipient who decided what kind of help should be performed during the allocated time. The caregiver's competence corresponded to that of an experienced housewife. At present, delivering services that closely fit the preferences of the care recipient is no longer a fundamental principle in the organisation of home care. Recent research has drawn attention to the deepened gap between care administration and the 'shopfloor' of care. Melin-Emilsson (2004) has identified this gap in terms of two different languages for care. One is the 'everyday language' of care and the other is the 'steering language' of care organisation, found in the documents written by politicians and officials in leading positions. The dominance of the steering language is reflected in increasing hierarchies and complexities in the institutional structures shaping care work. The power and decision making activities have moved upwards in the organisation. An increasing number of occupations have reached professional status and compete with each other about who should provide the attractive work tasks (Wreder 2005).

There are many ambiguities resulting from the ongoing reorganisation of care which have consequences to the legitimacy of knowledge. The professionals whose task is to act as case manager (*biståndsbedömare*) for the care recipients in need of social care have undergone a cultural transformation. When they earlier were 'housewife' professionals directly involved with clients, they are now educated academics with no direct contact to the care recipients. When social care managers are working as part of a team with representatives for other occupations such as nurses, physiotherapists and occupational therapists, the fact that they lack client-centred social knowledge undermines their professional legitimacy. Yet it is the case manager who makes the decisions concerning help.

Another new element concerning the competence structure in care work is the ambition that all care workers should have the auxiliary nurse competence. Formal education has replaced life experience as the ideal foundation for a career as a care worker. In future, young people are supposed to pass an improved Upper Secondary Health Care Programme (USHCP) and adults are to be offered adult education, a strategy expected to result in an elevation of the quality of care, referred to as the 'Care Lift'. Chapter 12, authored by *Petra Ahnlund* and *Stina Johansson*, presents an analysis of these developments, shedding light on the problems involved in the formalisation of the competence for social care.

In concrete terms, recent developments in care work organisation mean that individual occupations, like case managers, have an extensive responsibility for the organisation of elderly care. Municipal policymakers determine the economic frame within which they are able to operate. Within this framework the power that case managers wield in the organisation has increased. Andersson (2007) argues that they show greater responsibility for the municipal economy than could be expected of a professional group. But increased power does not necessarily mean complete control. As recruitment has become an increasingly important issue, managers have had to spend more and more time on administration and personnel management. The greater part of the case manager's time is spent on the recruitment of staff, which reduces the amount of time that can be spent on, for example, development tasks (Törnquist 2004). In other words, organisational changes have widened the gap between clients and management (Ingvad et al. 2006).

The development discussed has multiple consequences to the organisation of care for the elderly. Care organisations are steadily drained of competence, at the same time as the managers have too little time to investigate better strategies for holding on the existing staff. Furthermore, the time available for the social aspects of care work has considerably diminished. How will time for development be created? In Chapter 13 *Katarina Andersson* explores this theme further, arguing that care routines are a vital element in care work. In her view, care organisation should include both sufficient allocation of time for routines and time for unforeseen needs.

Together the remaining chapters that constitute the Swedish section contribute to an understanding of the diverse elements in the current crisis of care work as it is expressed in the context of public social care in Sweden. The authors examine the underlying dynamics giving rise to some of the concerns identified above. The focus is on highlighting features of care organisation that could be defined as the 'social' element in the social care services.

Notes

1 An often observed phenomenon is the Swedish tradition of state intervention in the development of professions (see Evertsson 2002).
2 The statistics refer to the year 2003.

References

Andersson, K. (2007) *Omsorg under förhandling—om tid, behov och kön i en föränderlig hemtjänstverksamhet.* Diss. Department of Social Work. Umeå university.

Evertsson, L. (2002) *Välfärdspolitik och kvinnoyrken.* Diss. Department of Sociology, Umeå university.

Franssén, A. (1997) *Omsorg i tanke och handling. En studie av kvinnors arbete i vården.* Lund: Arkiv.

Ingvad, B., Olsson, E., Bondesson, K. & Arndt, C. (2006) Organisationsförändring, omsorgsklimat och kvalitet i hemtjänsten. *Socialvetenskaplig tidskrift* (4), 331–349.

Melin-Emilsson, U. (2004) Gruppboende för dementa—en omsorgsform eller ett begrepp i försvinnande? *Socialvetenskaplig tidskrift* (3–4), 252–274.

Socialstyrelsen (2004) *Investera nu!—Handlingsplan för kompetensförsörjning inom vård och omsorg.* Stockholm.

Szebehely, M. (2005) *Äldreomsorgsforskning i Norden. En kunskapsöversikt.* Copenhagen:. TemaNord 2005:508.

Törnqvist, A. (2004) *Vad man ska kunna och hur man ska vara. En studie om enhetschefers och vårdbiträdens yrkeskompetens inom äldreomsorgens särskilda boendeformer.* Diss. Lärarhögskolan i Stockholm: HLS Förlag.

Wreder, M. (2005) *I omsorgens namn. Tre diskurser om äldreomsorg.* Diss. Karlstad University.

TEN

Academic Strength
and Boundary Work:
Contextualising Elderly Care

Stina Johansson

Changes induced by external forces will affect the interrelations of members of professions and supporting institutions. Policy makers have searched for new organisational solutions which should guarantee a better or more efficient use of resources. As mentioned in the introductory chapter the Swedish authorities propose ten targets and ten measures in a ten year plan of action designed to support investment in better working conditions and qualification levels in elderly care. One proposed solution is a higher theoretical standard of occupational qualifications. As a minimum, all personnel are to have basic formal knowledge. Besides a more creative space for learning and reflection, another outcome could be that the work gains a higher status and a corresponding lower staff turnover. A high performance of quality care, which demands a long and prestigious education, is something to strive for. The authorities propose training on both upper secondary level and higher education.

In the analysis of the crisis the work is focused in literature, and more precisely what kind of qualification is needed in order to perform the work tasks. In this chapter the focus is on the link between the profession and the work, what Andrew Abbott (1988) calls the jurisdiction: 'To analyze professional development is to analyze how this link is created in work, how it is anchored by formal and informal social structure, and how the interplay of jurisdictional links between professions determines the history of the individual professions themselves.' (Abbott 1988, p. 20).

There is tension between external and internal forces and Abbott shows that external forces sometimes disturb the system by opening new task arenas for jurisdiction and by replacing old jurisdictions. A weaker form of jurisdiction is therefore the 'intellectual jurisdiction'. One question I want to discuss is how intellectual jurisdiction over a professional field relates to the demands from outside powers of a praxis-relevant knowledge base in a field where the demographic change has created a need for a creative rethinking.

I use Abbotts (1988) definition of jurisdiction. He argues '[I]n claiming jurisdiction, a profession asks society to recognise its cognitive structure through exclusive rights; jurisdiction has not only a culture, but also a social structure. These claimed rights may include absolute monopoly of practice and of public payments, rights of self-discipline and of unconstrained employment, control and professional training, of recruitment, and of licensing, to mention only a few.' (p. 59).

This chapter deals with elderly care and the transformation of formal knowledge within higher education. From a broad introduction of the subject I will narrow down my focus to care work and its link to the organisation of knowledge. I will show how the professional agents of knowledge differ in their perspectives and needs of recognition in academia. The story I relay has its origins in my own personal experiences of a struggle for change within the academic discipline of social work.[1] The theoretical frame that I use to present my story is professionalisation theory. In a report from the National Agency for Higher Education the two educational degree programmes of social care (*sociala omsorgsprogrammet*) and social work (*socionomprogrammet)* were suggested to become integrated (Högskoleverket 2003). The material used is selected from the negotiations about the future boundary between the two fields of knowledge related to social care and social work. In this chapter I further describe the efforts to change the balance between those knowledge areas through changes in the educational system, and the struggle around the intellectual jurisdiction. I will end the chapter by discussing two contradictory strategies of support to the research field.

Academic strength and boundary work

The position of manager of care work is focus of this chapter. Two key concepts, 'academic strength' and 'boundary work', are used in my analysis in relation to work and to the formal structure of the profession. I argue that the higher demands on formal education, which are due to a more complex job situation, has created a boundary struggle for the intellectual jurisdiction over the field, in which 'academic strength' is one factor that has to be accounted for in a boundary struggle. It can therefore be argued that the suggested raise in competence levels will be a too 'down-to-earth' solution to the crisis. Following an academic logic of expansion, academisation has become a goal among professionals classified as so-called professions with a middle-to-long education (academic education about 3–4 years, which is less than the educations of physician, veterinary or dentist.)

The ongoing processes for change are manifold and difficult to describe as they are also contradictory (Johansson 2006). Demands come from external forces, for example, The Board of Higher Education, trade unions, The Association of Swedish Municipalities (*Kommunförbundet*) and The Association of Directors of Swedish Social Welfare Services (*Föreningen Sveriges Socialchefer*). Demands for research and evidence-based teaching have become an issue which professionals have to relate to. Visibility on a market is important and education and research have become strategies for survival (Freidson 1994). The increasing importance of control over the application and production of knowledge has led to consequences concerning the legitimating of professional work. As professions, they have the power to decide how resources are used and power over the inclusion and exclusion of clients.

Academic strength can be measured in many ways, and in this paper I use as one method of analysis the number of persons who hold a PhD within the field. I believe that the implementation of a national policy will reveal other and competing rationalities. One way to identify otherwise hidden contradictions is to focus on the different gaps between target formulations related to national and local levels respectively. One gap is visible between those who work with organisational strategies and the realities that the staff who work close to the care recipient have to adapt to (Törnquist 2004). The boundaries between targets and the concrete work are both strict and diffuse. There is also a gap between national targets and professional ambitions concerning involvement or escape from the field. The profession's strategies may have a wider scope of influence than they were planned for, as their resolutions can affect public opinion in, for example, determining how 'need' and 'help' are conceptualised. The strategies also influence the view of which profession should do the work, and which competence is relevant.

Thomas F. Gieryn has studied boundary struggles in different disciplinary settings. He discusses different situations where boundary work (the protection or control of a scientific arena) takes place. It can occur in situations of expulsion; a contest between rival authorities, with both proclaiming themselves to be scientific. It can also occur in situations of expansion if two or more rival epistemic authorities compete for jurisdictional control over a contested ontological domain (Gieryn 1999 p.15). A slightly different kind of boundary work results from efforts by outside powers, who, although not presupposed to dislodge science from its epistemic authority, exploit that authority in ways that compromise the material and symbolic resources of scientists inside. Gieryn calls his type of boundary work 'protection of autonomy'.

Care work and the link to the organisation of knowledge

Abbott interprets knowledge as an external force that shapes interprofessional competition. Knowledge is an internal resource which can be used against other professions. Abbott also argues that the growth of knowledge, which also can replace old knowledge, can have different effects on a profession. It can cause subdivisions or internal adjustments. Career patterns, for example, can cause adjustments while others can be caused by direct competitive strategies (Abbott 1988 p.179).

Borderlines between professions and different areas of knowledge are always under negotiation and often in tension.

In this chapter I describe the competition within academia in order to reach the intellectual jurisdiction of the social work field. I use Gieryns concept 'boundary work' and I look for struggles between rival authorities within academia. The aim of the struggle could be the protection of autonomy against newcomers in the academic arena. Sometimes a profession retains control over the cognitive knowledge of an academic field, but such a jurisdiction is extremely unstable, because there is little preventing outsiders from developing academic, cognitive programs of their own (Abbott 1988, p. 75): A new or potential clientele can be such a factor of disturbance. Abbott also argues that a strong profession can ignore a potential clientele. Elderly care is a new arena for trained social workers (*socionomer*). Some professionals interpret this expansion as a factor of disturbance, and some social workers and university teachers want to ignore the fact that elderly care can become a field for them to professionalise.

Sector/administrative boundaries

The occupations incorporated within the field of social care, and particularly in elderly care, have undergone an academisation process. Also other environmental changes have brought the arena of social care/elderly care into a very dynamic position, which has applied pressure to a more abstract body of knowledge. The need for broad competencies among care workers develops parallel with the fact that an increasing number of potential care recipients with health and social inadequacy survive the age of retirement. The need for changes in the preparation for social work is obvious.

Legislation is inconsistent and occupational roles are involved in a scenario of rapid transformation. For example young and middle-aged disabled persons have their own legislation. When they pass the age of 65 their situation is unexpectedly unclear. A similar lack of clarity can be found in the treatment of persons with so called double diagnosis, as different diagnoses are treated by different professional groups.

Persons working in the field must adapt to the new situation and broaden their competence, The message is clear, elderly persons also challenge the traditional fields of social work, as also alcoholics and drug addicts live longer than before.

Three borderlines to negotiate

There are three main borders to be aware of for a social care worker, borders which help to define and determine care work with older people. These borders may involve conflict and protection, or negotiation and cooperation—or both: in Sweden, at least, the protection of these borderlines has often been quite burdened by contradictions (Forsgärde & Westman 2002). They may be differentiated or indistinct. There is the border with social work with its emphasis, at least in Sweden, on delinquency and deviant behaviour. There is the border with health care, with its negative effects of medicalisation or hospitalisation (Trydegård 2000). And there is the border with informal care performed unpaid by family members or voluntary organisations (Trydegård 1996; Johansson 2001).

SOCIAL CARE AND SOCIAL WORK

There is a need for clarification of the concepts 'social care' and 'social work'. Working with elderly or disabled persons does not normally involve the notion of curing or the reversal of the person's life course. Professionals should be guided by the idea of keeping intact as many capabilities as possible. Life quality, not liberation from symptoms, has been defined as the goal for work with elderly people. Administratively the borderline is, in principle, drawn between work with elderly and disabled people on one side and socially delinquent persons on the other. The borderline is, however, difficult to maintain in a welfare society where also delinquent persons like alcoholics, drug addicts or poor people live until they become old. According to theories, social care includes emotions, engagement, individualisation and a unique meeting. Many of the aforementioned ingredients are also central in social work. In rhetoric, social work has come to include more distance, autonomy, rules, standardisation and justice, which has replaced the perspective of caring. In consequence the social care perspective, which includes dependency, asymmetry and reciprocity, has been questioned, and learning, influence and power have been introduced to the agenda. In elderly care practice the social care theme has become unclear due to standardisation and justice orientation. The relation between the school of social work and the expectations of the labour market on a relevant professional knowledge is vital. Law studies hold a strong position in the traditional education for social workers (*socionomprogrammen*), which is not the case in the social care education. The resultant problem is that there is a high level of variation when it comes to social service universalism (Rauch 2005). Social work is often performed outside the home, while elderly care is usually preformed within a private home.

SOCIAL CARE AND HEALTH CARE

Elderly people spend shorter periods of time than before in hospital care and many people with greater care needs are cared for in ordinary housing accommodation. At the same time, the municipalities, which are in charge of care for older people, have prioritised the provision of help and support to those with the greatest needs. This means that there are fewer elderly people today than there were 15 years ago that receive help from the municipalities, whereas the ones that do receive help are provided with more frequent or more extensive services.

During the 1990s, the boundaries between health care and social care have involved a great deal of tension. The management of the operations / activities has become a more multifaceted task. It is no longer a question of just supervising the work of subordinate staff, but of supervising the work of equally important professionals, for example registered nurses, physiotherapists and occupational therapists, who have advanced qualifications. The middle manager (*hemtjänstassistent* or *områdeschef*) no longer necessarily has her knowledge base in social care. The manager may instead be a registered nurse, an occupational therapist or a physiotherapist. There can indeed be competition for this role from other professions, who often have a health perspective in their training. Generally speaking, it can be said that registered nurses (*sjuksköterskor*) have a stronger position than they had previously due to the establishment of a medically answerable registered nurse (*medicinskt ansvarig sjuksköterska (MAS)*).

Professions that involve elderly care in medical settings, like nurses, physiotherapists, occupational therapists, nutritionists et cetera have reached a degree of intellectual jurisdiction over the field, which is not experienced as reasonable by social workers, because it seems to have excluded social thinking from the work agenda (Johansson 2006). Physicians and other health care staff, who have a monopoly of labour (*legitimation*), promote a medicalisation of the field, which results in a form of language use that describes the aged and ageing in the conceptual terminology of medical diagnosis and treatment. Professions with a background in social occupations are weaker—as negotiators—as the traditional Swedish social workers have not included elderly care into their area of competence and therefore lack a base of knowledge for work with elderly people (Sauer 2007). Consequently the possibilities for the social care workers to influence knowledge production and knowledge use are limited because their knowledge base has, interpreted in this theoretical frame, a relatively loose link to academia.

FORMAL SOCIAL CARE AND INFORMAL CARE

The present trend in Sweden is that informal care has increased in volume and importance (Sand 2005). New boundaries will be the outcome. An anxiety for loosing interesting but time-consuming caring tasks is reported from care workers.

Academic strength. System of professions

An educational programme has to meet the demands of academia and the labour market, which means that the boundary conflicts can be manifold and complex. I have chosen to focus on what happens within academia on educational programmes for social workers (*socionomprogram*) who train for professions in elderly care on the managerial level (middle managers/ supervisors) in order to illustrate that complexity should become integrated in the curriculum. This means that the relatively broad perspective presented above will be narrowed down to a more specific arena of the boundary struggle.

There have been two educational programmes for social workers in Sweden: social work education and social care education. Following the administrative borderline, the former educates social workers (socionomer) for work with delinquents or poor people with the normalisation principle in mind, while the latter educates social care workers in different positions in elderly care and care for the disabled.

During the late 1990s, Swedish middle-to-long care educations have undergone a radical change. The 1977 reform made it possible to tie research and PhD-studies to the vocational training that was previously configured as training for apprentices. Some of the education programmes, for example social work, had entered the academia already in the early 1980s, and started independent PhD programmes. Many middle-to-long care educations like social work physiotherapy, occupational therapy et cetera organised post-graduate courses for their students with the ambition to develop these into a PhD programme. PhD studies for nursing were arranged through collaboration with academic disciplines, like social medicine. The only vocational training programme which did not arrange any independent post-graduate education was the social care education (*social omsorgsutbildning*).

Recently the *Board of Higher Education* and the *Board of Health and Welfare* inspected the two educational programmes for social workers and suggested their unification. At a few universities there were already social work programmes with a special direction towards social care. The best from each one should be kept and the aims of the training should be adapted to the changed demands for professional knowledge in a global society with social work standards built on evidence and quality assurance. A competence raise was suggested for elderly care staff as the demands on their services have become more complex. The proposition brought together two very different approaches to social work. The suggestion from the National Boards was that the more prestigious title '*socionom*', should improve the expectations and protect the reformed education.

The strict demands of academic standards expressed by the Board of Higher Education (*Högskoleverket*) have accelerated a move into the universities and an adaptation to academic culture. Different forms of knowledge—experience-based, vocational and evidence-based—will then compete within the educational programmes. Those changes are part of an even greater change, which aims at a greater complexity in relation to individual responsibility, disposition for change and career tracks.

After their integration the contradictory orientations of social care and social work have, caused interdisciplinary conflicts, but also stimulated fruitful discussions about what these areas of work are. What kind of joint or unifying knowledge should underpin social workers' basic education? At certain schools of social work the tensions have resulted in unsuccessful attempts to integrate the two educational goals, which have resulted, in some cases, with total disintegration. One cause of the conflict is that social workers who begin to include older people in their client group fear that a degree of status will be lost.

Boundaries of knowledge/academic disciplines

Through participation in the structuring of knowledge, a profession has the power to decide what should be included and what should be excluded from the knowledge base. The possibilities to defend an intellectual jurisdiction have partly to do with the strength of the academic discipline, and partly to do with the volumes of the voices from work places that articulate the need for relevant competence. In the lobbying for and against the new and broader social worker exam, the unbalance in academic competence between the academic teaching staff has become obvious. The unbalance of academic competence between teachers who represent traditional social work and the teaching staff who are representative of the social care programmes has had consequences for social care professional's possibilities to influence the knowledge base.

In comparison with other professions the social care programmes had a week position within academia, at the time of the reform. The academic strength of the closest collaborators on the 'medical' and the 'social' sides can be measured through the publications of scientific knowledge within the field. I will focus especially on the competition between academics who represent traditional social workers and the academic staff who represent the social care programme and its struggle for acceptance.

Through a comparison of the number of dissertations it is possible to rank the professions. In her investigation Alice Hermansson (1999) found that 411 persons had passed their PhD in the new academic disciplines occupational therapy, biomedical laboratory science, nursing, reproductive and neonatal nursing and physiotherapy up to 1998. The nurses were first out. Already in the 1960s they had contacted their British and American counterparts and started research on their own. The Medical Research Council and The Council of Social Sciences funded the nursing sciences which strengthened their position. Swedish nurses have a relatively high status. By 1995, the number of nurses who had passed their

PhD numbered 65. The development thereafter has been extraordinary. In 2001 more than 300 nurses held PhDs and the number of professors in nursing was 18.[2] By 2005 the number had increased to 550 PhDs and 34 professors in nursing.[3] In physiotherapy 69 dissertations were written between the years 1977–1997 and 185 physiotherapists had passed their PhDs before May 2005. At that time there were 12[4] professors in physiotherapy. In September 2005 there were 68 occupational therapists who had passed their PhD, and there were five professors plus three associated professors in the field.[5] The discipline of social work held 167 PhDs and 27 professors in December 2004.[6]

In the field of 'social care', the two first persons who trained as the managers of old peoples homes (*ålderdomshemsförestån-dare*) passed their PhDs in 1999. They were the first ones who linked their professional training and experience in social care to research. By 2005 the number had increased to four persons, which included two who had passed their PhDs in social work.

These are the findings if we arrange data with respect to the professional background of the researchers. However, if we were to enter research on social care with more generous inclusion criteria, we will arrive at another conclusion. There are a great number of persons unrelated to the professions who made research on elderly care and disabled people. Around the millennium shift there were around 30 persons who had passed their PhDs on social care related subjects. Eliasson-Lappalainen, Wœrness and Tedre found that there were 44 dissertations related to elderly care (2005). They were spread over several disciplines, but the majority was written within sociology and social work. There has been a constant increase of dissertations in the field since 1995.

Professional structure in relation to intellectual jurisdictions

The occupations in the field of social care are not possible to rationally classify according to professional theory. The links between research, education and praxis are loose or even non-existent. In international curriculum of social work educations, work with elderly and disabled people has also a subordinate position in the literature (Sauer 2007). The same pattern is evident all around the western world. Work with elderly people is not an integral part of the curriculum and the students tend not to choose the electable courses in elderly care.

a) None of these professions or the professions close to them voices an interest in the monopolisation of the research arena of social care. This is an odd situation as medically oriented professions on the same academic level (similar length of education and same possibilities to academise the field) have created research areas of their own.

b) There are no corresponding professions on the international arena—social care workers' organisations—to which research could be linked.

c) Signals from the field indicate that the employees are locked in traditional roles that are of questionable relevance to the care recipients.

At the universities where the integration of the two programmes already have started, some problems have already become obvious. The intellectual jurisdiction is protected by the lecturing staff, who had all written their PhDs with a traditional perspective on social work. This does not create a climate where integration is attained on equal terms.

As mentioned above, I have assessed the power to create an intellectual jurisdiction through the number of dissertations passed in each field. The fact that more than 170 persons who were trained as traditional social workers have passed their

PhD, while the corresponding figure for social care workers is four, would indicate that the chances for the negation of the curriculum on equal terms are limited. The state of inequality has consequences for the chances to procure supervision for a PhD thesis about elderly care and for the student's chances of being recognised as qualified for post-graduate studies. It also has consequences for the competition concerning the curriculum within the social work programme, and for how the qualifications will be valued on the labour market. Finally, it has consequences for our view of old people and their specific needs.

Consequently, recruitment to post-graduate studies has become a problem. Does a social care oriented background qualify for acceptance as a PhD student within a department of social work? Is a care worker with complementary academic competence in research methods and theory of science more acceptable? Or could a social worker with a traditional exam (*socionom*), or a social scientist without practical experience, but with a research interest in the area, be qualified? Within the social work programmes the hierarchy has been threatened.

The labour market has adapted too slowly to the new system with social work programmes with a special direction and many students with a broad education have become confused concerning the value of their education. A hierarchy has emerged, and traditional social work content score higher than the social care-related. The resultant weakness of academic recognition and, lack of vocal power, is clearly related to cutbacks and the low status of social care in practice as well as in research. Employers have been uninformed. Furthermore elderly care managers have preferred persons with a traditional training rather than social workers with a broader and relevant competence.

The question is how to enter and become accepted in an arena where the roles are already defined. The number of persons who hold a PhD defines the direction and structure of the knowledge production and the intellectual jurisdiction.

Contemporary strategic discussions focus on how to strengthen a field in need of renewal and modernisation. At the present time, students are being educated for professions that have no equivalent in an international setting. Furthermore, new working tools for present social problems are needed; already existent problems need remedying, and new solutions need to be developed (Johansson 2005).

Two contradictory strategies

There has been little discussion concerning societal strategies to strengthen research with a social care perspective. Two different strategies can be discussed: support could either be given to a professionalisation of the field through a special profession, or the support could be given more directly to the research field.

Support to a profession. To provide support to the building of research within the frame of an academic discipline based on professional knowledge.

Long before the 1977 reform, actors within most middle-to-long educations had started research in order to develop and make their area of knowledge evidence based. One possibility for social care in social work would be to copy that strategy even if it involved a considerable time factor. For some the aim is to surpass the goals that other professionals have already accomplished. Occupations in social care, then, have to compete not only with social work educations and their struggle for legitimisation but also with the hundreds of academically titled nurses, physiotherapists and occupational therapists.

Support to a research field. To give support to an already existing arena of research, an arena that is open to persons from a variety of professions and disciplines with various development and interest needs.

Universities have supported the development of many professions, which have developed PhD programmes of its own and a special exam: nurses, physiotherapists, occupational therapists et cetera. However, one glove does not fit everyone, and the social care educations may be well advised to choose a different way. Today, the best strategy may well be to follow the trend towards multiprofessionalism and cooperation which transgress disciplinary borders. One line of argumentation could be to focus on intersectional processes in order to achieve something better and more significant than just an addition of one piece of knowledge to another. Instead of following the trend that confines subjects in narrow fields, the principle of unlocking could be the alternative that creates bridges between different fields. This is not meant as a temporary strategy but as a permanent one. The point is openness with all its potentials for enrichment.

In sum, in the first scenario it is important to build and police professional borders, in the other to open them.

Conclusion

There is a great need for social care workers with high degree competence in elderly care. This demand from outside powers should be considered in relation to ongoing boundary work within the educational system. Even if the borderline between social care and social work is blurred, the struggle for the intellectual jurisdiction is hard. A fight between those who want to keep the demarcation and those who, with some support from outside, want a broader definition of the field of social work is well known. There are also some factors within academia that complicate the situation.

1 Educations in social care have both a social and a medical/ nursing orientation. The educations linked to medical sciences have a longer tradition in academia and have, consequently, accumulated a stronger position than the social work/ social care disciplines. The career paths are different in the two faculties.
2 The social care educations have a weak position within the social work programmes. The weak position is partly

due to relatively low course applicant level, and partly due to research competence among lecturers. It also depends on the conflicting foci described above.

These two factors should be balanced with external powers who have made huge economic investments on research and slowly a change can be recognised. Research on elderly care and ageing is the field most increasing within the discipline of social work (Dellgran personal communication). One complication is that there still is a lack of researchers with specific competence in social care. Therefore there is a risk that the unbalance between different professional bases of knowledge will remain.

THE DISCIPLINE IS BROADER THAN THE PROFESSION

The two ideas presented above clarify that in the development of a field we have to differentiate between professionalisation and academisation. Professionalisation has to do with the labour market role, whereas academisation refers to the role within academia. The two ideas can be implemented either as a number of professionally defined boxes or as one open research arena where professionals from different professions meet and create an arena with fruitful meetings concerning joint research problems.

Social care, which often refers to every day life and a social dependency that most of us will experience during our lifetime, could with preference, develop in other directions than the well worn paths of professionalisation and academisation. It also refers to a specific professional ethics. Professional authority is a kind of power which is contradictory to caring. The ideal is reciprocity which is in juxtaposition to a division between 'we who have the rights to decide over your life' and 'those who have to change their lives'.

In an open research arena the same ethics that could become an ideal for care practice could also guide research practice. That means an ethics built on openness, balance, dialogue, reflexivity and response, and not on monopoly, boundaries and authority. It should be a great challenge to build a research arena that theorises social care from many, and sometimes contradictory, perspectives. With a clear leadership a knowledge base with a social content could be created, an arena for co-operation between different professions, which unlocks isolated academic arenas. The same ideals could also guide the recruitment strategies to the direct care work. Instead of one basic education for all, the melting pot could be the ideal. Staff with different educational backgrounds, experiences and ages could better fulfil the intentions of care work.

Notes

1. In 1999 I was appointed professor with the mission to integrate social care research into the field of social work. I have worked with post-graduate supervision of PhD students in order to create a team of researchers in the field. I have also taken part in a national project in order to integrate social care into the curriculum of social work educations. I have chaired the committee of The Board of Higher Education who examines the applications from former social care educations who want to convert their educational programme into one in social work.
2. Information from *Vårdförbundet* (The Swedish Association of Health Professions) October 2001.
3. Information from Annika Rickardsson, *Vårdförbundet* 3/10 2005.
4. Information from Eva Höjer, *LSR*, (Swedish Association of Registered Physiotherapists) 22/9 2005.
5. Information from Sofia Segergren, *FSA* Swedish Association of Occupational Therapists), 22/9 2005.
6. Information from Dellgran och Höjer, see also their chapter in Blom et.al. 2006 (ed.).

References

Abbott, A. (1988) *The System of Professions*. Chicago and London: The University of Chicago Press.
Dellgran, P. & S. Höjer (2006) Kunskapsbildning som praktik och politik—om socialt arbete som forskningsämne. In B. Blom, S. Morén & L. Nygren (Eds), *Kunskap i socialt arbete*. Stockholm: Natur och Kultur.
Evertsson, L. (2002) *Välfärdspolitik och kvinnoyrken*. Diss. Department of Sociology, Umeå University.
Forsgärde, M. & Westman, B. (2002) *Att skapa rum för reflektion*. Diss. Department of Social Work, Umeå University.

Freidson, E. (1994) *Professionalism Reborn. Theory, Prophecy and Policy*. Oxford: Polity Press.

Gieryn, T. F. (1999) *Cultural Boundaries of Science*. Chicago and London: The University of Chicago Press.

Hermansson, A. R. (1999) Chapter 8 in SOU 1999:66 *God vård på lika villkor. Om statens styrning av hälso- och sjukvården*.

Högskoleverket (2003) Social omsorgsutbildning och socionomutbildning. Högskoleverkets rapportserie 2003:29R

Johansson, S. (2001) Den sociala omsorgens akademisering. Stockholm: Liber.

Johansson S. (2005) Att följa strömmen eller öppna eget? *Social omsorg* nr 5–6, 4–7.

Johansson, S. (2006) Social.omsorg, jämställdhet och kompetens. In K. Ekberg, J.Eklund, P-E. Ellström & S. Johansson (Eds), *Tid för utveckling?* pp. 81–106. Lund: Studentlitteratur.

Lappalainen-Eliasson, R, Wœrness, K. & Tedre, S. (2005) Perspektiv i forskning om äldreomsorg. In M. Szebehely (Ed.) *Äldreomsorgsforskning i Norden. En kunskapsöversikt*. Köpenhamn: Nordisk Ministerråd.

Rauch D. (2005) *Institutional Fragmentation and Social Services Variations. A Scandinavian Comparison*. Diss. Department of Sociology. Umeå University.

Sand, A-B, M. (2005) Informell omsorg i de nordiska länderna. In M. Szebehely (Ed.), *Äldreomsorgsforskning i Norden. En kunskapsöversikt*. Köpenhamn. Nordisk Ministerråd.

Sauer L. (2007) *Socialt arbete bland äldre*. Stockholm: Socialstyrelsen.

Socialstyrelsen (2004) *Investera nu!—Handlingsplan för kompetensförsörjning inom vård och omsorg*. Stockholm.

Socialstyrelsen (2006) *Vård- och omsorgsassistenters kompetens—en litteraturgenomgång*. www.socialstyrelsen.se, september 2006.

Trydegård, G-B. (1996) Från kommandora till driftchef. In R. Eliasson (Ed.), *Omsorgens skiftningar*. Lund: Studentlitteratur.

Trydegård, G-B. (2000) *Tradition, Change and Variation. Past and Present Trends in Public Old Care*. Department of Social Work, Stockholm University.

Törnquist, A. (2004) *Vad man ska kunna och hur man ska vara*. Diss. Lärarhögskolan i Stockholm: HLS Förlag.

ELEVEN

To Organise for Care Work—Work Environment and Relational Aspects of Care Work in Sweden[1]

Petra Ahnlund

The recruitment of care workers to work in the areas of health and social care for the elderly and people with disabilities has been a problem for Swedish municipalities already for some time. The combination of large-scale retirements among care workers and a declining interest in health and care education among students has led to a more general and national concern for future recruitment (Socialstyrelsen 2002, 2004). In order to retain and attract care workers, the creation of a good working environment is essential (for an overview of work environment issues within Nordic welfare research, see Trydegård 2005).

Demands, control and social support are concepts that are frequently used to describe employee's psychosocial work environment and experience of work (Karasek & Theorell 1990). They highlight that a good working environment must be organised so that the employees are able to obtain control in their working life, for example, through the allocation of time for reflection and participation in the planning of the work. Other important factors are social and collegial support. Fisher and Tronto (1990) foreground specific ability factors as fundamental for social care actions. According to Fisher and Tronto, time, material resources, knowledge and skill make up the framework for meaningful social care work and that there should be a balance between them. If care workers have the skills that are required for the job, but not the time nor the resources, the work can indeed be carried out, however, 'these imbalances lead to many of the ineffective and destructive patterns we encounter in caring activities' (1990:41). This places demands on the organisation of social care work.

The focus of this article is on the psychosocial work environment of care workers; care workers' educational levels; collegial relations and the relations between care workers and care recipients. In relation to a recruitment problem within municipalities' care work sectors, these aspects must be discussed in relation to care workers' experiences of the psychosocial work environment. This chapter aims to *examine how care workers in the eldercare and care for people with disabilities experience their psychosocial work environment.* A central question is how the educational level among care workers connects to the perception of work environment and work relations?

The analysis in this chapter is drawn from material that was collected from two different care domains: elderly care and care for persons with disabilities. The comparison of two care services provides a deeper understanding of, in this particular case, the dynamic work environment than a study that encompasses only one care domain (cf. Alvesson & Sköldberg 2000). These services can be seen as two different sectors in the Swedish welfare system, as many municipalities have divided their services into two different organisations. Another reason is that the age 65 constitutes a decisive factor in whether one can be included by the Social Service Act (*Socialtjänstlagen, SoL*) or the Act concerning Support and Service for Persons with Certain Functional Impairments (*Lagen om stöd och service till vissa funktionshindrade, LSS*). Persons who are 65 years or older are automatically included in the service of SoL when they get their functional impairment (Szebehely & Trydegård 2007, see also Lewin 1998).

The working environment: some definitions

There are different models for what affects human's experience of their work conditions. This article highlights Karasek and Theorell (1990) model of how the psychosocial work environment is affected by 1 the *demands* that employees experience in their work, 2 the degree of *control* the individual has at work and 3 the amount of *social support* the person experiences in his/her work. Demands refer to the physical exertion that is required to be able to carry out the work and the mental work demands: aspects of the work's scope and time pressure. The ability to control depends partly on the knowledge that is required in order to carry out the work and partly on the individual's possibilities to make decisions in his/her work situation. In this study, social support is divided into formal and informal social support. Formal support deals with support from management and informal support deals with support from colleagues and care recipients. Karasek and Theorell's model discusses other factors of social support, however, in this study, formal and informal support fit in well with the empirical material.

The basis of the model is that the experience of work conditions is affected by and interacts with the control a person has over his/her work, the demands the work places on that person and how the social support is perceived. Using a matrix of combinations where stress and activities are included, different types of work are classified on a scale of bad health and health depending on how great the demands are in relationship to being able to have control in relation to the ability to command the work. In summary, one can state that high demands are experienced as stressful, and especially so if one has little control over one's work situation (Eriksson 1998). Control is a core factor for the experience of one's work situation; the more control, the better the employee can manage psychosocial stress (Karasek & Theorell 1990). However, we live in an ever-changing society and the connections are not always so simple. Research shows that even in work where employees have considerable control, there are many who suffer from bad health and stress (Bäckman & Edling 2000). Women in the public sector report the highest degree of bad health related to work conditions. The theoretical model has had to endure criticism from researchers who reason that it cannot predict the psychosocial strain for personnel (Beehr et al. 2001). The model, though, has shown to be useful in identifying differences between different work groups and I believe it can be useful as an indicator of what care workers can or cannot cope with in their work. Research on care work and the working environment is important, especially if we take into consideration the municipalities' need to recruit and retain competent care workers and thereby create attractive and goal-oriented work places.

Care work: a relational job

Working life of today is often described using concepts such as increased flexibility, ability to adapt and client focus, and working life is to a large extent about understanding, problematising and analysing (Grönlund 2004). From this, Döös (2004) highlights the importance of 'competent others' i.e. that knowing is a relational phenomenon and it is in communication with others that knowledge becomes available for reflection and development through *competence-bearing relationships*. Such relationships develop through conversations, interaction and commonly shared experiences.

What characterises these competence-bearing relationships? Ellström (2002) discusses two forms of learning: adaptation-oriented and development-oriented learning, and it becomes obvious that different types of learning require different strategies and relationships. Adaptation-oriented learning focuses on the reproduction of established knowledge or routines. It is about being able to master and adapt oneself to known situations and is referred to as quick learning. In contrast, the development-oriented learning focuses omit on possibilities, learning to formulate and solve problems and learning to question prevailing structures. It is about focusing on possibilities to discover and develop new knowledge. This presupposes that there is time for reflection and that there is room provided for informal learning activities, for example, experience exchange and dialogue in the work group.

Specific to the field of social care is that care workers also have to relate themselves to the care recipient (Hasenfeld 1992) and research about work environment and work satisfaction within the social care field clearly demonstrates the complex and contradictory nature of care work. Firstly, work in the care work sector is experienced as both mentally and physically demanding and feelings of stress and inadequacy are common. Secondly, the work is also experienced as meaningful and stimulating. The complex co-existence of both positive and negative aspects is not surprising. The majority of

Nordic eldercare research has shown that the relationship with the elderly care recipients is an important aspect of the work. Not having time to create and maintain these relationships is experienced as unsatisfactory (Gustavsson & Szebehely 2005, Astvik 2003, Ingvad 2003, Szebehely 1995, 2005).

The result of a more individual-based care and service ideology also emphasises the importance of good relationships with the care recipients within care for persons with disabilities (Olin 2003, Tideman & Tøssebro 1996). Research in the disability field, and especially among personal assistants, shows that the relationships with care recipients is constructed through the work, but is often described as a personal relation that can be complex and problematical (Hugemark & Wahlström 2002). For example, the home of the care recipients is the care workers' work place, and, as a home is perceived to be a private place, the relationships between the actors are constructed through other norms than those found at a 'normal' work place. The question is how the relationships with colleagues and care recipients are part of the experience of the psychosocial work environment and to what extent the educational level is significant?

Methodological considerations and ideal types

The empirical material is presented in the form of three ideal types, which are based on how the care workers relate to their work, i.e. positive and negative aspects. The purpose is to describe the different attitudes towards care work in relation to how the work environment is perceived. These aspects will then be placed in relation to the theoretical concepts: demands, control and social support.

An ideal type can be described as a case, an abstract description that is constructed based on the emphasis of certain characteristic patterns in theoretical or empirical material. These cases become analytical models that can be used as tools in order to enable further analysis (Giddens 2003). According to Weber, an ideal type is an abstraction of theoretical relationships and is associated with historical descriptions of different phenomena (Weber 1904/1977). However, ideal types today have even come to be used to present and analyse empirical material (Waara 1996, Widerberg 2002). An advantage with presenting one's empirical material in this manner is that the analysis becomes clear and manageable and that the analytical properties that an ideal type constitutes are a summary of the material and abstract in character (Widerberg 2002).

The study has a qualitative approach and is based on an interview study of care workers working in elderly care and the care of persons with disabilities.[2] The care workers have also answered a questionnaire about meetings, levels of education and relations to other professions in the care sector. A total of 37 care workers from different care work settings have been interviewed, see table 11.1.

Table 11.1 The distribution of the informants according to type of work and gender

	ELDERLY CARE		DISABILITY CARE			TOTAL
	RESIDENTIAL CARE	HOME HELP SERVICE	RESIDENTIAL WITH SPECIAL SERVICE	DAILY ACTIVITIES	PERSONAL ASSISTANT	
Female	10	8	4	5	2	29
Male	4	1	1	1	1	8
Total	14	9	5	6	3	37
Total	23		14			37

As described in table 11.1, the article is based on a material in which care workers from different kinds of care sectors are included: home help services (*hemtjänst*) and residential care (*särskilt boende*) in eldercare and residential with special support (*boende med särskilt service*), day care services (*daglig verksamhet*) and personal assistance (*personlig assistent*) in the care of persons with disabilities. The construction of ideal types enables me to gather those who reply similarly to a number of central concepts. I can then acquire valid data irrespective of whether they belong to elderly care (EC) or disability care (DC).

The educational background of the care workers shows that many of them have an education which is related to health and social care. In the elderly care sector, care workers are employed as nurse assistants (*vårdbiträde)* or auxiliary nurses (*undersköterska*). The nurse assistants have a more diversified educational background than the auxiliary nurses in elderly care. The nurse assistants either have an upper secondary general education, health care support training (*sjukvårdsbiträdesutbildning*) or nursing assistant training (*vårdbiträdesutbildning*). The ones that work as auxiliary nurses have undergone the Upper Secondary Health Care Programme or a 32-week supplementary course (see also Ahnlund & Johansson in Chapter 12 for more information about the educational programmes).

In the care for persons with disabilities, the care workers have an even more varied educational background and they are employed as carers (*vårdare eller vårdarinna*), as occupational therapists (*arbetsterapeut*) and personal assistants (*personlig assistant*). A number of the carers have university degrees, one is, for example, a teacher, others have a upper secondary health care education or a upper secondary education within a more general area, for example, the humanities programme. The personal assistants also have a varied educational background and one have undergone the upper secondary health care program, one has a university degree in pedagogy and one has a general upper secondary education.

The hermeneutic process described by Alvesson & Sköldberg (2000:58) inspired the analysis, which concisely means that I have alternated the reading of the interviews with theoretical interpretations for a deeper understanding of the data. On the basis of the analysis, I have constructed different themes from which the ideal types have been constructed. The aim of constructing ideal types is to show differences between groups, in this case of care workers. The quotations presented in the ideal types are chosen to demonstrate these differences, but are simultaneously representative for more than one person in the ideal type.

Ideal types: the care recipient controlled, the organisational abandoned and the environmentally supported

THE CARE RECIPIENT CONTROLLED

In this ideal type, care workers from the care of persons with disabilities are represented: care workers from residential with special support, day care services and personal assistants. They have a diversified educational background. The care workers have either an education in health and social care, both at the upper secondary school and higher education level, or no upper secondary school education at all. They work as carer (*vårdare och vårdarinnor*) or as personal assistants.

The work demands in this ideal type are substantial due to the fact that the care recipients have a considerable need for help and the care workers often work alone. Working alone is described on the basis of two aspects: difficult in relation to being without colleagues and unproblematic because staff and care recipient(s) work together. The difficult part originates from the fact that the care recipient(s) can be very demanding and that care workers are left alone with considerable responsibility for individuals: 'Yes the worst is that they are so demanding. And if you are not fit yourself, you become very tired and down. And especially when one is working alone.' (Female, carer 10DC).

Care workers have considerable possibilities to influence their schedule and work task contents together with the care recipient(s). One negative aspect for this group, and especially for the personal assistants, is the restriction of their possibilities to exercise control over the work. For example, if the care recipient does not want to propose fun activities or if conflicting interests occur, the staff experience that they are 'in the hands of the care recipients'. In extreme cases, this can be expressed in terms of being a slave without rights: 'Some are very burdensome to work with where one can't go out, many are of course depressed and are sitting at home, smoking all day and yes then those are long workdays. (...) some care recipients in this branch are 'demanding machines' (...) don't understand that I need to go to the toilet and things like that. I am just a slave.' (Male, personal assistant 17DC).

Due to the fact that many work alone, it varies how often the care worker has meetings together with colleagues and management and they do not have regularly scheduled discussions about the work's values and pedagogical methods. They experience that they do not have relevant training in relation to the care recipients' problems and that it is up to themselves to read up on this: 'I have received information for half a day about MS, but there is often literature at home with the person one works for, so then one can look at that' (Male, personal assistant 17DC). They ask for further education but realise that the municipalities' economical situation makes make it impossible for them to participate in courses: 'When the municipality needs to save, then they take away all further education, cut down on staff. It is like panic.' (Female, carer 11DC). The result is that the work can sometimes be experienced as boring because development remains at a standstill: 'Not too much happens. It's the same routines every time. It's like, how should I say, not boring but it easily becomes very routine' (Female, personal assistant 16DC).

Care workers in the care recipient controlled, work to a large extent alone and have few opportunities to discuss their work with colleagues. In those cases where the personnel work in integrated day care services (*integrerad daglig verksamhet*), the approach is that the 'regular' staff at the workplace provide good support in the work but only in relation to the work tasks. They cannot help with information, for example, about problems related to the care recipient(s) or other confidential information: 'I can't talk about a problem regarding the group, the employees. I have to separate between what is about the job and what is about them.' (Female, carer 10 DC). Most have weak formal support and state that they rarely receive any appreciation from persons in managerial positions, whether it is verbal or material appreciation: 'I have worked here for eight years and I have never received any praise from

my work supervisors. Earlier we would get a Christmas present, but yes even the Christmas lunch has been cancelled.'
(Male, personal assistant 17DC). 'If I want to quit work? Yes,
sometimes because you never get any feedback from our so-
called supervisors' (Male, carer 21DC). They are not offered
supervision (*handledning*) and they seldom have contact with
relatives.

To sum up, 'the care recipient controlled' are characterised
by weak informal support as well as weak formal support in
relation to management and colleagues. Their work is highly
demanding, and control is either minimal or considerable,
depending on the relation to the care recipients. They often
have a close, and for the work fulfilment, crucial relationship
with the care recipients. When these relations do not function
well, the work is experienced as less stimulating.

THE ORGANISATIONAL ABANDONED

In this ideal type, eldercare personnel from residential care
and home help services are represented. They have a diversified educational background: some are employed as auxiliary nurses (*undersköterskor*) but most have a nursing assistant
education (*vårdbiträdesutbildning*), alternatively no theoretical
educational regarding health or social care.

The personnel in this ideal type has also a heavy workload and high demands in their work due to the care recipients' urgent need of assistance and organisational problems,
for example, a shortage of staff and difficulty in getting substitutes when necessary. Lack of time is a pressing issue. The
care worker experiences difficulty in managing all their work
tasks: 'It becomes stressful because one has to take on more
work when there are many who are sick' (Female, nursing assistant 5bEC). They are motivated to do more during their
working hour, for example, engage the elderly in different
ways, but are frustrated by organisational problems and continuous time pressure: 'I promise that there are not many who
would be able to cope with working in this unit. There are always things to do. The downside is that the elderly are not

activated by us because we don't have enough time' (Male nursing assistant 16EC). 'We haven't been out for a walk in a long time, we haven't.' (Female, nursing assistant 1EC). The work is perceived as being mentally straining and physically demanding, for example, the elderly have lost many of their social and bodily functions that the staff has to compensate for. This influence how they feel about the elderly: 'One becomes stressed and a few cry out for attention and one becomes irritated, I have to admit.' (Female, auxiliary nurse 18EC) 'Sometimes the work is boring when things are the same all the time, a few pensioners say the same thing every morning' (Female, auxiliary nurse 8EC).

The staff can control their work to the extent that they can plan how the days are to be arranged and they are also responsible for the work group's schedule. However, the influence on scheduling does not always benefit the staff: 'one does not have any regularly scheduled coffee breaks and sometimes one does not have lunch either, (laughs) if it's really bad' (Female, nursing assistant 5bEC). They have regularly scheduled morning meetings where the work distribution and practical work tasks are discussed. However, much of the responsibility to solve daily occurring problems is left to the individual, both in regards to organisational problems and problems in relation to the elderly: 'Last Monday, if I followed my schedule, then there was no time to go and get lunch boxes (for the elderly), I had to do that during my lunch' (Female, nursing assistant 5bEC). They do not have many opportunities to discuss pedagogical issues or ethical values at work: 'It is not that often that we sit down and talk about this and that' (Female, auxiliary nurse 17EC). The care worker is worried about the municipalities' economical programme and its negative affects on the elderly care. In their opinion, this is a factor that prevents further training: 'Further education? I don't think that I have seen so much of that' (Male, nursing assistant 13EC). It is also difficult to obtain substitutes when needed.

Care workers in the ideal type 'the organisational abandoned' have informal support, and colleagues are described to be the number one reason for remaining at the workplace: 'Really great work mates, I get along with them really well.' (Female, auxiliary nurse 8EC) 'I have great colleagues and they are in fact the reason why I remain at this workplace' (Female, nursing assistant 3EC). But problematic situations are in best cases discussed with colleagues, it is also common that difficulties are not discussed in the work group. This can lead to feelings of loneliness at work: 'When one walks out to the elderly, you are all alone with the responsibility and one has to be clear about what you have to do.' (Female, nursing assistant 4EC). They are not offered supervision (*handledning*) and there is no specific time set a side for discussions about the work's values and methods. There is cooperation with actors outside the eldercare sector, for example, district nurses, and a satisfaction from being rooted in the local community where persons are known by shopkeepers and public actors: 'It becomes very social in some way, the stores know that one works at home help services. The pharmacy and the post office, they say hello when we meet on the street' (Male, nursing assistant 5aEC). They seldom receive appreciation from persons in supervisory positions, whether it be verbal or material appreciation: 'Our registered nurse is better at encouragement, the supervisor isn't here so much.' (Female, auxiliary nurse 17EC). Relatives are described as somewhat uninformed about the social care sector and therefore make unrealistic demands on the staff's work: 'One can cope with the dement person but I have a hard time managing with the relatives if they can't behave.' (Male, nursing assistant 16EC).

To sum up, 'the organisational abandoned' are characterised by having a strong informal support, but a weak formal support in their work. Their work is highly demanding and their control over how the work is organised and planned is minimal. This leads to time shortages and feelings of inadequacy which are stressful factors at work.

THE ENVIRONMENTALLY SUPPORTED

Care workers from both eldercare and care for persons with disabilities are represented in this ideal type. The majority of those who work with elderly care, work in residential care. Those who work in disability care service work with persons who have a learning disability, either at housing with special support for adults or at day care services. The care workers have either a higher secondary education with a specialisation in social care or a university degree, specialised in pedagogy or health and social care, for example, occupational therapist (*arbetsterapeut*) in the care of persons with disabilities. A number of care workers are employed as auxiliary nurses (*undersköterskor*), a few as nursing assistants (*vårdbiträden)* in elderly care and others as carers (*vårdare*) in the care for persons with disabilities.

This group has a heavy workload due to the care recipients' urgent need of assistance as well as organisational problems, for example, a shortage of staff and difficulty in getting substitutes when necessary. These two factors have a negative impact on the staff, and they experience difficulty in managing all their assigned work tasks. As a result, personal relationships suffer, which exposes the group to psychological stress: 'One should be there mentally for others and if it is then a person with a physical handicap one for example must lift, then it is extremely hard if one does not get a substitute.' (Female, occupational therapist 5DC). They state that the work is physically demanding, and that it requires psychological presence all the time.

In this group there are clear routines for how the work should be carried out and the staff has considerable control over the planning of work tasks. They have regular scheduled meetings where colleagues and management participate, and where the organisational aspects of the work are discussed. The meetings can include discussions concerning finances, scheduling and the delegation of responsibility in the work: 'He has given us a lot of responsibility. I mean, we can take care of this with holiday schedules, finding substitutes, all those things we do ourselves. We also cut cost, it's us who decide what when it is needed ourselves, it is we who decide what.' (Female, auxiliary nurse 15EC). There are also meetings to address how the work around care recipients can be developed, and different pedagogical models for the work are discussed: 'It is about having the feeling for, when one begins in the morning, that one makes plans. How shall we do it today? How will we make sure that Margit does not have to wait for us for so long?' (Male, auxiliary nurse 9EC). They organise their work around the elderly and care recipients from a 'support person' (*kontaktperson*) model, where continuity and relationships are highly important: 'Every care recipient has a support person in the staff group who is more responsible for this person. It can be about finances or purchases and arranging with authorities, medical services.' (Male, carer 3DC). They see the need for further training and courses at the workplace, which all care workers have the possibility to attend: 'We have had courses here in the house. They are about dementia illnesses, elderly that have difficulty in swallowing. We have had different lecturers, its good.' (Female, auxiliary nurse 10EC).

Care workers have substantial informal support in their work, i.e., they have a functioning cooperation and emotional support from their colleagues and others, for example, from the local care centre and staff from other care organisations: 'It is such a great staff group here. Many mornings or nights, when one is tired I think about that. I think about the care recipients, I think of those I am meeting the next day and it gives me so much energy.' (Female, carer 4DC). The informal support means that they often discuss work with colleagues in the work group, both at meetings and during the course of work: 'I have to be able to say 'oh God I think I am going to strangle him'. Because then I won't do it. Then I can go in and give the man a hug instead. We discuss a lot of ethics and our morale.' (Female auxiliary nurse 15EC). They have strong, formal support from management, supervisors (*handledare*) and other staff and discuss the power they have as care workers: 'A work atmosphere where it is all the time permitted to reflect 'are we doing the right thing now, should we do it like this? Or is there another solution' so one does not just move forward.' (Female, occupational therapist 5DC). The management and care workers 'speak the same language' and the management has a good understanding of what the work's purpose is and its advantages and disadvantages: 'How one copes and how one works, it matters a great deal who one has for a supervisor. And we have a really good one. He has worked as a nurse in the psychiatric ward and knows exactly what it is about.' (Female, auxiliary nurse 10EC). They receive guidance when needed and support from different expert groups, for example, the dementia team. The personnel's view of relatives is that they are a resource that can help them arrive at a better understanding of the care recipient and the recipient's relation to a (eventual) dementia illness: 'We have something that is called life story, a form that we send with relatives. Then they get to write as much as possible about the care recipient to us.' (Female, auxiliary nurse 15EC).

To sum up; the environmentally supported are characterised by strong informal and formal social support in their work. Their work is highly demanding but they have a high degree of control over their work. This helps them to organise the work so that they have time and opportunity to discuss and reflect upon the work together.

Conclusion

The purpose of the chapter is to examine how care workers in eldercare and care for people with disabilities experience their psychosocial work environment in relation to how the relationships are expressed and educational levels among care workers. Based on the analysis, we can see that all care workers who fall within the three ideal types state have a substantial workload, i.e., high demands in their work. What separates the ideal types is how they handle work demands and how relationships to the care recipients and colleagues are expressed, i.e., the level of control and social support.

The competence-bearing relationships, which Döös (2004) views as important elements in a work group, appear in different ways in each ideal type. 'The environmentally supported' have a work environment that permits them to exercise control over the work sectors' planning and organisation; they have supervision and regularly scheduled meetings where social care recipients and work methods are discussed. They have a work climate where it is possible to express that the relational aspects can be burdensome. At the same time, they have support in the work group and from supervisors, and this helps them deal with problematic situations, for example, via pedagogical methods, supervision and reflection in the work group. The substantial work demands are, in other words, facilitated because there is a dialogue regarding the work's different aspects where social care recipient, colleagues and management are involved in development-oriented learning.

In contrast, the work environment for the ideal type 'the organisational abandoned' is an adaptation-oriented type. The work needs to be carried out in a sector where time pressure and care-burdened elderly are made out to be problematic. This leads to a hard work climate where there is almost nothing organised for collective reflection at work. There are established work models where all the elderly receive help with basic needs, but there is no time for engagement, i.e., to do things together with the elderly. The substantial work demands make it easier for colleagues to cope and appreciate one another in a learning environment that includes the mastery of the institutional rules that are constructed by the work team. On the other hand, there is no common dialogue regarding pedagogical methods or guidance regarding work in formal situations.

For 'the care recipients controlled', the central aspect that is explicitly expressed is the relation between the care worker and the care recipient. This relationship is one of the main reasons that the work is considered to be satisfying, but also problematic. It appears that working alone is difficult to handle if these relationships do not function satisfactorily. When

the care recipient has a moderate need for help, the care worker can experience her- or himself to be in a more subordinate position than when the need for help is more urgent
(Christensen 1991). Learning occurs in relation to the needs
of the care recipients but the relationship between the parties is often left unreflected upon. They rarely have meetings,
whether they be with formal or formal actors, in which these
aspects of work are discussed.

According to Ellström (2006), in order to learn and to make
changes in one's working life, there either has to be an interest, or the learning has to have already begun. In the ideal
type 'the environmentally supported' most of the care workers are well-educated. Furthermore, they are also shown to be
the most balanced when it comes to the application of different aspects of care work, to make the complexity visible. One
can ask oneself whether it is educated people who demand
that the work should be organised so that a relational perspective exists, or whether it is a certain type of person who
applies for a position at such work places. It can also be asked
whether it is more knowledge or more time that is necessary
to receive a good working environment in today's eldercare
and care of people with disabilities.

Certainly, a development-oriented learning demands a
great deal from management and the organisation of the
work. If the employer want care workers who can develop in
their work and who are satisfied with the working environment, it can be worthwhile to invest in making social care's
complex nature visible.

Notes

1 I want to thank the two anonymous reviewers, whose comments had
substantial impact on the text.
2 The study is part of a European project, for a more detailed description see Hansen and Jensen (2004), Johansson (2003), Ahnlund and
Johansson (2006).

References

Ahnlund, P., & Johansson, S. (2006) Omvårdnadsutbildning som mål eller medel? Om legitimitetsproblem och kunskapssyn. *Socialvetenskaplig tidskrift*, 13(3), 212–227.

Alvesson, M., & Sköldberg, K. (2000) *Reflexive Methodology*. London: SAGE Publications.

Astvik, W. (2003) *Relationer som arbete. Förutsättningar för omsorgsfulla möten i hemtjänsten*. Diss. Department of Psychology. Stockholm University. Stockholm: Arbetslivsinstitutet.

Beehr, T A., Glaser, K. M., Canali, K. G., & Wallwey, D. A. (2001) Back to Basics: Re-examination of Demand-Control Theory of Occupational Stress. *Work & Stress*, 15(2), 115–130.

Bäckman, O., & Edling, C. (2000) Arbetsmiljö och arbetsrelaterade besvär under 1990 talet. In Marklund, S. (Ed.), *Arbetsliv och hälsa 2000*. Stockholm: Arbetslivsinstitutet.

Christensen, K. (1991) Hjemmehjælperen—en ny offentlig omsorgsrolle: et kvindesyn på ældreomsorgen. *Social Kritik* 2 6–18.

Döös, M. (2004) Arbetsplatsens relationik. *Arbetsmarknad och arbetsliv*. 10(2), 77–93.

Ellström, P. E. (2006) Tid för utveckling? In Ekberg, K., Eklund, J., Ellström, P. E., & Johansson, S. (Eds), *Tid för utveckling?* Lund: Studentlitteratur.

Ellström, P. E. (2002) Lärande—i spänningsfältet mellan produktionens och utvecklingens logik. In Abrahamsson, K., Abrahamsson, L., Björkman, T., Ellström, P. E., & Johansson, J. (Eds), *Utbildning, kompetens och arbete*. Lund: Studentlitteratur.

Eriksson, B. (1998) *Arbetet i människors liv*. Diss. Göteborgs universitet: Sociologiska institutionen.

Fisher, B., & Tronto, J. (1990) Toward a feminist theory of caring. In Abel, E. K., & Nelson. M. K. (Eds), *Circles of Care. Work and Identity in Women´s Lives*. Albany, N.Y.: State University of New York Press.

Giddens, A. (2003) *Sociologi*. Lund: Studentlitteratur.

Grönlund, A. (2004) *Flexibilitetens gränser. Förändring och friktion i arbetsliv och familj*. Diss. Department of Sociology. Umeå University. Umeå: Boréa Bokförlag.

Gustafsson, R. Å., & Szebehely, M. (2005) *Arbetsvillkor och styrning i äldreomsorgens hierarki*. Stockholms universitet: Institutionen för socialt arbete.

Hasenfeld, Y. (1992) The nature of human service organisation. In Hasenfeld, Y. (Ed.), *Human Services as Complex Organisations*. Newbury: SAGE Publications.

Hansen, H., & Jensen, J. (2004) *Work with Adults with Severe Disabilities: A Case Study of Denmark, The Nederlands and Sweden*. Roskilde universitetscenter.

Hugemark, A., & Wahlström, K. (2002) *Personlig assistans i olika former.* FoU Rapport 2002:4 Stockholm Stad.

Ingvad, B. (2003) *Omsorg och relationer.* Diss. Lunds universitet: Socialhögskolan.

Johansson, S. (2003) *Work with elderly people. A Case Study of Sweden, Spain and England with additional material from Hungary.* www.umu.se/socw/forskning/WP9%20consolidated%20report.pdf

Karasek, R., & Theorell, T. (1990) *Healthy Work. Stress, Productivity and the Reconstruction in Working Life.* New York: Basic Books.

Lewin, B. (1998) *Funktionshinder och medborgarskap.* Diss. Uppsala universitet: Socialmedicinsk tidskriftserie nr.55.

Olin, E. (2003) *Uppbrott och förändring.* Diss. Göteborgs universitet, Institutionen för socialt arbete.

Socialstyrelsen (2002) *Kompetenskrav för personal inom vård och omsorg om äldre.* Art nr: 2002-124-14.

Socialstyrelsen (2004) *Investera Nu! Handlingsplan för kompetensförsörjning inom vård och omsorg.* Art nr: 2004-103-10.

Szebehely, M., & Trydegård, G. B. (2007) Omsorgstjänster för äldre och funktionshindrade: skilda villkor, skilda trender? *Socialvetenskaplig tidskrift,* 14(2–3), 196–219.

Szebehely, M. (2005) Sammanfattning. In Szebehely, M. (Ed.), *Äldreomsorgsforskning i Norden.* TemaNord 2005:508 Köpenhamn: Nordiska ministerrådet.

Szebehely, M. (1995) *Vardagens organisering.* Diss. Lund: Studies in Social Welfare.

Tideman, M. & Tøssebro, J. (1996) Levels of living for intellectual disabled people in Sweden and Norway: Changes during the first half of the 1990´s. In Tøssebro, J., Gustavsson, A. & Dyrendahl, G. (Ed.), *Intellectual disabilities in the Nordic Welfare States.* Kristianstad: Norwegian Academic Press.

Trydegård, G. B. (2005) Äldreomsorgspersonalens arbetsvillkor i Norden—en forskningsöversikt. In Szebehely, M. (Ed.), *Äldreomsorgsforskning i Norden.* 2005:508 Köpenhamn: Nordiska ministerrådet.

Waara, P. (1996) *Ungdom i gränsland.* Diss. Department of Sociology. Umeå University. Umeå: Boréa Bokförlag.

Weber, M. (1904/1977) *Vetenskap och politik.* Göteborg: Bokförlaget Korpen.

Widerberg, K. (2002) *Kvalitativ forskning i praktiken.* Lund: Studentlitteratur.

TWELVE

Upper Secondary Health
Care Programme as Means or
Measure?

On the Problem of Legitimacy
and the View of Knowledge

Petra Ahnlund and
Stina Johansson

Training and qualifications of health care personnel are questions of current concern which are under discussion at various levels of society. This chapter deals firstly with the question of how the middle managers and staff of certain elderly care units in two Swedish municipalities approach current formal training requirements, and secondly with what is regarded as relevant qualifications for working in the health care field. Has the internal divisions of labour played a role in the recruitment crisis?

Care work is presented at central administrative level in Sweden as a complex task for which personnel require special qualifications. In elderly care, questions of training and qualifications form the highly topical theme noticed by central actors [see e g. Regeringens proposition 2005/06:115, The National Board of Health and Welfare (*Socialstyrelsen*) 2002, 2004, The Swedish Association of Local Authorities [(*Svenska Kommunförbundet*) 2003]. According to The National Board of Health and Welfare (2002), the manpower supply is the most important factor in ensuring high quality care for the elderly. The lowest level of formal training is defined by The National Board of Health and Welfare (2001) as the care and welfare equivalent to an upper secondary qualification level. The report on Everyday Ethics in the Care of Elderly People of 1997 (*Bemötandeutredningen*) considers the above mentioned qualification requirement to be insufficient. Personnel need at least a basic qualification in accordance with the Upper Secondary Health Care Programme [USHCP (*Omvårdnadsprogrammet*)] along with advanced courses and specialisation in relevant areas (SOU 1997:51). This is a recommendation on which the National Board of Health and Welfare insists. The 'Invest Now!' ('*Investera nu!*') report states that all care workers, including basic staff of both care of the disabled and elderly care ought to have qualifications in pedagogics, medicine and the social welfare field as a base for their occupational qualifications and that these qualifications ought to be upgraded via the USHCP (National Board of Health and Welfare 2004).

At the local authority level, where the recruitment effort focuses on personnel in direct care work, the starting points for assessing qualification criteria and educational requirements are somewhat different. Swedish managers at local level manifest[1] an ambivalence confronting what they regard as the best qualification (Johansson 2004). They are aware that their staff members are keen to gain more qualifications while at the same time they declare that experience-based knowledge is more important than formal education. It may be easier for the caregiver to understand the elderly if the person has experience of looking after a home or is not too young.

> We have experienced, you see, that a person who is not that young, who encounters a pensioner, gets on a bit more easily than if it is a really young girl or boy that turns up. Well of course that can work too, but generally speaking it is easier to set up a dialogue and an exchange of ideas if the person is not a spring chicken. (A high-level local authority manager, quoted in Johansson 2004 p. 108)

Other studies have shown that even care workers declare that experience is the heart of their occupational competence and that anyone is able to perform the work tasks (Wahlgren 1996, Wreder 2005). Staff sees no need to verbalise what they do, because the work is guided by the needs of the elderly and how they want the work to be performed (Christensen 1997).

The contradictory opinions we have presented so far regarding the way in which different actors in elderly care view formal training, have evoked our interest in analysing what significance terms such as qualification and formal education and training have for personnel working in elderly care. The aim of the chapter is to analyse and consider how middle managers and personnel can discuss training and qualifications of care workers in relation to the field of activity in which they are involved and the duties which they perform.

In our analysis and discussion we shall make use of Abbott's (1988) professionalisation theory, which differs from others in many ways inasmuch as it sets processes at the workplace in the foreground. Controlling and supervising work tasks usually form part of a professional culture. Scholars researching professions have focused on external organisation aimed at clarifying the line of demarcation to other occupations. Abbott believes that '... relatively less organised professions have certain distinct advantages in workplace competition. Because they lack clear focus and perhaps a clearly established cognitive structure, they are free to move into available tasks.' (p. 83) How knowledge is applied in practice, and how knowledge gains legitimacy in the cultural context of the workplace, thus become challenges in studying an occupation in which formalisation of qualification requirements has not arisen from competition for tasks but has been something demanded from external sources.

Training as a professionalisation strategy

Training, knowledge and qualification are terms which have been examined theoretically in terms of professionalisation theory. The knowledge base is of great importance to any professional group. The professional group itself often assumes responsibility for ensuring that members are trained to a certain level and also for offering its professional skills on the market. This is not the case with the occupational groups presented here. Instead, their training and qualifications have been determined by external requirements and expectations (National Board of Health and Welfare 2005). Nevertheless we believe that some of the concepts developed in professionalisation theory may be of use in analysing statements made by health care personnel and their managers/supervisors about qualification requirements for the work.

One way of considering knowledge and qualifications is to view these categories in their relation to the occupational group's own interests. Abbott (1988) uses terms such as *abstraction* and *legitimacy* to describe the role of knowledge in the fight for turf. Abstraction—the ability to talk about what one does—can be used as an argument for a place on the labour market, often so as to strengthen it. The terms then used are intended to make clear that one is in command of something which it is not given to everyone to understand. This confers legitimacy on the occupation.

To communicate successfully with the surrounding world is necessary and advantageous to the occupation. Despite the fact that Abbott does not discuss the knowledge base of occupations but of professions, we shall nonetheless make use of his terms in order to analyse statements about training and qualifications. We shall focus especially on what Abbott regards as limitations on abstraction. He believes that if knowledge is presented in communication with others so abstract that the unifying idea is unclear, the occupational group's position is undermined. In other words if the spokesman of the occupation cannot explain how the body of occupational knowledge corresponds with key values in the surrounding culture then the link between the profession and the work is attenuated. Abbott mentions two such forms of abstraction. One form of abstraction emphasises mere absence of concrete content. To speak about work content without being able to show effective practical results, weakens its significance. 'With no effective treatments, abstractions are simply generalities without legitimacy' (p. 103).

The second form of abstraction emphasises formalisation, in which the application of knowledge is routinised or seized by limited groups and requires specific qualification.

The two types often coincide, but they must be clearly distinguished in practice, Abbott argues (1988). Abstraction in the first sense—lack of content—can weaken the occupation because there is no clear-cut connection between an input and an outcome. This encourages the impression that anyone can perform the work tasks involved. In these circumstances the occupational group's *legitimacy* is undermined when the field stands open for others to establish themselves in it. Abstraction in the second sense—formalisation (p. 102)—may have the effect of strengthening the occupation, especially if the links between input and outcome are strong. Viewed in terms of a medical discourse, success is associated with effective treatment. But if formalisation takes place without such effectiveness, this may signify impairment of the occupation's credibility. Abbott (1988) cites examples from the world of business management (p. 103) where such effectiveness cannot be demonstrated.

Externally induced changes, along with drastic financial cuts, have been implemented more or less successfully by representatives of the elderly care sector. Medical diagnosis has increasingly become the determinant of whether or not home help services can be provided (see e.g. Andersson 2004). Abbott would surely have argued that no one was able through abstraction, whether as to content or formalisation, to legitimise contributing to the social element of health care. Bearing in mind that a medical diagnosis is an important factor for justifying the granting of home help services, one would expect medical knowledge to become a key feature for elderly care personnel.

Quality assurance via training?

Changes in the base of knowledge may enforce changes in several other aspects—in work tasks, in the division of labour and in hierarchical order. Changes in the social environment, such as reforms, demographic change, economic or legislative changes, may also produce such effects. Scholars studying social care have taken a critical stance towards the idea of professionalisation. Knowledge is not neutral, says Wærness (1995). Different aims come into collision with practical restrictions. The consequence of a long formal education is that it may lead to a more or less far-reaching specialisation and hierarchisation with staffing cuts as a result. Employers are not willing to pay the costs and meet the specific demands which a profession makes for all employees but only for the smaller group whose special training is a necessity (Wærness 1995). What is more, academic knowledge estranges the professionally active away from practical work, drawing them instead towards other careers in administration and research. Many researchers have instead thought it necessary to draw attention to women's experience and advocate an upgraded evaluation of it. One of these is Wærness (1984, 1999) with her term 'housewife competence', which refers to the skills which women have acquired within the family circle as mothers, daughters and daughters-in-law. Also Davies (1995) belongs to the group which wants to accord recognition to gendered competence. She argues that the emphasis on the impersonal power of bureaucracy, the rational, formal, emotional distance, causes both creativity and flexibility to be lost. Other scholars (see e.g. Astvik 2003 and Johansson 2001) maintain that one must look beyond normative descriptions of women's lives and work, emphasising instead training for health care personnel groups. The view of personnel competence can be said to reside at a breakpoint between formal training and common sense (Wreder 2005) where different occupational groups advocate different knowledge requirements.

At an epistemological level one can discuss what kind of knowledge is relevant in a particular context and how it is formed. Dewey & Bentley (1950) hold that theory and practice cannot be treated as two distinct elements; it is more a matter of an approach in which knowledge is regarded as a bit of both. In other words they advocate a dialectical approach to knowledge, with the individual learning in interaction with his/her (changeable) environment, and in which the everyday know-how of everyday work is regarded as the foundation for a scholarly approach. By stimulating the individual to commitment and emphasising the intersection between environment, training and experience, knowledge is made available which also becomes a necessary condition for actively influencing the individual's own situation (Hartman & Lundgren 2002).

The administrative structure

The organisation of work is important for how care work can be performed. Work routines could either strengthen or weaken cooperation, or they could increase standardisation of care. Franssén (1997) explains how routines in an emergency ward and at a long-term care ward at a large hospital were planned from the top by the medical administrative system. Franssén noted the fragmentation of the different occupation's specific work tasks and areas of responsibility. The registered nurses, due to their higher formal education, were delegated greater responsibilities in medical and administrative areas. Franssén also observes the competition and the struggle to gain respect by the colleagues in one's own occupational group through the demarcation of group boundaries (p. 281). Also Wreder (2005) finds a struggle going on in elderly care between nursing assistant and auxiliary nurses, who are to perform different work tasks. The auxiliary nurses want to establish an occupational border towards the nursing assistants, in order to increase the value of their qualifications.

The formal delegation of work tasks from one group to another is therefore a relevant discussion topic in relation to the concept of formalisation and abstraction in the second sense. One interpretation could be that the delegation of work tasks and the choice of delegees is an obstacle for auxiliary nurses to form an occupational role of their own. As the system works today, the auxiliary nurses have to carry out their delegated and routinised tasks before they are able to pay attention to the more specific needs of the client. The knowledge that is attained from the performance of delegated routine tasks qualifies differently than that acquired from the experiences of the clients' needs.

The statement by Wærness, as by Abbott, Dewey and others, to the effect that knowledge is not neutral, can be interpreted to mean that whether it is to be classified as one thing or the other depends on the context. In the light of the foregoing we will study the attitudes of elderly care personnel in direct care work and middle managers of necessary qualifications and educations for their positions[2]. In this study no registered nurses are included; therefore the organisational conditions and the power relation between registered nurses and auxiliary can only be indirectly discussed.

The material: nursing assistants and auxiliary nurses

In our study we interviewed twenty-three care workers (18 women and 5 men), working day-to-day with the elderly. Of the care workers 9 worked in home help services and 14 in residential care housings along with six middle managers. For a more detailed description see Ahnlund & Johansson (2006). The personnel who took part in the study had different educational backgrounds. Some were employed as nursing assistants (*vårdbiträden*) and others as auxiliary nurses (*undersköterskor*). Nursing assistants had a variety of upper secondary qualifications in, for example, social services or the humanities programme. Three persons had undergone health care support training (*sjukvårdsbiträdesutbildning*) which is no longer available for care workers and eight had completed nursing assistant training (*vårdbiträdesutbildning*). The aforementioned programs vary in length and differ from one municipality to another. They are forms of basic level vocational training that attract, for the most part, those that are already employed in care services. Two individuals had studied at university and others had lower secondary school qualifications.

The individuals who work as auxiliary nurses have either undergone the USHCP or a 32-week supplementary course. The USHCP is part of the national upper secondary education which is a three-year programme. The programs offer a broad education and the basic eligibility for higher education. The national programs include eight obligatory core subjects: English, the Arts, Physical Education and Health, Mathematics, General Science, Social Studies, Swedish (or Swedish as a Second Language) and Religion. Each programme has specific subjects, which are in concordance to the specific programme's aims and learning outcomes (The Swedish National Agency for Education, *www.skolverket.se*).

The USHCP has no national specialisation areas. In examining what different municipalities classify as main areas for the USHCPs, we could identify four subjects that were prioritised; health, environment, nursing and social care (*hälsa, miljö, omvårdnad och social omsorg*). Theoretical courses vary with vocational training being carried out in health care and social care. The programme is also given for adults at the municipal adult education (*KomVux*). The municipal programme can vary in length and from one municipality to another. The aim of the education at *KomVux* is to provide adult pupils with the basic skills necessary for work in the public care services, and to prepare them for further study. The level at which pupils at KomVux begin their studies is determined according to a pupils´ existing knowledge. The rate of study is chosen by the pupils themselves. This makes it possible to combine studies with work (The Swedish National Agency for Education, www.skolverket.se).

Six middle managers, five female and one male, working in various sectors were interviewed. Their backgrounds were diverse. Several had no experience of working in elderly care before being appointed to supervisory posts while others were well experienced, firstly as care workers and then as supervisors.

The analytical themes we have identified are concerned with *formal training* versus *personal experience*, i.e. which of these qualifications is more desirable among staff.

Middle managers in elderly care—formal training versus personal suitability

Middle mangers in elderly care declared that they want all care personnel to have formal training in health care and social welfare, preferably from the USHCP. They also addressed the issue regarding what sort of qualification is to be preferred. They were not always certain that the auxiliary nurse qualification was the best basis for employment. What is clear is that in many respects personal suitability was higher ranked than formal training when staff is being recruited (cf Törnquist 2004). When middle managers have to choose between recruiting an applicant who has passed an examination in USHCP or another applicant without formal training who is considered to be better suited personally, the latter is chosen. Personal suitability means being empathetic, able to listen to old people and sense their feelings. Some middle managers maintain that they do not look for applicants with formal training at all but have other criteria for what constitute relevant qualifications for care workers, e.g. that they shall not be too young. They prefer to recruit women over 30 years of age, when experience and commitment to the work tasks are more likely. Other middle managers declare that they welcome men and immigrants as applicants for jobs because diversity among the workforce is desirable. They regard training as an auxiliary nurse irrelevant since primary health care (*primärvården*) is responsible for the medical health care required.

In this way it emerges that middle managers do not take it for granted that all personnel ought to be qualified auxiliary nurses. They refer instead to what Wærness (1984, 1999) calls 'housewife competence', i.e. personal qualities and experience of work tasks traditionally regarded as 'woman's work'. Other alternatives for improving qualifications are suggested, pedagogical methods designed to make work easier for the staff and to improve the situation of persons suffering from dementia. Some managers use other strategies for tackling improvement of staff qualifications. One stresses the importance of further training being closely related to the needs of staff. They should be trained in pedagogical methods for which they have a use in their day-to-day work, this means in this instance as training in the reminiscence method[3]. In relation to the national recommendations established for care personnel with regard to training, it seems that middle managers in elderly care are not entirely opposed to the idea that all should have the auxiliary nurse qualification. But in the practical work of recruiting staff, training lacks legitimacy because it is not that skill which takes priority. Abbott (1988) believes that legitimacy makes its appearance when there is correspondence between rhetoric and praxis, and such correspondence seems to be missing among middle managers working in elderly care.

Personnel in direct care work in the elderly care sector

On the question of the importance of formal training and what qualifications are relevant to elderly care, one clear theme that emerged concerns who is best qualified to deliver care and supervision of the elderly. This question has been raised in several studies (see e.g. Törnquist 2004, Wreder 2005). Whereas the Swedish Board of Health and Welfare (2004) advocates a general improvement of the qualification level, the debate within the personnel group has been more disparate. The question revolves around whether or not one needs to have an auxiliary nursing qualification in order to do a good job in elderly care. The empirical material shows that most of the personnel, including both auxiliary nurses and nursing assistants, believe it is unnecessary to be an auxiliary nurse when you are not allowed to perform such duties as part of your job anyway. Others, but fewer—again including auxiliary nurses and nursing assistants—consider it of the highest relevance to possess an auxiliary nursing qualification in order to do a good job.

The persons who argue that it is unnecessary to be an auxiliary nurse point to the absence of duties of a medical character. For instance they do not administer injections, fill dossette packs, renew dressings or other medical duties.

> I am an auxiliary nurse and I think that as an auxiliary nurse you don't get much out of a place like this, there are no dressings to be changed, nothing like that, so it can be a bit boring, you get the feeling that in about a year you'll perhaps be on your way from here so you can do a little bit more.

(Female, auxiliary nurse, residential care)

> It's a lot to do with attitude, I think. It's sort of like diligence and a good spirit at work and being kind to the care recipients and having patience (…) There's a bit of self-deception in this business. You have to pretend you can get on, like a sort of career path. Of course a nursing assistant can get to be an auxiliary nurse. But auxiliary nurses often do exactly the same things as care workers in elderly care.
>
> (Male, nursing assistant, residential care)

The above citations reflect a frustration expressed by several of the interviewees over the fact that auxiliary nurses are not allowed to carry out duties for which they are qualified. Employees feel that the job does not broaden their experiences. Nor does it seem necessary to be qualified as an auxiliary nurse when prohibited from using the knowledge acquired and confined to doing exactly the same things as the nursing assistants. There is an observable tendency for those who graduate from the USHCP to value their medical knowledge more highly than anything else they learned on their course of training (SOU 1997:170).

Those individuals who in turn believe it necessary to have passed the USHCP cite other aspects of their work. Through training—it is said—one understands the body and temperament of the elderly better and in that way gets a different insight into what is healthy aging and what is considered to be sick.

> Ordinary nursing competence, of course that's important. Then you need to have a large helping of patience. You need a lot of imagination too. That's the most important. (laughs). For an auxiliary nurse it's both nursing and caring. Here it's mostly nursing but I do need the other aspect as well.
>
> (Female, auxiliary nurse, residential care)

These persons underline the view that it is important to have both auxiliary nursing competence (i.e. knowledge of caring and nursing of the sick) and personal aptitude (i.e. humour and imagination). They see no contradiction between the different skills.

On the basis of our analysis we believe that the arguments for or against formal training are also based on different understandings of what is meant by having passed the USHCP. The occupational skills which follow from health care training leads many auxiliary nurses to feel frustrated at not being permitted to carry out a certain type of duty; the expectations they had of their occupational work are not fulfilled in the elderly care sector. Many of them have a limited view of what an auxiliary nurse should do, and they do not include other duties than the medically-orientated ones. We believe that there is a lack of balance in the view of how general knowledge can be applied in concrete terms and of how the concrete knowledge can be used. Expressed in Abbott's (1988) terminology, the restriction of the scope for performing auxiliary nursing tasks implies that auxiliary nurses regard this as a devaluation of their knowledge. That it does not pay to undertake training implies that working in the elderly care sector is within the capability of anybody at all.

Conclusion

We have studied the attitudes adopted by middle managers and personnel of some elderly care institutions towards questions involving training and qualifications. From national level it is laid down that health care personnel ought to have at least an auxiliary nursing qualification. Yet we can see from the empirical material that the USHCP lacks legitimacy in the eyes of the majority of the participants in our sample. The link between the knowledge base that the auxiliary nurse considers vital and the work-task priorities set in actual health care practice is weak. The knowledge which the environment regards as legitimate is rejected in the workplace. In other words the legitimacy problems are in the workplace, not the public arena. Using Abbott's and Dewey's theories of knowledge and qualifications as our point of departure, we shall discuss how the attitude of personnel to training and qualification issues can be understood.

The majority of personnel interviewed agree that the auxiliary nursing qualification serves no purpose in elderly care. This is surprising as elderly care has changed character over the most recent decades (see Johansson's introductory chapter to the Swedish section in this book) with the result that the work has come increasingly formalised to cover the care of the older old. The work amounts to more than just carrying out medically-related tasks, the personnel involved argue. The approach of middle managers to the question of what constitutes a relevant skill qualification for personnel in elderly care lacks the balance which Abbott (1988) advocates.

Commitment to the principle that care workers should have passed an USHCP has not led to a balance between different actors' wishes. The qualification requirement recommended from central authorities is not supported by the way middle managers and care workers within elderly care look at what constitutes relevant qualification. But as we have shown there are also personnel in elderly care who assert the usefulness of other forms of knowledge than the purely health oriented. Many in our study believe that consumers of elderly care services need personnel with a broad range of skills, and many advocate both concrete care-specific knowledge and also what are called 'personal qualities'. On the basis of Dewey's and Bentley's (1950) reasoning with regard to knowledge and pedagogy it could be argued that it is just as relevant for health care personnel to adopt an attitude to theoretical knowledge about both care and nursing as it is to bring in practical experiences from work with the care recipients. We wonder why the majority of personnel in elderly care fail to accept the usefulness of both forms of knowledge. A dialectical approach to knowledge in relation to health care duties does not solely embrace 'housewife competence' based on gender and experience of home-like tasks. Neither is a purely health oriented approach being advocated of which the central feature is the gaining of permission to carry out medical procedures. Instead, it is a matter of taking advantage of different kinds of knowledge and broadening the scope for using one's skills in the context of the target groups. By appreciating the usefulness of different qualifications rather than focusing on the lack of relevant work tasks one emphasises diversity and an enlarged view of what kind of knowledge is relevant. This reasoning enables us to identify two aspects which may become a reality in the future social care sector.

The formalisation trap. The first of these aspects has to do with an extreme formalisation which depends on processes implemented from a national top-level. The formalisation arises when certain aims and aspirations relating to training and qualifications represent a political drive rather than actual needs. Another formalisation process is the delegation of responsibilities in medical and administrative areas from registered nurses to auxiliary nurses. This splitting procedure can be an obstacle for auxiliary nurses in their development of an autonomous occupational identity.

The emptiness trap. When an extreme formalisation as described above becomes a reality, this has consequences at local level. If the qualifications of staff are expressed in excessively abstract terms (lack of content) and the qualifications being advocated at national level lack legitimacy in the operational realities, a gap emerges between the attitudes of different actors and the demands for qualifications. As we have shown in the chapter, there are differing opinions as to what knowledge is most relevant to personnel working in elderly care, where the national aims do not always correspond to what the personnel within elderly care regard as vital. Has, perhaps, an excessively one-sided emphasis been mandated advocating a particular type of medical knowledge? Those workers in elderly care who claim to be frustrated by not being allowed to perform medical duties are expressing one aspect of this issue. They have had training which makes them suitable for certain work tasks, which in practice they are not allowed to perform. Their medical skills seem irrelevant.

There is a need for further discussion of what are relevant qualifications for personnel in elderly care. There is also a need to discuss ways of learning other than medical and social qualifications, e.g. pedagogical methods. The needs and preferences of user groups ought to be examined. That is what, in the end, confers legitimacy on the knowledge base.

Notes

1 The chapter is based on material assembled in an EU-financed project: *Care Work in Europe. Current understandings and future directions,* with data collected in six European countries. The project covers different occupational groups in the care of the disabled and the elderly. The chapter includes interview material with health care personnel and middle managers in Sweden.

2 The study takes a qualitative approach and consists of an interview study, those interviewed being personnel and middle managers involved in elderly care. The studies were carried out in two cities and in various elderly care institutions in those cities. The study forms part of a European project and the selection criteria were established in collaboration with other participating countries (Johansson 2004, Hansen & Jensen 2004).

3 The reminiscence method is a pedagogical model focusing on helping people with dementia to communicate (Gibson 2004).

References

Abbott, A. (1988) *The System of Professions.* Chicago: The University of Chicago Press.

Ahnlund, P. & Johansson, S. (2006) Omvårdnadsutbildning som mål eller medel? Om legitimitetsproblem och kunskapssyn. *Socialvetenskaplig tidskrift,* 13(3), 212–227.

Alvesson, M. & Sköldberg, K. (1994) *Tolkning och reflektion.* Lund: Studentlitteratur.

Andersson, K. (2004) Det gäller att hushålla med kommunens resurser. Biståndsbedömares syn på äldres sociala resurser. *Socialvetenskaplig tidskrift,* 11(3–4), 275–292.

Astvik, W. (2003) *Relationer som arbete.* Diss. Arbetslivsinstitutet (National Institute of Working Life).

Care work in Europe Contract no. HSPE-CT-2001-00091. European Comission Fifth Framework Programme.

Christensen, K. (1997) *Omsorg og arbete.* Diss. University of Bergen.

Davies, C. (1995) *Gender and the professional predicament in nursing.* Buckingham: Open University Press.

Dewey, J. & Bentley, A. F. (1950) *Knowing and the known.* Boston: Beacon Press.

Franssén, A. (1997) *Omsorg i tanke och handling.* Diss. Lund: Arkiv förlag.

Gibson, F. (2004) *The Past in the Present*. Baltimore: Health Professions Press.

Hansen, H. & Jensen, J. (2004) *Work with Adults with Severe Disabilities: A Case Study of Denmark, The Netherlands and Sweden*. Roskilde universitetscenter.

Hartman, S. G & Lundgren, U.P. (2002) *Individ, skola och samhälle*. Stockholm: Natur och Kultur.

Johansson, S. (2001) *Den sociala omsorgens akademisering*. Stockholm: Liber.

Johansson, S. (2004) *Work with elderly people. A Case Study of Sweden, Spain and England with additional material from Hungary*. www.umu.se/socw/forskning/WP9%20consolidated%20report.pdf

Regeringens proposition 2005/06:115 *Nationell utvecklingsplan för vård och omsorg om äldre*.

Socialstyrelsen (2001) *Nationell handlingsplan för äldrepolitiken*. Lägesrapport 2001. Art. nr: 2001-103-7.

Socialstyrelsen (2002) *Kompetenskrav för personal inom vård och omsorg om äldre*. Art. nr 2002-124-14.

Socialstyrelsen (2004) *Investera Nu! Handlingsplan för kompetensförsörjning inom vård och omsorg*. Art.nr: 2004-103-10.

Socialstyrelsen (2005) *Omvårdnadsassistentens kompetens. Grundläggande kompetensnivå*. Remissversion. Art.nr: 2005-110-8.

SOU (1997) *Brister i omsorg*. Socialdepartementet 1997:51.

SOU (1997) *Bemötandet av äldre*. Socialdepartementet 1997:170.

Svenska kommunförbundet (2003) *Aktuellt om äldreomsorgen*.

Törnquist, A. (2004) *Vad man ska kunna och hur man ska vara*. Diss. The Stockholm Institute of Education.

Wahlgren, I. (1996) *Vem tröstar Ruth?* Diss. Stockholm University, School of Business.

Wreder, M. (2005) *I omsorgens namn*. Diss. Karlstad University.

Wærness, K. (1984) The rationality of caring. *Economic and Industrial Democracy*. 5, 185–211.

Wærness, K. (1995) En offentlig tjeneste i spenningsfeltet mellom ulike kulturer. In S. Johansson (Ed.), *Sjukhus som hem och arbetsplats*. Stockholm: Bonniers utbildning och Universitetsforlaget.

Wærness, K. (1999) Et personalperspektiv på eldreomsorgen i den senmoderne skandinaviske velferdsstat. In *2000-talets äldrevård och äldreomsorg*. Spri report nr: 491, Documentation from a conference.

Internet page: www.skolverket.se (The Swedish National Agency for Education) (information retrieved 2007-04-18).

THIRTEEN

The Neglect of Time as an Aspect of Organising Care Work

Katarina Andersson

In the Swedish context as well as in the other Nordic countries, the managerial reforms of elderly care in the public sector have commonly involved the creation of a new position in the organisation of care; the care manager. The care managers were to be pure administrators and in this capacity they were made responsible for the task of assessing the care needs of an elderly client. The argument made in this chapter is that when the care managers focused on the needs of the client, they simultaneously lost sight of the time a care worker needs to perform the care tasks required to meet those needs. Therefore, the allocation of time for carrying out care tasks has become neglected as an aspect of organising care. This chapter examines the ambiguity of time organisation in elderly care, which arose from the simultaneous neglect of time at the level of care administration, and the use of time when measuring the work input carried out by care workers. Despite of its centrality, attention to the organisation of time in care work has been more or less invisible in both theory and practice. The aim of this chapter is to highlight time as a key perspective of care work. I further argue that the commonly held definition of care as a mutual relationship, based on moral obligation, makes time invisible.

The purpose of home help services is for care workers to attend to the daily needs of the elderly in relation to the care of the home and the body. Work in the home help service includes interaction with the elderly who are in need of care. This need for care makes this relation between the caregiver and the recipient essential. Nordic theorising on care posits the notion of the 'care relations' between the care-needing elderly and the staff working closely with them as a vital issue (see e.g. Eliasson 1992; Szebehely 1995; Wærness 1984, 1990). A recurrent perspective in this literature is that caring is based on a personal commitment and reciprocity in the relation between the care-needing elderly and the caregiver. The research further emphasises the emotional interaction between the caregiver and the recipient, who are related to each other through reciprocal dependence; both parts influence each other's actions and experiences (e.g. Ingvad 2003).

Today's elderly care is undergoing organisational restructuring, which includes new forms of organisation and downsizing. These changes, in combination with the increasing ill health among the elderly who receive home help service, raise questions about the significance of time in care work. How is the actual time handled and experienced by different participants in the increasingly strained elderly care? How has the issue of time been handled in the theories that focus on care work and care relations?

In theories of caring that focus on the relation between giver and recipient, time has an obscure role. The implicit message is that personal involvement; closeness and reciprocity cannot be restricted in terms of time. In other words, care relations appear to take place beyond time and space, even though, in practice, care work needs a real time frame in order to satisfy the needs of the elderly. A gap between theory and practice is apparent. On the basis of the empirical material, I will point out more gaps, which can be related to time in the current home help service. In home help service there are gaps on different levels, within and between different groups, and these, I believe, are vital to the understanding of organisational changes. Work in home help service is carried out in other people's homes. This kind of work is often underestimated in society and this may be one reason why this field appears to be contradictory and full of gaps.

Public elderly care in transformation

In recent decades, public elderly care has been in a state of continual change (cf. Johansson 2006). I would like to emphasise two major changes, downsizing and new forms of organisation, which have led to increased time pressure in this field. At the same time, the elderly who receive some kind of help from the municipality today are older and require more care than before (Blomberg et al. 1999; Szebehely 2000,

2003). The managerial reform that separates care management from the practice of caring has become widespread in Swedish as well as Norwegian municipality strivings for economic efficiency (Blomberg 2004; Christensen 1998, 2001). 'Needs assessment' has become *separated* into a particular task that is carried out by care managers. In the last few years, the process of conducting need assessments has been formalised and standardised to a great extent, which makes it more difficult for the individual to influence the decision making process concerning care tasks. (Blomberg & Pettersson 2003). In the 'traditional organisation' the care administration was *integrated* with the actual task of caring, which meant that the administrator acted as both manager and supervisor of the care workers. In contrast, the new system administration is separated from the practical care work and the administrator who grants too little time for care work does not see the consequences of this neglect in practice (Lindelöf & Rönnbäck 1997). The traditional integrated organisation has been pushed into the background, as the divisive managerial reform constitutes the organisation model in many Swedish municipalities.

In the municipality of the study on which this chapter is based, the managerial reform is applied. However, it is not the organisation of home help service as such that is dealt with. The focus is instead on time and the use of time in the actual care work situation. Qualitative interviews with a focus on care relations have been carried out with the care managers, the care workers and the elderly, who receive home help service. Elderly care is traditionally 'women's work' (cf. Johansson 1999, Szebehely 1998). Even though my ambition was to create a gender balance, the majority of the informants in my empirical material are women. The six interviewed care managers are all women. In the group of care workers there are twelve women and four men, and in the group of six care recipients there are four women. The empirical examples in the text have been chosen from the all-embracing analytical question; *when and how is time reflected in public home help service?* In other words, the answers given by the caregivers and recipients are presented and analysed in this chapter.

It is obvious, however, that the restructuring of public elderly care has led to changes in the administration of time in the current organisation. For example, the time available for various social activities has decreased. The Swedish sociologist Malin Wreder (2005) shows that when care workers describe problems in care work their statements are remarkably homogenous, and include stress, lack of time and understaffing. The care workers discursively posit these problems as the enemy of 'good' care. My argument is that the organisation of care in most municipalities makes time invisible. The care managers` focus was consistently on help-activities given to the elderly, and not on time. This neglect of time has real consequences for the staff who work closest to the elderly and for the elderly who receive the care. These consequences demand closer attention, as the displacement of time in the organisation of home help service threatens to render care relations invisible.

Other issues discussed later in this chapter concern how relations between the elderly and the staff are affected by time pressure. What different meanings lie in the talk about time within the different groups, and how can care be interpreted and understood in relation to this? Furthermore, questions concerning theories on caring will be problematised in order to elucidate on aspects of time, for example, an increased time pressure in home help service.

According to one of the care workers, public elderly care is beset with problems: the lack of sufficient numbers of well trained staff and a noticeable shortage of time. She made this comment about her experiences of the changes in public elderly care:

> I have to say that, I think it has become, it is falling apart. Too few of the staff is sufficiently well trained; they do not have enough experience, while the elderly become sicker and sicker. There are cancer patients, their mental... often do these elderly have mental problems. It is fairly common. Not only dementia but also anxiety,

they get depressed, some stop eating because of it. The ageing process involves so much. It is not only something that happens to them. It is terrible to see this development, how it has become. I think there is a huge difference... In the seventies, then we had the time to sit and talk with the elderly and the sick and that part is also very important. To make them feel good and be able to stay in their home.

The care workers in home care service commonly hold this lack of time space. According to the care workers, it is very important for them to show the elderly that they have the time to sit down and talk, but today that is not feasible.

Care beyond time and space

In the literature of today, the notion of care can be defined in innumerable ways and depends on the discipline and the field of study. It also depends on the approach to the discussion (for a detailed outline, see Johansson 2002). Issues concerning time have been largely neglected in the literature on caring. However, the relation between the caregiver and the recipients is covered extensively. A prominent approach in Scandinavian research about care from a social science perspective, which has its origins in American philosophy, is to view care as a reciprocal relationship. The American philosopher Nel Noddings (1984) emphasises relations instead of loneliness in human existence and acting. She looks upon the ontological base of care as a female way of approaching the concepts of ethics and moral. Furthermore, she dissociates herself from the rules and principles for how care should be performed. Noddings proposes that caring is characterised by taking a stand in each individual case, facing the other person morally and maintaining what is unique in human encounters. The subjective experiences of the parties involved are therefore of vital importance (Noddings 1984, p. 5).

When care is regarded as a relationship and a moral standpoint, time becomes fairly insignificant. In my opinion, this

346

lack of interest in time seems problematical in times of down-sizing. Qualities such as empathy and the ability to create genuine and close relations with the elderly are idealised and regarded as inherent qualities that are mainly possessed by women. The aforementioned scenario also becomes complex when looked upon from a feministic point of view (Johansson 2006). As an ideal, I think an ethically defensible perspective may be important in care work, but not at all costs. There is a dimension of power involved in care relations, which Noddings apparently ignores. In Scandinavian research a great deal of written material can be found that focuses on asymmetrical care relations. Kari Wærness (1984) argues that there is a degree of asymmetry in relations where the person in need of care is at a disadvantage. It may, however, be questioned whether the care recipient is always at a disadvantage. The dimensions of power involved in care work are complex (Ingvad 2003).

Even if Scandinavian care research has problematised care and care relation in a more profound way than the American Noddings, a certain problematic idealisation remains. In my view, the idealised focus on closeness and reciprocity entails the risk that theories of caring will stagnate and become immune to changes in the surrounding world. Care appears to be something that takes place beyond time and space. An important change in public elderly care is an increase in time pressure. A focus on time structures and work makes time visible, whereas a moralistic point of view does not. In addition, the idealised care relation—the 'good' care—is not always a given companion in women's daily care work. There are also traces of monotony and gloominess, which appeared in my interviews with care workers (cf. Wreder 2005). The Swedish sociologist Agneta Franssén (1997) observed that even when there was a time space, the care workers often preferred the routine work instead of using the time to care for the elderly people. Her findings indicate that care work is hard work and that a critique of 'good' care work is overdue. Today, care work seems to become more complex over time and more difficult to define in terms of time and space. It may not only be about work routines anymore, but also about how to handle the unpredictability of care work.

It appears to me that time is invisible, in theory and in practice. According to my analysis, care work seems to be based on the activities (not the time) that care managers allot to the elderly. In theories of caring it is mainly the relation that has been visible in care work. Time has not been considered relevant in theory, and especially if it is as concrete as real time (Davies 1989). One reason for this is that care is supposed to be carried out beyond time and space. I consider this to imply a trivialising of the actual lack of time. In other words, theories of caring have neglected time and the use of time as elements that structure care work. Theories of caring widely promote the idea that care work would run the risk of becoming a routine job if it was subjected to rules and principles of how to perform it. I believe that ignoring time in care work may lead to the opposite effect. The particularly relational and unpredictable nature of care work, as emphasised in theories of caring, would thus run the risk of being rendered invisible. In the next section I will examine the role routines play in care work and explore how the routines relate to time.

Time and routines

Time and the use of time may have different meanings for those involved in elderly care. One way of representing care work is to estimate or measure the real time used for the recurrent activities carried out in home help service.

ROUTINES ARE NECESSARY AND MAKE TIME VISIBLE

A recurrent activity is usually described as a routine. The concept of routines can have different meanings depending on the context. In an every day sense in a Swedish context, 'routine' means 'skill that has arisen from experience' (Norstedts svenska ordbok 1990). However, there is also another meaning of the word 'routine'; an ability that has become mechanical—a routine work—something that is repeated time and time again. A routine can also mean something that must be adhered to; a procedure that is determined in a certain situation, for example a routine measure or a routine check. These definitions indicate a lack of spontaneity, creativity and fresh ideas. Routine work seems to be defined by a lack of flexibility.

Even if routines need not necessarily be interpreted negatively, it is often the case. In theories of caring, work routines are frequently perceived in a negative light. A care relation is a genuine encounter and it cannot be restricted to routines (see e.g. Noddings 1984). The question is whether routines should be regarded in this negative way and for whom are they negative. Franssén (1997) is sceptical when female caregivers prefer routine work to a personal and emotional approach towards the care recipient. However, my point is that these attitudes do not have to be in opposition to each other. An encounter, or an activity, which is followed by a fixed procedure, may also create a form of security, particularly for the elderly. In that sense, the repetition of routines creates a certain form of positive predictability. Furthermore, routine work may help to make care work visible, as routines need visible time in the organisations of home care service.

RENEGOTIATION OF ROUTINES IN EVERYDAY CARE WORK
What kind of work do care workers carry out, and is this work only a matter of routine? The staff consider their work to be all but perfunctory. The tasks vary according to the working hours. At the time of the interviews in the municipality under research, there were stationary daytime groups, groups working in the evenings or during the nights and mobile emergency groups. Work in the mobile emergency groups also includes everyday tasks in the homes of the elderly. These tasks may include everything from helping the elderly to get out of bed in the morning to helping them to go to bed at night. Depending on the needs of the elderly, the work is characterised by around-the-clock care. The close direct and recurring

contact with the elderly is a very important part of the work. This involves being a support for the elderly in their every day life and to interpret the signs of changes in their health and well-being. According to the staff, the elderly are less healthy, more decrepit and more demented than before; an observation that is in accordance with current research (Szebehely 2000; Thorslund 2002). This situation tends to make the work very trying. In the staff's opinion, quite a few of the elderly should not be living at home at all. As a result, the working situation becomes more unpredictable and the daily routines cannot be maintained in the same way as before.

My interviews with care workers show that a considerable percentage of their working hours are used to change the schedule and the working routines, as there are often staff shortages that have to be dealt with on short notice. The number of elderly persons requiring help is constantly rising: 'it becomes like doing a jigsaw puzzle.' The elderly often just sit and wait for the care workers to come, with their eyes on the clock. According to the care workers, the elderly are often obsessed with time: 'Because they often look at the clock, yes, now they will be here in five minutes, and then we might come in twenty minutes.' When unexpected things occur, like an alarm call at night, the staff may have to change the planning for the entire night, and this can be very tough: 'Some people need their medicine at a certain time; we have to do that first. Someone wants to go to bed early, so we have to do that first. This means that we have to reschedule the whole evening.' The staff often try to contact the persons next in turn to tell them that they are delayed. However, a lot of the elderly are too ill to understand and some of them are not able to use the phone. In these circumstances, the question is whether it would be possible to plan the work on the basis of time.

In the 'jigsaw puzzle' of daily routines that the staff has to manage, there are a lot of unforeseen tasks where time is always present but still not visible. This unpredictability is difficult for the staff to handle, as every activity takes time. They also point out that the elderly have the right to expect some degree of continuity with reference to the time that the activity will take place. A person who needs to take his medicine four times a day also needs a very detailed schedule, which has to fit the working hours of the care workers.

The members of staff who work closest to the elderly must adjust to the times and routines of the entire activity, while simultaneously taking into consideration the needs and routines of the elderly. Problems concerning task-coordination may cause a conflict between different tasks. Whose time and routines are given priority? Is it possible to talk about routines at all when the routines are continuously renegotiated? Of what importance is time pressure in terms of the amount of real time in care work, and how do the elderly feel about this?

TAKING CONTROL OF TIME REQUIRES FLEXIBILITY

If the word 'routine' has an unpleasant ring to it, flexibility is looked upon as something positive. The Swedish sociologist Anne Grönlund (2004), who has examined the current rhetoric of working life, questions the discourse of flexibility. She argues that flexibility mainly serves a purpose of adjusting the organisation to the fluctuations between the production and staff of the market. At the same time, flexibility is presumed to favour the employees in terms of good and improving work conditions. Flexible working hours are also presumed to give the individuals an increased opportunity to balance a career and family life. However, according to Grönlund, flexibility for the organisation does not necessarily mean the same thing for the staff. Increasing demands for constant changes between different tasks, may, in contradiction of the presumptions concerning flexible working hours, lead to a more stressful working situation (Grönlund 2004, pp 15).

The care workers spend a considerable part of their time planning and devising schedules—to establish routines— which they cannot pursue. There is not enough time and this leads to stress: 'In theory it may seem like we are overstaffed.' She means that time is often distributed per day and per employee and this is not how it really works: 'But it might work if we could start showering Clare on Monday morning and finish her on Thursday afternoon.' She points out that it is not possible to gather the remaining quarters and half hours when the schedule is made. This proves that it is not possible to divide time as the work consists of human relations.

The main task for the administrators of the organisation is to carry out an individual assessment of the needs of the elderly and to allot the help activities that are called for. The care managers repeatedly emphasise the importance of *not* talking to the elderly about time but about 'help activities': 'And then the time is not devoted to the users. It is extremely important that they get activities, but the staff has not always realised that.' The elderly are supposed to get the help they need anyway. One of the care managers believes that the work tasks carried out by the care workers are quite unrelated to time. It is all about *how* to perform them.

The main concern of the care managers is the economy and resources of the municipality. They therefore consider it important not to waste time, even though they are well aware of the understaffing of home help service (see Andersson 2004). Moving a task to another day, even if it involves a deviation, can solve the problems that may occur as a result of understaffing. One of the care manager's points out. 'There is a certain form to fill in.' The care managers stress that the care workers should be flexible: 'I believe they are there for the pensioners and not the other way around.'

The care workers, on the other hand, feel that the constant reprioritising of their tasks makes them lose control over time. The variety of flexibility that the care workers refer to is not the same as the care managers are talking about. There is a form of flexibility that is not concerned with obtaining power over time, but about flexibility in relationships. Working in the elderly people's homes requires constant adaptability, as no one is exactly like someone else. According to the care workers, time is an essential ingredient in the switch from one recipient to another.

My conclusion is that flexibility has different meanings depending on one's perspective. The question appears to be related to what opportunities the elderly have to harness the power over time and anticipate the help they can expect to receive.

EXPERIENCES OF TIME PRESSURE—GAPS BETWEEN THE
ADMINISTRATION OF CARE AND CARE WORKERS

Although the care workers, according to the interviews, consistently need to piece the time together and conduct themselves in as flexible a manner as possible, time is a constant topic of conversation. It is difficult to constantly have to look at the clock without the elderly noticing: 'You cannot just come and tell them to jump out of bed.' Several of the care workers stress that it is difficult to have to explain the lack of time to the elderly. According to the care workers, the problem is that the care managers calculate that the performance of 'help activities' (defined by the needs assessment document) and the social contact with the client are conducted simultaneously: 'I have been in one of those meetings and what they can grant is dressing and undressing, help with personal hygiene, help to go to the toilet, cooking, cleaning...but it is included in this, in a way.' Even though the tasks themselves may be simple, the interpersonal context in which they are performed takes time. According to the care managers, the staff is not supposed to act as companions. 'But they are lonely people with anxiety,' as one of the care workers stated, then it does not feel right to have to look at the clock all the time. According to the care workers, the elderly people are older and frailer than before. They sometimes get up during the night, and the police find many elderly people who are out wandering about.

Not only is there a considerable element of unpredictability in the work in home help service, but also less time for social interaction with the elderly than before. However, according to the care managers, this is not related to time, but about how to perform an activity: 'The care workers can go in without taking their coats off, just go in and heat the food in the microwave for five minutes, put it on the table...that takes no more than ten minutes. The quality is non-existent.' However, the care managers are well aware of the lack of resources and understaffing in the organisation. According to the care managers, there is less time for the needs-assessments and less freedom of choice for the elderly. It seems as if the separated organisation and the strivings for efficiency affect all the actors within the organisation.

ON WHOSE TERMS IS FLEXIBILITY CREATED?

The constant restructuring of routines in home help service creates noticeable anxiety, insecurity and annoyance in the elderly. One elderly lady was apparently annoyed because she had to wait for home help service: 'Because in quarter of an hour, I would have had the opportunity to do something if had I not been waiting for them. It is not nice, but sit down and start eating, they say. Why? I want to eat my dinner or lunch in peace. I need that.' This lady's annoyance is due to the staff's lack of planning. Besides, it is always difficult to depend on help: 'Why can't they leave me alone and let me have a lie-in once in a while?' However necessary it may be, there is an act of interference in the ordinary routines, the lady continues.

It appears as when the elderly people's routines are interrupted by rescheduled visits from the home help service, they lose control of time. They do not know when to expect the help they need. It seems to me that the staff has probably not even considered that the lady needs to be left alone at times. But even if she is old and in need of help, she might still have her own routines and needs in life other than waiting for the home help service. In my opinion, this reflects a stereotyped perspective on the elderly, by regarding them as passive and always available.

Another lady stated, 'There is so much to talk about, but the care workers do not usually have the time,' and 'they keep looking at the clock and say that they have to go.' According to the elderly, the home help service sometimes arrives at other times than those that were agreed upon. One lady, who expressed a desire to gain an insight into the routines of the home help service, states, 'There is not enough supervision.' She also points out that the staff does not have enough time. Another lady who lives in a housing facility for senior citizens does not think that the staff has sufficient contact with the care recipients. The staff does not do enough and they are under constant stress: 'In a place like this, there should be more time for talking and having a cup of coffee.' The main reason why she chose this housing arrangement was to be able to receive help around-the-clock, but now the building is unattended by night. She is very worried about what might happen to her: 'Now I feel insecure even in my sleep.'

An elderly man is annoyed by the numerous changes in staff that he has been subjected to, without having been previously informed: 'Those working in that area moved here. I became quite annoyed so I phoned the supervisor. I asked what they would gain by making these changes but I got no answer.'

Many of the statements made by the elderly reveal an anxiety and a lack of social interaction with the staff. The elderly also indicate that there is confusion among the staff, which they interpret in terms of a lack of supervision. Many statements also show a discontent with the administration of home help service. Apparently, several gaps can be traced on different levels between groups in the existing organisation.

Is care work still a question of personal chemistry and a given time space?

The current separation between administrations of publicly provided elderly home care and the actual performance of home help leads to a sharp contrast between organisational guidelines and actual care practice. Making time the focus of an analytical perspective that tries to bridge this gap has its risks. To demand that the organisation of care should be based on the time in the time needed to perform tasks may under-mine the idea of the vitality of the care relation and the idea of care as an activity that cannot be restricted by time. When we discuss care, time should possibly be of secondary impor-tance, but this is hardly the case. On the level of care manage-ment, it has been emphasised above that the elderly in need of care are allotted activities instead of time. Could this trans-formation of time into activities in home help service be a profound way of making relations in care work invisible?

In this section, I move on to examine the subjective pro-cesses that shape care and care work performed by staff in home help service. I analyse how the staff portrays the condi-tions under which they carry out their work. I further explore their perceptions of the wishes of the elderly and of the care relation. Finally, I will compare the views of the staff with those of the elderly and examine whether the two sets of an-swers are in harmony or not.

When I asked the staff in home help about what they con-sidered to be important qualities for working with elderly, I received the following answers: the ability to feel empathy, sympathy and human feeling. Previous research also reports similar statements, identifying them as elements in a dis-course on 'good' care (Wreder 2005). According to the care workers, it is of vital importance to be sensitive to the needs of the elderly and to be a good listener: 'I would not work here if I was not happy with it. It is essential to like people.' From the analysis it may be inferred that an essential part of this is about 'taking the time' to show that one cares about the el-derly. This part of caring could mean everything from doing a little extra shopping or putting someone's hair in curlers, to taking one's coat off when coming inside. These practices may be translated as a human feeling that cannot be restricted in time and space: 'I care a lot about them. I feel responsible. Perhaps more than what can be shown on paper.' The care workers emphasised that it is essential to feel responsible to-wards the elderly; a responsibility that extends beyond work-ing hours and set routines.

Another important aspect that was raised in the interviews is that the personal chemistry has to be right. One male care worker put the question of personal chemistry in perspective: 'Then everything works.' This is a common argument held by the group of care workers. If the chemistry is not right, a member of the staff cannot be forced to attend to that particular person.

The importance of the right personal chemistry was raised also in the interviews with the elderly, although they did not bestow it as much importance as the care workers. According to one lady, 'If the chemistry is not right, the best thing is to avoid getting involved [...] I do not have to like everyone around me. It works out anyway.' Another lady pointed out that it could sometimes be difficult not to get too closely acquainted with the staff: 'I would not want that. But I am more comfortable with some than with others.' There is a human side to the relation with the caregiver that cannot be avoided, even if it is not ideal to create excessively close relations with the staff. A relation that becomes too close can be difficult to handle, and not only for the care workers: 'The most important thing is that they can manage the work in our homes,' the elderly pointed out, 'to see what is needed to be done and to take initiatives.' Several of the elderly stressed the importance of the staff having the right kind of education. In order to take care of medical complaints, certain knowledge is required. An elderly man who had suffered a stroke means that it is easy to see whether the staff is educated or not.

As work in home help service involves human relations, it is not surprising that both care workers and the elderly emphasise the issue of personal chemistry. Problems related to personal chemistry sometimes make the contacts more difficult, both for the staff and the elderly. Both parties need to strike a balance concerning the closeness of the care relation and both struggle with the problem of not being able to like everybody equally. The emphasis care workers laid on personal chemistry imply that the concept of the 'good' care with ideals such as reciprocity and closeness is a shared representation of the staff (see Wreder 2005). In my interpretation it seems like the care workers keep holding on to the image of the care relations as ideal, even if it is not firmly established by the elderly. As we have seen, there is an indication that the elderly do not prioritise close relations with the staff. What is important to them is to control over the help received; to foresee when it is coming and that the staff knows what to do.

The consequences of the neglect of time

This chapter has examined the implications of the recent processes of downsizing and reorganisation in the elderly care services. I have identified time as a central feature in the organisation of care work, and argued that this centrality has been ignored. In order to understand why such neglect is possible, it is necessary to take contextual considerations into account. In theories of caring, time aspects have an obscure role, whereas there has been more focus on the relation between giver and recipient. Care cannot be restricted in time or arranged in terms of routines. Care is perceived as an activity related to personal commitment within which reciprocity and closeness are central. This kind of idealised vision of care that places care more or less outside the formal organisation and above economic considerations, underpins theories on caring, and hampers its use as a frame of interpretation in the study of the organisation of care work. When examining elderly care provision in the context of the reorganised public elderly care services in Sweden, I believe it is necessary to turn one's attention towards issues regarding time and its organisation. In order to understand organisational changes in home help service, it is vital to regard aspects of both time and care in theory and in practice.

Empirical examples indicate a complex and partly contradictory picture of elderly care. The care managers demonstrate an indirect attitude towards time for care. They seek more flexibility in the work carried out by care workers and prefer an administrative solution to the problems with lack of time.

The administrative solutions offered by the care managers is to fill in reports of deviation, when there is not enough time to care for all the elderly people. My analysis of the current working situation of the care workers demonstrates that the problems in the care of the elderly are related to the neglect of time at the level of administration and the increased unpredictability of care needs related to the increasing frailness of the elderly. In the statements of the care workers, sufficient allocation of time for both routines and for coping with unforeseen needs is emphasised. The unpredictability of care needs cannot be solved through further standardisations. In the daily work with the elderly, set routines are vital. The organisation of care work through routines does not necessarily mean to act in a standardised way vis-à-vis the elderly. My point is that routines constitute a way to handle the unpredictability. At the same time, the unpredictability of the work in home help service implies that daily routines need to be constantly renegotiated, and this does affect the elderly. For one thing, the staff seems to consider the elderly always to be available and grateful whichever time they come.

Is more time the solution to the problems in elderly care? If we compare the prevailing attitudes of the staff towards the elderly with the situation before the downsizing in the 1990s, when there was more time available, then answer to the question is no. When asked, in the past and the present, the staff consider empathy, human feeling and compassion to be the most important qualities in their work (see Wærness 1984, 1990). My analysis suggests that the degree of closeness in relations constitutes a complex thinking pattern, and especially so for the staff. It is vital to balance demands with needs for the recipient, the working team and the individual caregivers. To grant a recipient extra time may be looked upon as a betrayal within the working team; a way of not following the current norm for how to handle the elderly. Apparently, there is tension between closeness and distance, for the care workers and the elderly. There is always a risk of providing in excess and becoming too absorbed. My analysis shows, however, that the elderly appreciate routines and working skills more than social interaction with the staff. Furthermore, more time does not automatically lead to reciprocal relations. The way personal chemistry is debated in my material demonstrates the frailness of the care relations. It is apparent that personal chemistry between the elderly and the staff stands for complex issues related to the organisation of care. The care relations are considered to be something familiar and close. I consider these ideals to be problematic when applied to care relations between strangers with no obvious reciprocity or closeness. More theoretical and empirical attention is needed to examine what happens in care relations between strangers in formally organised care.

References

Andersson, K. (2004) Det gäller att hushålla med kommunens resurser—biståndsbedömarnas syn på äldres sociala behov. *Socialvetenskaplig tidskrift*, 11(3–4), 275–292.

Blomberg, S. (2004) *Specialiserad biståndshandläggning inom den kommunala äldreomsorgen. Genomförandet av en organisationsreform och dess praktik*. Socialhögskolan, Lunds universitet. Diss.

Blomberg, S. & Petterson, J. (2003) Offentlig äldreomsorg som del i ett socialt medborgarskap. *Socialvetenskaplig tidskrift*, 10(4), 303–318.

Blomberg, S., Edebalk, P.G. & Petersson, J. (1999) *Äldreomsorg utan service, en framgångsrik strategi?* Lund: Meddelanden från socialhögskolan. 1999:1

Christensen, K (1998) Andre-orientering og offentligt omsorgsarbejde. *Tidsskrift for Velferdsforskning*, 1(2), 82–96.

Christensen, K (2001) Mellem politikken og folket. De sociale tjensters græsrodsbureaukrater og deres fordelingspraksis. *Tidsskrift for Velferdsforskning*, 4(4), 222–238.

Davies, K (1989) *Women and time. Weaving the strands of everyday life*. Sociologiska institutionen, Lunds universitet. Diss.

Eliasson, R. (1992) Omsorg och rationalitet. In R. Eliasson (Ed.) *Egenheter och allmänheter. En antologi om omsorg och omsorgens villkor*. Lund: Arkiv.

Franssén, A. (1997) *Omsorgs i tanke och handling. En studie av kvinnors arbete i vården*. Lunds universitet, Lund studies in social welfare, Arkiv. Diss.

Grönlund, A. (2004) *Flexibilitetens gränser. Förändring och friktion i arbetsliv och familj*. Sociologiska institutionen, Umeå. Universitet. Diss. Umeå: Boréa bokförlag.

Ingvad, B. (2003) *Omsorg och relationer. Om det känslomässiga samspelet i hemtjänsten.* Socialhögskolan, Lunds universitet. Diss.

Johansson, S. (1999) Kvinnan som norm—om omsorg och jämställdhet. In K. Christensen & L. J. Syltevik (Eds), *Omsorgens forvitring?Antologi om utfordringer i velferdsstaten.* Bergen: Fagbokforlaget.

Johansson, S. (2002) *Den sociala omsorgens akademisering.* Stockholm: Liber.

Johansson, Stina (2006) Social omsorg, jämställdhet och kompetens. In K. Ekberg, J. Eklund, P.-E. Ellström & S. Johansson (Eds), *Tid för utveckling?* Lund: Studentlitteratur.

Lindelöf, M. & Rönnbäck, E. (1997) *Behov, bedömning och beslut i äldreomsorgen. En studie i 27 kommuner kring handläggningsprocessen.* SoS-rapport 1997:8, Socialstyrelsen.

Noddings, N. (1984) *Caring, A Feminine Approach to Ethics & Moral Education.* Berkeley & Los Angeles: University of California Press.

Norstedts Svenska ordbok (1990) Språkdata, Göteborgs universitet: Sture Allén och Norstedts förlag.

Szebehely, M. (2003) Den nordiska hemtjänsten—bakgrund och omfattning. In M. Szebehely (Ed.), *Hemhjälp i Norden—illustrationer och reflektioner.* Lund: Studentlitteratur.

Szebehely, M. (2000) Äldreomsorg i förändring—knappare resurser och nya organisationsformer. In M. Szebehely (Ed.), *Välfärd, vård och omsorg.* SOU 2000:38, Socialdepartementet.

Szebehely, M. (1998) Hjälp i hemmet i nedskärningstid, hemtjänsten och anhörigas insatser för gamla kvinnor och män. In A.-M. Sandqvist (Ed.), *Åt var och en efter behov.* Stockholm: Kommentus förlag.

Szebehely, M. (1995) *Vardagens organisering. Om vårdbiträden och gamla i hemtjänsten.* Lund: Arkiv. Diss.

Thorslund, M. (2002) Dagens och morgondagens vård och omsorg. In L. Andersson (Ed.), *Socialgerontologi.* Lund: Studentlitteratur.

Wreder, M. (2005) *I omsorgens namn. Tre diskurser om äldreomsorg.* Karlstad University Studies 2005:2. Diss.

Wærness, K. (1984) The Rationality of Caring. *Economic and Industrial Democracy* vol. 5, s. 185–211.

Wærness, K. (1990) 'Omsorgsrationalitet'. Reflexioner över ett begrepps karriär. In R. Eliasson (Ed.) *Omsorgens skiftningar. Begreppet, vardagen, politiken, forskningen.* Lund: Studentlitteratur.

EPILOGUE

The Unheard Voices of Care Workers and Care Researchers

Kari Wærness

I have been engaged in sociological research on care since the 1970's. For many years my main research field was the public home care services in the Nordic countries. Much of the research was defined as applied or policy research and the goal was all the time to do research that could really matter in policies and practices. My research was based on my experiences as a politician in my home municipality. These experiences made me recognise that dominant scientific perspectives in the political planning discourse on public care services were defective and inadequate. They did not describe the problems in the everyday world of care in a way that could give new ideas on how to organise public care services to make them better both for clients and carers.

This book documents that the problems facing the public home care services in the Nordic countries today are probably at least as great as they were more than thirty years ago. The research done by those of us who used what is called a 'bottom-up' or an 'everyday life' perspective on these services seems to have had very little, if any, influence on the many reforms and on the ideological changes these services have gone through during more than three decades. Instead *the care friendly ethos* guiding the Nordic welfare state, as discussed in the introduction, has weakened during the last decade. In this short epilogue, I will present a short historical overview of the changes that may contribute somewhat to the understanding of why a multifaceted 'care crisis' as described in this book has become a problem even in the Nordic 'care friendly' modern welfare states. At the same time such crises are discussed in most other modern societies, and in many developing countries the care problems are even greater.

The 1950s and the 1960s: homemaking as a new ideology in public care for the elderly

When public home care services for the elderly became an issue of rapidly increasing interest in Nordic social policy in the in the 1950s and 60s, what we could call 'the homemaking culture' became a dominant ideology behind the organisation of these services. At this time there already existed a public home based service for families in the Nordic Countries. In this family care service some professional education and full-time positions for all employees was an ideal that to some extent was realised (Simonen 1990, Wærness 1995). The new public home care service for the elderly was not, however, made a part of this earlier established and to some extent professionalised home care service, and the dominant ideology behind it was quite different. In Norway and Sweden middle-aged housewives willing to take part time work were explicitly called upon to go into this new service. Informal rather than formal competence was emphasised. The following statement of the leader of the Public Poverty Care Administration in Stockholm in 1953 is indicative of commonly held ideas of the needed qualifications for workers in this service: Home helpers were to have 'the ordinary competence of a housewife and a honest will to help one's fellow-beings' (Szebehely 1995:58). Another key aspect was that home help should preferably be organised as part-time work. Male Norwegian Parliamentarians expressed similar views in the 1960s, and even if some female members of the Parliament expressed different views, the Norwegian public home help service for the elderly became established on the basis of this same ideology (Nordhus et.al. 1987:77). Also in Finland, where the home care service for families with children was more professionalised than in the other Nordic countries, former housewives taking a short training course for household tasks were the preferred labour force in the new public service for the elderly. In contrast to the other Nordic countries, however, this service became in Finland organised as full-time work.

The homemaking ideology implied that each home helper gave versatile help to a few clients who she learned to know personally. The individual client was allotted a certain amount of hours of 'home help' the content of which was not specified. There existed however some written rules about a few household services and tasks that were not to be provided.

In practice, the clients' immediate needs became decisive for which kinds of help were given. In order to give good care the home helpers often had to provide services that according to the written rules were not to be given. They also often used more time than the clients were allotted and the home helpers were paid for.

The welfare of the individual elderly person had in the 1950s and 1960s become a new and important explicit premise in the political discussions on how public care services for the elderly should be organised (Nordhus et al. 1987: ch 4). The public home care service was the enterprise that was supposed to realise this new premise. In addition the question of how to organise the home care services to make the most efficient use of resources became an issue of steadily growing importance for the political authorities in all Nordic countries from the 1970s. Both the premise of economic efficiency and of individual welfare had resulted in very negative evaluations of public institutional care. Public home help and home nursing services were defined as an alternative to institutional care—an alternative that was evaluated as being both more cost-efficient and more humane for most elderly unable to care for themselves in everyday life. Good public care was defined as care so 'homelike' as possible. The organisational changes of the public care services that were needed according to this new ideology were not based on any solid empirical analyses. No one had tried to fathom out if it was economically and socially possible to organise public care services according to this ideal of good care, independent on how much help the individual elderly needed and what was their family situation. Another neglected question was to what extent this ideal was possible to realise in a situation where the public home helpers would have labour contracts in line with those available to other employees in a modern welfare state. For some years this public service was able to meet the increasing demand without major problems by continually recruiting new home helpers among the middle-aged housewives who were willing to work without regular labour contracts.

The 1970s and the1980s: increasing bureaucratisation, standardisation, professionalisation and institutionalisation of the home care services

After some years it became evident that the goal of organising a public home care service fulfilling traditional norms for good individual care came into conflict with the general norms and rules for modern working life. These included regulated working hours and tasks, possibilities for specialisation and professionalisation and for moving up in a job hierarchy. Empirical studies (Liljeström & Özgalda 1980, Wærness 1978) had shown that the first generation of home helpers, the middle-aged and elderly housewives, did not seem to want their work to change according to these dominating norms in working life. What they wanted was more time with each client and more regular contact with other home helpers. In their view the personal commitment to their clients and the autonomous judgments they did in their daily work were the most satisfying elements of the job. In general they wanted the public home help service to be organised in such a way that they could give versatile and personal help and care to individual clients and at the same time belong to a strong collective of equal home helpers. After a few years, however, the home help services began to change in a direction very different from what this first generation of front-line workers wanted. A generational crisis in the home help service emerged first in Sweden, when the elderly and middle-aged housewives gradually became replaced by a younger generation of women who had got some special education for the job. The younger women found that the realities of the job did not fit the descriptions they had got through their education. The result was that they did not become a stable labour force. Great organisational problems arose when the traditional housewives gradually disappeared from the service and the home helpers' rights as normal employees had to be taken into consideration.

Reforms of public management and the organisation of municipal health and care services began in the 1980s. A pioneer study by sociologist Ritva Gough (1987) documents the great problems of implementing the new public care policy in one of Sweden's most 'innovative' municipalities. Many of the same problems have over the years been documented in a lot of other studies. I therefore want to present some of the main findings of this study. These results tell us that to a great extent the problems we are struggling with today and which are presented in more chapters in this book are not new. They have lasted since the Nordic public home care services started to be organised as normal wage labour.

Gough (1987) shows that contrary to the intensions of the new ideology of public care, the new services introduced new divisions of labour based on greater collectivisation and specialisations of functions, as well as increased the time used for planning, administration and coordination of activities. These tendencies, which were basic reasons for the severe criticism of the traditional institutional care services, could now be observed in the new community service program. This finding, which later has been confirmed in so many other studies of the public home care services, documents that many of the negative traits in institutional care should not be seen as a result of institutionalisation per se, but as a result of a greater problematic connected to managing and organising effective care for the elderly with the greatest needs for help and care.

The statistics pointed to that the number of elderly who received home help as well as the total number of paid working hours of home helpers increased during the 1980s. Still the home helpers tended to experience a decrease in the amount of the personal assistance they were able to give the individual elderly. This was to a large extent due to the changing nature of the care needs of the elderly. During these years, placements in institutions were put off longer. Thus, there was a steady increase in clients who were in need of more care and help due to increasing age. In addition, new clients with complex problems ranging from alcohol abuse to other psychosocial concerns were included in the service. This would have presumed a professional competence and guidance to the home helpers whose formal qualifications to cope with such problems often were lacking. *'Use of time, making priorities among clients, adjusting demands to available resources and especially developing continuity in the social relations between home helpers and the elderly are factors that have contributed to a highly problematic organisation which cannot be overlooked in future programs.'* (Gough 1987: 216, my italics). Continuity in these social relations could be seen as a core value in a care service that should be 'homelike'. This value is most easily realised when the elderly client's need for help and care is not too comprehensive; i.e. for those whose need for public care mainly consist of help with specific household tasks and regular shorter visits to satisfy needs for personal care, social contact and security, and help with more irregular errands or small practical problems in everyday life. Homelike care becomes much more difficult to realise when clients become dependent on help with daily personal hygiene and eating. When a growing proportion of the clients over time become dependent on more comprehensive care and the home helpers at same time are supposed to become normal wage workers this value of continuity became nearly impossible to realise.

The changes in the public home care in this Swedish municipality during the 1980s (Gough 1987:197–198), listed below, are much the same as those we find documented in studies from other communities in the Nordic countries in 1980s and 1990s (see for instance Christensen 1997, Szebehely 1995):

1 Home helpers' personal knowledge of her clients is no longer a self-evident quality of the service. It becomes lost as the individual home helpers have a larger number of clients, work more often outside their own local community, and because the distribution of work and the regulation of working hours make it impossible for the majority of home helpers to have 'their own pensioners'.

2 The home helpers are exposed to the same kind of organisational- and efficiency- trials as the rest of the public administration services, and their division of labour is developed according to patterns similar to those found in large health care institutions. The work methods evolve in more professional directions, in spite of the intentions to avoid this.

3 The occupational roles in the professional organisation are made distinct, and different work tasks become decided for different personnel groups. This creates inequalities among the personnel groups in salaries and employment conditions.

4 One implicit consequence of this change is new divisions between personnel on the one hand and clients and their relatives on the other.

More studies which documented an increasing gap between ideals and realities in public home care argued for trying to find new ways of organising these services. I myself argued (Wærness 1984) that care work is based on a logic or rationality different from the logic in production of goods or administrative work—a rationality of caring—that should be taken into consideration when organising public care. These studies have not had any influence on the planning and political authorities. And, as documented in this book, the new educational programs for care workers have still not solved the problems of recruiting enough care workers that could become a stable work force in this sector. During the 1980s an increasing bureaucratisation and standardisation of the services and different organisational reforms took place, and some new occupational education programs for care workers were established. However, lack of recognition and status for the first line care work and for the knowledge and experiences of the care workers continue to be an important characteristic of the whole public care system. These characteristics seem immutable. The professionalisation of care has implied first and foremost better education for administrators and leaders and not for the first line care workers lowest in the hierarchy. Instead, management ideas from the private sector have been taken in by planners and politicians, and these ideas continue to have an increasing influence on the public care organisations in all Nordic countries (Vabø 2007).

The 1990s and beyond: the pace of organisational changes increases and 'new public management' is introduced

The public care services for the elderly in the Nordic countries can be said to have been under constant organisational change since these services became a part of the welfare state. The pace of change has however varied both between countries and over time. During the 1990s it also became evident that the changes in ideology take place much more rapidly than the changes in everyday practices. Several qualitative studies documented great variation as to how much 'the homemaking ideology' still influenced the organising and practicing of this service, as also is shown in this book. The culture of care can vary even in the same community, as shown by Szebehely (1995), Christensen (1997) and Vabø (2007). At the same time the tendency toward less autonomy and greater subordination in the home helper's job seems to happen everywhere. An increasing medicalisation of the services takes place in all countries as public home care to a greater extent becomes reserved for the most helpless elderly and help with housework becomes a shrinking service. The tasks related to personal care and medical needs have higher prestige than the household tasks. This may be one reason to the fact that 'the disappearance' of the housework did not meet much resistance from the home helpers as a group, even if it resulted in that they to an increasing extent became assistants to the professional nurses rather than autonomous helpers. The impact of the changes in the working conditions—greater time pressure and less contact with each client—has, however, been documented. As a result, it becomes increasingly difficult for the home helpers to acquire the most satisfying and meaningful aspects of the job, that is, the feeling of giving good care to individuals who they get acquainted with (Næss & Wærness 1996). The dilemma in their work situation seems to be the same as the dilemma Gough described in her study: 'We are not respected as competent care workers as long as we carry the wash-tube in one hand and support the pensioner with the other. To get recognition for the 'invisible' work we are doing, we have to let go of both the wash-tube and the pensioner' (Gough 1987:212). Many of the chapters in this book show that this evaluation is still very relevant, maybe more relevant than ever.

As discussed in the introduction, concominant with the neoliberal turn in welfare policy, a new disciplinary order of managerialism has been imposed on the care workers. This new managerialism which has taken somewhat different directions and had some different consequences in the different Nordic countries has been given name 'New Public Management'. What I here will underline is that following these new principles of retrenching, rationing and restructuring of care service delivery, the tendency that Eliasson (1992) characterised as the Taylorisation of the care services in all Nordic countries has increased during the recent years. By Taylorisation we mean a horizontal splitting up of the different tasks and an increasing hierarchisation of the organisation. These processes strengthen the separation of the 'work of the hand' and the 'work of the head'. This means also that the gap between clients and management has widened. But as *Stina Johansson* argues in her introduction to the Swedish section, the increased power to the managers does not necessary mean they have complete or better control than before, as the problems of recruiting enough care workers take more and more of the time resources. As documented very well in Chapter 8, efforts to improve the recruitment situation by educational reforms can easily become 'a story of failed modernisation'. Chapter 4, again, documents in a convincing manner that the neoliberal ethos has been a legitimating ideology behind setting up a hierarchical task-oriented work culture in Finland which have many of the characteristics of Taylorisation: The work that frontline care workers have access to is curtailed by an organisation that blurs their work role through an unclear system of task transferrals. At the same time, the system does not value the socially defined care they provide. On the other hand new individual career opportunities have appeared for the more educated professionals. Not to be better in care work, but to become managers or experts in a more specified fields.

On the basis of the content of all chapters in this book I find that, in spite of the differences between the national problems which are discussed, there is a common core in what is documented. This core finding should be strongly argued to all political and planning authorities in our countries: The modernisation of the public care services in all the Nordic countries has been on a wrong track for quite a long time now. It is therefore high time to try to reform the services from the bottom up. One strategy to do this is by building on the knowledge that can be acquired from listening to the yet unheard voices of the care researchers who have tried to analyse these services from such a perspective. In addition and still more, reform should build upon the knowledge resources of the experienced frontline workers who may still be found in our public care organisations. For such a long time, diverse management ideas have been sought from other types of work organisation in order to make the services 'more efficient'. It is high time that the important knowledge resources to be found within the care field come into focus in the planning process. When I say that it is high time, it is because we have good reasons to assume that the proportion of experienced frontline care workers is steadily decreasing. They are substituted by streams of less stable care workers, and this tendency threatens to rapidly exhaust the relevant practical knowledge resources in the field.

Epilogue

References

Christensen, K. (1997) *Omsorg og arbejde, En sociologisk studie af ændringer i den hjemmebaserte omsorgen*. Dr.polit.avhandling. Sosiologisk Institutt, Universitetet i Bergen.

Eliasson, R. (1992) Omsorg och rationalitet. In R.Eliasson (Ed.) *Egenheter och allmänheter en antologi om omsorg och omsorgens villkor*. Lund: Studentlitteratur.

Gough, R. (1987) *Hemhjälp till gamla*. Stockholm: Forskningsrapport 54 Arbetslivscentrum.

Liljeström, R. & Özgalda, E. (1980) *Kommunals kvinnor på livets trappa*. Stockholm: Svenska kommunalarbetarforbundet.

Nordhus, I.H., Isaksen, L.W. & Wærness, K. (1987) *De fleste gamle er kvinner*. Bergen.: Universitetsforlaget.

Næss, S. & Wærness, K. (1996) *Bedre omsorg?Kommunal eldreomsorg 1980–1995*. Bergen: SEFOS.

Simonen, L. (1990) *Contradictions of the Welfare State, Women and Caring*. Doctoral Diss., University of Tampere.

Szebehely, M. (1995) *Vardagens organisering. Om vårdbiträden och gamla i hemtjänsten*. Lund: Arkiv Forlag.

Vabø, M. (2007) *Organisering for velferd. Hjemmetjenesten i en ideologisk brytningstid*. Oslo: Dr.philos- avhandling. Institutt for sosiologi og samfunnsgeografi, universitetet i Oslo.

Wærness, K. (1978) Hjemmehjelperne-den moderne velferdsstats hushjelper. *Tidsskrift for samfunnsforskning*, vol 19.

Wærness, K. (1984) The rationality of caring. *Economic an Industrial Democracy*, 5, 185–211.

Wærness, K. (1995) En offentlig tjeneste i spenningsfeltet mellom ulike kulturer. In S. Johansson (Ed.) *Sjukhus och hem som arbetsplass* Stockholm/ Oslo: Bonniers/ Universitetsforlaget.

© The authors and Studentlitteratur

Printed in the United States
141038LV00005B/12/P

9 789144 052533